# Unconditional Honor

# UNCONDITIONAL HONOR
*Wounded Warriors and Their Dogs*

## CATHY SCOTT

## PHOTOGRAPHY BY CLAY MYERS

Guilford, Connecticut

An imprint of Rowman & Littlefield

Distributed by NATIONAL BOOK NETWORK

Copyright © 2015 by Cathy Scott
Photographs © 2015 by Clay Myers

British Library Cataloguing-in-Publication Information Available

Library of Congress Cataloging-in-Publication Data Available

ISBN 978-1-4930-0329-7

♾™ The paper used in this publication meets the minimum requirements of American National Standard for Information Sciences—Permanence of Paper for Printed Library Materials, ANSI/NISO Z39.48-1992.

*To all the wounded warriors for their heroism and sacrifice, and to their service dogs, heroes, one and all, who show more dedication to their human teammates than words can ever describe.*

# CONTENTS

# FOREWORD

I'm Bill Walton. It's my unconditional honor, good fortune, and privilege to be Lance Weir's best friend. Lance's story about life with his service dog is found in this book.

Words and phrases allow us to drill deep into the core of our unspoken emotions, passions, loyalties, and experiences.

*Honor*: Just do what's right.

*Unconditional*: without hesitation, reservation, limits, doubt, or uncertainty.

The combination of these two powerful words makes for an unbeatable force. Without them, we simply cannot win—at anything.

I know Lance through our dogs. My wife and her team raise service dogs, and through her programs and organizations I have been able to meet, know, and learn from the finest people in the entire world. People like Kevin and LeAnn Buchanan; David and Rhonda Gruca; Betty and Tom Drumm; Andy, Caroline, Chase, Izzy, and Zoey Boyd; Nurse Ronnie and her husband, Jack Feehan; and, now, Lance Weir.

More recently, I am humbled to now be on the same team as Cathy Scott and Clay Myers through this magnificent book, *Unconditional Honor*.

This army may be small, but it is huge in its vision, dreams, and accomplishments. Through this remarkable group of people, I have become a better, happier person. I am the luckiest guy on earth to be happily married to Lori. As great as that is, however, I'd rather be her dog. The four pillars of happiness in life are health, family, home, and the hope and dream that tomorrow will be better.

*Unconditional Honor* is the ultimate story of achieving happiness in life, despite hardships. We can be going along just fine, and then all of a sudden, something awful happens. It's by struggling through the ensuing journey, to get back up and going in the right direction, that we can find joy and fulfillment again.

Lance Weir was born in Walnut Ridge, Arkansas. He is named after Lance Alworth, one of the greatest all-around athletes our country has ever known. Alworth, nicknamed Bambi because of his powerful abilities to bound over this most bountiful land, burst onto the national stage at the University of Arkansas, which is heaven on earth to all the young dreamers from the Natural State. "A natural" is what each Lance turned out to be.

Lance Weir grew up immersed in the culture of sports as both a participant and a spectator. He loved all that it gave him—a sense of accomplishment, self-esteem, and being part of something special, with grander horizons than he could have ever imagined.

He too went to college in Arkansas, and continued chasing his dreams—including everything that sports and education meant to him: discipline, sacrifice, focus, determination, persistence, and perseverance.

From there, Lance made the ultimate commitment: He joined the US Marine Corps. He was a champion there as well, recognized as an expert marksman with a variety of weapons.

But then one day, twenty-one years ago, Lance got hurt, suffering an injury to his spine. He has been in a wheelchair as a quadriplegic ever since.

I met Lance about twelve years ago, and my life has never been the same either. Lori and I connected with Lance on the day he arrived in San Diego to be matched with Satine, his first service dog.

*Unconditional Honor* is the story of many people just like us—people with dreams, hopes, aspirations, and plans—but also with problems. We all have intractable challenges and issues. Some of you just don't know it yet.

This book captures the lives and resilient nature of these people, and what happens when the ball bounces the other way in the biggest game of all—the game of life. It is the story of what it means to be part of a special team. Through her brilliant and creative prose, Cathy Scott makes you think long and hard, at times bringing you to tears. Clay Myers's touching pictures tie the stories together. As a team, these kind and generous souls have memorialized the pride and satisfaction of the countless numbers of soldiers who have given every bit of themselves for a greater calling, only to find themselves up against true adversity.

When the bad stuff first happens, the overwhelming sadness of this simple twist of fate often leads to dire and fatal consequences. Lance Weir knows this well, and so do I. We have both been there, done that.

But then the lucky ones—again, like Lance and me—have something, or someone, in our lives that enables us to find a way back into the game, back onto the team, back onto the long, hard climb that is the best part of this game of life.

In this book, Cathy and Clay tell the story of our military veterans and service personnel who have risked everything, often with devastating results. Some come home with little else but their fearsome and daunting challenges. They need our help. Pairing them up with a service dog is often the answer.

Service dogs, like their ultimate partners, don't just happen. There are incredible levels of sacrifice, selfless love, determination, and friendship involved. From the fund-raisers and donors to the breeder-caretakers, from the puppy raisers to the volunteer staff and professional trainers—this is an overwhelming commitment and solemn responsibility, all undertaken with unconditional honor. Although service dogs are able to perform a phenomenal number of physical tasks that are of incalculable value, that's the easy part. What they do emotionally is beyond description.

Lance is now the proud teammate of a second-generation service dog named Auggie. His first dog, Satine, who did her job masterfully, has since passed on. Her ashes are buried at the base of a beautiful Buddha fig tree in my family's backyard. The heart-shaped leaves are a direct reflection of the magnitude of Satine's—and Lance's—love of life.

Never think for a moment that it's easy to tell these wonderful stories. For those who struggle with disabilities and challenges, it takes all they have just to stay on the beat.

Whether it's Auggie or Satine, and other service canines like them, or my own service dog, Cortez, there is no way to assign a value to what they do for us. This is because, at the end of the day, our service dogs make us happy. And that's the best place to start—as well as finish—just about anything.

—Bill Walton

# PROLOGUE

We walked into a suburban backyard in San Diego County and were instantly surrounded by happy, bouncing puppies from three months to about a year old. The first thing that came to mind was the song, "Who Let the Dogs Out?"

And then there was an older dog, twelve-year-old Shakai, who was one of the first to greet us. Years earlier, he had been released before graduating from service dog training.

"Shakai went to advanced training for three weeks," said Cyndy Carlton, who raised Shakai through the Canine Companions for Independence (CCI) puppy-raiser program. "He didn't adapt well."

Cyndy took Shakai back home with her, and that's where he's been ever since.

"He is exactly where he needs to be. Not every dog was meant to do this. He's my forever dog—the light of my life," she said. Instead of being a service dog, he has spent his working life going to libraries and sitting with children as they read, and to a VA hospital in Southern California as a visiting therapy dog for veterans.

After basic training with puppy raisers, the organization these puppies are with—in this case, CCI—puts them through an advanced program at their Southern California center, which follows Assistance Dogs International (ADI) guidelines, approved by the Americans with Disabilities Act of 1990. They require dogs to respond to commands 90 percent of the time, whether in public or at home.

As for the puppies from a variety of organizations that go on to advanced training, and eventually graduation, where they're matched and placed at no cost to the veterans, it is as if they were born to work.

The puppy meet-up we attended happens once a week, to keep the service dogs in training socialized with other dogs, and to give them some downtime.

On this particular day, on command, the puppies sat in a row for a group photo on a retaining wall in Cyndy's backyard. They did not leave that position—except for Tamera, the youngest of the bunch, at three and a half months, who leapt to the ground. On command, she quickly returned. The others sat until the puppy moms said, in unison, "Release." Off they went, running and romping around like the puppies they were. Not a growl could be heard. It was all about friendly play, along with some downtime as volunteer Heidi Badger-Chrisman took time sitting with her puppy in training, Stanza, and two of Stanza's playmates, yellow Lab pups Lois and Nira.

Meet the class of 2015, hoping to graduate from CCI's Southwest Division. They're in Cyndy's yard for their weekly playdate as part of their socialization to prepare the dogs, one at a time, to move on to the next step in a series of training exercises at CCI's facility in North San Diego County.

"They're working dogs," said Kathy Bennett, who's raising Meeko, her latest service canine in training, "but they're also just dogs. They need this playtime to blow off steam."

And blow off steam they did, chasing each other around the yard, wriggling and rolling on their backs, and bouncing around.

The weekend gathering is representative of thousands of service canines in training across the country who are being socialized, taught basic and advanced skills, and then trained to perform specific tasks to become service dogs for troops, active-duty and retired, from every branch of the military who find themselves wounded, whether in combat, or on or off duty. These puppies in training are examples of the scores of dogs across the United States who work hard daily to one day stand at the sides of wounded veterans as their helpers and best friends. While not all of the puppies at the weekly playdate we observed will go on to assist wounded warriors (some will assist children and disabled adults), a large number will.

It's serious business, preparing dogs to perform specific tasks for disabled people in real time, the training for which begins when they're pups and continues until after the dogs are matched with a disabled person, with refresher training for the rest of the dogs' lives.

The goal for service dogs, whether mixes or purebreds, is to reduce the disabling conditions of their handlers' health, mobility, moods, social interactions, and employment. The dogs, often by their presence alone, increase the veterans' levels of functioning, overall well-being, and confidence.

The earliest use of guide dogs—by soldiers who had been blinded during battle—was documented in Germany following World War I. But only since mid-2000 have service dogs been used in the United States specifically for veterans and active-duty military members who have psychological conditions and physical injuries, and need more than traditional medical treatments.

The definition of a service dog, gleaned from a variety of groups, is a dog that is specifically trained in obedience, manners, and public behavior to perform tasks or provide assistance to one individual to help mitigate a specific disability.

The journey of pairing these canines with wounded veterans begins when the dogs are young and rescued from shelters, donated by breeders, or bred in-house by their respective groups. The training and socialization often begin in foster care with puppy raisers. In some cases, inmates teach both bred and rescued dogs behind prison walls. Finally, the canines are placed with veterans, where they receive even more hands-on instruction from their new teammates.

Once the trained canines become a part of their lives, these wounded warriors are better equipped to navigate the rough road back to civilian life or the return to full military duty, whatever the individual case may be. With dogs by their sides, they no longer feel alone, they are better able to cope, and their futures are brighter. As Mary Cortani, a military veteran and a Top 10 CNN Hero of 2012, puts it, when veterans "have a service dog, there are immediate benefits right off the bat. They have a mission and a purpose again. It gives them something to focus on and to complete. It gives them a sense of security and safety."

"They know they're not alone," she continued. "They've always got their buddy at the end of the leash."

When it comes to service dogs in training that go on to graduate, one thing is clear: When the dogs' service vests are on their backs and around their chests, they are in full working mode. When the vests come off, it's playtime, and they become rambunctious dogs.

It doesn't get any better than this. For veterans who have returned from deployment overseas from Southeast Asia, East Asia, Africa, Panama, the Middle East, Guam, or Haiti, the dogs soon become their new battle buddies, their housemates, their best friends.

Observing these special dogs and people teaming together in daily activities and chores is something that's tough to describe. The emotional bonds they share are palpable. And watching the puppies with their foster parents is just plain fun. Knowing that many are going on to dedicate their lives to either veterans or active-duty personnel makes the playful moments even more precious.

Talking to puppy raisers, foster moms and dads, inmate trainers, veterans, and canine instructors, and visiting organizations and facilities across the country either in person or by telephone to photograph and hear their stories, has been a privilege and an honor. We've talked with veterans as well as those directly involved in the process, from raising and training the dogs to placing them. Photographing dogs that are treated well and held in such high esteem is priceless, and it provides a stark contrast to other assignments where we have observed and photographed canines housed in shelters, puppy mills, or hoarding situations, where the dogs' pleading eyes have said, "Get me out of here."

It is our hope that this book will help to raise awareness of the unmistakable impact service dogs have on improving the daily lives of wounded warriors with both physical and mental injuries.

A common thread with the wounded warriors and those involved in service dog programs is that they pay it forward every day. From the people who raise the dogs to those who give breed-specific puppies or homeless dogs to groups to be trained—from the instructors themselves to the puppy parents who donate and devote their time to teaching the dogs basic cues—everyone involved in the process wants to share the love. This includes the state prison and federal penitentiary inmates who raise and train the puppies, to give them the necessary tools to become service dogs; the advanced trainers who teach them specific tasks and skills; the people who match them with veterans; the veterans who take them into their homes and treat them like one of the family; and the veterans' families, who also welcome the dogs. Each is dedicated to the cause of canines helping wounded warriors. Each pays it forward every day.

In a somber turn of events, one veteran, Brian Coutch, passed away the night before he and photographer Clay Myers, who had driven four hours to meet Brian, could photograph him and his dog, Slate, for this book. Clay recounted learning the bad news upon his arrival at a VFW center in New Kensington, Pennsylvania.

"I was looking forward to meeting Brian," Clay said. "He called me within five minutes after I sent my query e-mail to him. Brian was devoted to raising awareness about how service dogs can help veterans and wanted to tell his story. And what a story—Brian was a highly decorated twenty-two-year Army veteran and a true hero."

Clay walked into the center but did not see a veteran with a dog. He soon learned that Brian had been found dead in his home that morning. A couple of veterans expressed concern for Slate, who never left Brian's side. Clay attended Brian's service at Arlington National Cemetery, where Slate said his final good-bye to his human partner. Brian's story, as well as where Slate is today, is included in these pages.

We've come away from our travels understanding that there are three things veterans care about most: their country, their families, and their dogs, not necessarily in that order. Veterans and their service canines share a deep, symbiotic relationship.

We leave it to the individual service members and veterans in the following pages to describe, in their own inspiring words, the tales of these special relationships and the interactions they share with their dogs.

Those involved in placing service dogs with active and retired military personnel have one thing in common: They have seen firsthand how difficult civilian life can be for many returning warriors—what a challenge it can be for them to reconnect with society. For so many, the answer is a service dog. This book includes personal experiences that reveal just what these dogs mean to veterans and how their lives have been forever changed, enhanced, and even saved by service canines. It follows the journeys of physically as well as psychologically injured veterans in an examination of service and therapy dogs who are having a profound impact on the lives of active and retired military personnel injured in action. The veterans, who come from all branches of military service, often have such severe psychological diagnoses that they turn to alternative treatments, including assistance, companionship, and love from dogs.

Yet this is more than a collection of tales about veterans and their service dogs. It is also the story of people in a wide variety of circumstances paying it forward by giving back and expecting nothing in return. To these men and women across the country, heroes all, and those included in these pages who have returned from overseas assignments, we say, "Welcome home," and "Give your dogs a hug from us."

Through *Unconditional Honor*, we hope that more people will recognize the vital role dogs can play in making service members once again feel at home on American soil.

These are their stories.

# CHAPTER 1

# In Their Own Words

Calvin Smith suffered traumatic brain and spinal injuries after being cut down by an improvised explosive device, commonly called an IED. These homemade bombs are the leading cause of injuries and death in Iraq and Afghanistan. Calvin finds relief in his service dog, who helps with daily tasks that Calvin is no longer able to do himself.

Andrew Pike, a veteran paralyzed from the waist down, overcame some of his physical challenges with the assistance of his trained dog, Yazmin, who performs basic daily tasks for Andrew.

Army soldier Jesse Tanner experienced symptoms of traumatic brain injury, but the pain eased after Dakota, a boxer and Labrador retriever mix, entered his life.

Staff Sergeant Richard Gonzalez, an active-duty Marine who served multiple tours of duty, arrived home to find himself in the throes of post-traumatic stress, coupled with physical injuries he suffered while in Fallujah, about forty miles west of Baghdad, on the Euphrates River. Life for Richard improved once Charlie, a Labrador retriever, came on the scene. Richard went on to volunteer at the Wounded Warrior Battalion West to help others like himself.

And navy corpsman Melissa Jaramillo Ramirez had symptoms of post-traumatic stress so extreme she was frightened to leave her home—until she learned about Freedom Dogs and their canine training program for military personnel like herself.

Their stories are not unique; they each suffer with PTSD. And each found relief in the presence of their service canines.

According to a 2008 RAND Corporation study, approximately 14 percent of the 1.6 million military personnel who deployed to the Iraq and Afghanistan conflicts have screened positively for post-traumatic stress. The Department of Veterans Affairs' National Center for PTSD estimates that this number is between 11 and 20 percent. The RAND study notes that without treatment, combat veterans can experience extreme difficulty with social interactions and will often be unable to sustain personal relationships.

For the first time in American history, large percentages of wounded warriors returning from the battlefield—in this case, from Iraq and Afghanistan—have survived their injuries.

The Afghanistan War, which began in 2001, followed the September 11 terrorist attacks against the United States. President George W. Bush demanded that the Taliban, which had seized control of Afghanistan, hand over Osama bin Laden. When they refused, US forces invaded Afghanistan with the goal of removing the extremist Islamic regime from power. Much of the action demanded ground troops, and many of these soldiers returned home with amputations, traumatic brain injury, and post-traumatic stress.

According to *Encyclopedia Britannica,* the Iraq War occurred in two stages: The first began in 2003 with a US-led invasion force; the second stage involved lengthier fighting, where insurgents opposed the occupying forces and the newly formed Iraqi government. After nine years of war, the United States completed its withdrawal of military personnel in late 2011.

An estimated 30 percent of America's war veterans struggle with the invisible wounds of post-traumatic stress. Symptoms include severe depression, anxiety, flashbacks, and panic attacks related to the horrors of war and the difficulty of readjusting to civilian life. While many vets are able to adjust and handle the physical and emotional wounds of war, despite the treatments they receive, some still struggle to function as they face debilitating periods of anxiety, anger, nightmares, sleeplessness, and depression, along with unemployment, homelessness, and substance abuse as they try to assimilate back into everyday life. Many suffering from physical and psychological trauma need help resuming their normal lives.

Statistics show that one in eight returning veterans suffers from PTSD, and the problem does not appear to be going away. During times of conflict and war, some 30,000 troops return home each year from overseas. This translates to nearly 4,000 service members every year who could be beneficiaries of the various service dog programs available.

Canines not only provide assistance with the varied tasks they are trained to perform, but in many cases, they can help to prevent suicides. As of 2014, veterans account for 20 percent of suicides in the United States, according to Face the Facts USA, a nonprofit project of the George Washington School of Media and Public Affairs. For soldiers aged twenty-four and younger, their lives are taken at four times the rate of other veteran age groups.

When it comes to helping war vets who are experiencing post-traumatic stress, dogs are proving to be some of the best medicine. According to *Smithsonian* magazine, "The animals draw out even the most isolated personality, and having to praise the animals helps traumatized veterans overcome emotional numbness. Teaching the dogs service commands develops a patient's ability to communicate, to be assertive but not aggressive, a distinction some struggle with. The dogs can also assuage the hypervigilance common in vets with PTSD. Some participants report they finally got some sleep knowing that a naturally alert soul was standing watch."

Dr. Gina Simmons, a marriage and family therapist in San Diego for more than twenty years, agrees with this assessment. "When someone suffers from PTSD, their basic bond of trust with others and with the world is broken. They also lose trust in their own ability to assess threat accurately. Service dogs," she notes, "help mend that sense of trust by creating a bond and attachment. The dog provides feedback about danger that the owner can trust." This, she says, also gives them "a greater sense of safety, security, and bonding."

Growing numbers of troops returning from Iraq and Afghanistan are learning about service dog programs and turning to them for assistance. Not only do the dogs help wounded warriors deal with physical damage, especially traumatic brain injury—a blow or jolt to the head, or a penetrating head injury that disrupts the function of the brain—but they also help to address the hidden psychological consequences of combat conditions, namely post-traumatic stress. Both have become known as the signature combat wounds of the Iraq and Afghanistan conflicts.

One service dog group, Canine Angels, omits the word *disorder* altogether from the name of the syndrome, because the group's founder, Rick Kaplan, wants to avoid a possible social stigma attached to the word. "Rick refers to post-traumatic stress as a definable injury, not a disorder," said Jan Igoe, a volunteer communications manager for the group. "Our veterans and others who suffer from it respond better to the term 'injury.'"

⌢

From a distance, a scene at a local park of a man with a dog appears to be just that: a resident walking his pet. Take a closer look, and you'll see that it's former Marine sergeant Calvin Smith and his specially trained service dog, Chesney.

Life has been anything but a walk in the park for Calvin. He had an epiphany after his difficult journey connected him with Chesney, a calm, intelligent, and family-friendly black Labrador retriever. With this dog, he felt whole again. And Chesney appears to feel very much at home with Calvin.

Calvin's arduous saga began after the ambush in 2003 when he was struck in the back by a sniper's bullet. Calvin—muscular, athletic, and ready for anything—was riding in a military vehicle when snipers started firing.

"I was thrown from my seat into the top of the Humvee," Calvin said. "It had bars across the top, and my head hit the bars. A corpsman cleaned me up. I didn't see a doctor. There wasn't anyone there to help," he explained.

Calvin began having what he described as "major nerve sensations" in his legs, and it worried him. At times when he walked, his legs collapsed beneath him.

When he got home, he was diagnosed with herniated discs and had surgery to repair them. Once he had recovered from surgery, he was eager to return to Iraq. After he was medically cleared, he was deployed once again to the front line. While out on routine patrol in the streets of Fallujah, he was wounded once again, this time from what he called "a couple of IEDs"—improvised explosive devices. His injuries not only ended his combat duty, but also much of his independence.

It was 2005, and Calvin arrived home from the battlefield the second time a dramatically changed man. With migraines from the traumatic brain injury that made him dizzy, plus spasms from spine damage that caused sharp pain in his legs, he was no longer steady on his feet. He needed a cane to walk. He also had nightmares flashing back to warfare in the military theater. He continued to suffer from back and leg pain. During a second surgery, a doctor fused his spine, allowing him to be more mobile.

But because he was still unsteady on his feet even after the operation, his surgeon recommended something Calvin had not considered before: a service dog. He was told a dog would help him with basic and daily tasks he could no longer do himself—things that used to be simple, like bending down to pick up a shoe or a set of dropped keys. He could also use a dog to lean on to help him balance. But Calvin resisted. After all, he emphasized, "I'm a Marine. We're taught to be strong."

Eventually, however, Calvin, still muscular and looking every bit on the outside like the stoic, proud Marine he once was, swallowed his military pride and conceded that he needed help.

He found that assistance in Chesney, a larger-size service dog strong enough to physically aid him. Chesney has been Calvin's constant companion since 2009. Upon their first meeting, Calvin was using his cane. Unfazed, Chesney walked up to Calvin, sat at his feet, and looked up at him adoringly. Calvin had found his canine companion, and Chesney had found his human partner.

"Chesney changed my life," Calvin said. "If I drop my cell phone or keys, he picks them up. Once, I dropped my credit card at the bank, and I couldn't bend down to get it. Chesney picked it up, put his paws on the counter, and handed it to the teller."

In 2013, doctors had to amputate Calvin's left leg because the bone did not heal properly, and he now wears a prosthesis. To maintain his balance, he holds Chesney's harness, which is equipped with a handle.

"He helps me walk," Calvin said. "Chesney knows that once the harness is buckled on, he's in working mode." Throughout the day, Chesney regularly looks up at Calvin to monitor how he's doing. "Good boy," Calvin said to his concerned dog as the two, side by side, made their way safely down a flight of stairs.

Calvin cannot imagine life without Chesney. "In the morning, he's the first thing I see. He needs me to feed him, give him water, and take him outside. He helps me get up and out of bed. He's an amazing friend. If I'm having a bad day because my legs aren't working that well, my back is killing me, or I'm having a migraine because of the brain injury I got over there, he's here to help me overcome them.

"He knows when to be there and what to do. It's like having my life back. He gives me purpose."

❧

Andrew Pike's experience is similar to Calvin's. A wounded Iraq War veteran, paralyzed from the waist down from a sniper's bullet, Andrew has also overcome many of his challenges with the help of his service dog, two-year-old Yazmin.

Andrew, who uses a wheelchair for mobility, heard from a veterans' clinic about service dogs and applied to adopt a canine partner. Yazmin, a black Labrador retriever whose breed looks at learning tasks as fun and games, knows forty voice cues, can pick up keys and credit cards, push and pull doors open for Andrew, push an elevator button, and open and close appliance doors, cupboards, and file cabinets. He braces to assist Andrew as he gets in and out of his chair. He'll even lift Andrew's legs, one at a time.

A big boost for Andrew when he's in his nonmotorized wheelchair is when he needs Yazmin to tow the chair. All Andrew has to say is "Tug," and he gets a tow. Because of Yazmin, Andrew has reentered civilian life with a dog that has made everyday tasks easier and, as a result, made him more independent.

Jesse Tanner's life changed drastically after his discharge from the US Army's 82nd Airborne Infantry out of Fort Bragg, North Carolina. In November 2010, the former sergeant, when he wasn't home, frequented a neighborhood bar. "I would go to the bar, go home and go to sleep, and redo it the next day," he said. No longer part of the group dynamics of the military, he felt alone. He experienced panic attacks and debilitating headaches caused by a traumatic brain injury from daily exposure to incoming fire, mortar, and rockets.

His disposition after serving in the military was quite different from what it had been just a short time earlier. In high school, he had been all-conference in sports. He had considered college, but the thought of going into debt with student loans stopped him. Instead, he enlisted in the army.

"I didn't know what I wanted to do," he said. "So, right out of high school, I was off to basic training, and my first time truly out on my own." When confronted with making a choice as to what he wanted to do in the service, "I told them, 'Give me a gun and let me jump out of airplanes,' and that's what I ended up doing." His grandfather, who passed away in 2014, was a veteran of World War II, Korea, and Vietnam. The service was a part of his family history.

Jesse's infantry unit was the first on the ground in early 2007 for the final military surge into Baghdad and its borough, Sadr City, in what Jesse described as "the worst part of Iraq. We woke up most mornings to the sound of mortars hitting our motor pool, where we parked our trucks." They settled in for the rest of their tour at Combat Outpost

Callahan, which was set up at an abandoned three-story shopping center in Sadr City.

Jumping out of airplanes caused herniated discs in his back and arthritis and tendinitis in his knees. The rockets and mortars landing nearby as his unit patrolled caused trauma to his brain.

Once Jesse was back home in Euclid, Ohio, his longtime girlfriend Sarah Brown saw a big difference in his behavior. "I noticed a change in him," she said. "He stayed home a lot. He didn't have the outgoing, friendly personality he had when I first met him. He was always at the bar. It seemed to be the only place he was comfortable outside of his house."

In military parlance, he had become a "cave dweller" who rarely left the safety of his house or the bar.

Sarah read an article in a local paper about a nonprofit service dog organization called Veteran's Best Friend. She and Jesse attended an event where the organization's service dogs were training with veterans under the supervision of Lisa Slama, a trainer and one of the founders. "My girlfriend did all of the talking for me," Jesse said. "It was at a shopping center, and I wasn't comfortable. I was shaking."

Jesse's life began to turn around in October 2011 after Lisa matched him with Dakota, a then-six-month-old female boxer-terrier mix. Dakota had been found by an animal control officer at a local fairground after being dumped there by her owner. She was rescued and taken to an animal shelter and, after spending three months there, was placed in the Veteran's Best Friend's K9 Coaches training program.

At one point after he got Dakota, Jesse recalled, "I went to the emergency room because I was going to commit suicide," he said. "I checked into the psych ward. If it wasn't for Dakota, I wouldn't be alive."

As with so many wounded warriors with service dogs, Jesse feels a strong sense of responsibility toward Dakota. "She's the reason I get up in the morning," he said. "I have to take care of this creature, this animal who helped me."

When asked how she's changed his life, Jesse answered, "Wow, what *hasn't* she done for me?" When he gets migraines that immobilize him, Dakota is there for him. "Sometimes I get these headaches and I can't move. Dakota gets my medication for me," he said.

Besides the physical things—picking up items he's dropped, or bringing things he needs to him—Dakota also attends college with Jesse. "I take her to school and she sits in front of me. If someone walks up from behind, she nudges me. I know I'm not going to flip out with someone startling me, because she lets me know ahead of time. With a dog, you don't feel so sorry for yourself. She's always there. I've got Dakota, and even when people look at me funny, that's okay."

Jesse's advice for veterans struggling with similar issues: "They need to know there is a way out of it. You can live your life again." With the soothing presence of a dog, he no longer feels the need to sit next to the door in a classroom or to have his back against the wall at a restaurant. "Dakota is the reason I'm still alive," Jesse said matter-of-factly. His girlfriend Sarah agreed, saying, "They have a powerful bond."

Without Dakota, Jesse noted, "I don't know where I'd be right now. I don't know if I'd still be sitting at the bar. I might not be in school. Veteran's Best Friend and Dakota saved my life. Going from doing nothing to living my life again has been a blessing. I can see my life going in the right direction now."

Jesse's story is typical of what so many service members experience once their overseas tours end. They find themselves alone, without the companionship of their military brothers and sisters. A service dog, they learn, can fill that void.

Take Staff Sergeant Richard Gonzalez, the determined Marine who served multiple tours of duty overseas. He arrived home deeply immersed in the symptoms of post-traumatic stress while still healing from his physical injuries. Through a partnership between the Wounded Warrior Battalion West at Camp Pendleton in Southern California and the group Freedom Dogs, Richard began a training regimen with Charlie, an English Labrador retriever. Working together helped Richard deal with the nightmares that disrupted his sleep.

The goal of Freedom Dogs, along with other service dog organizations across the country, is to use the healing power of the human-animal bond to help wounded warriors recover from post-traumatic stress and traumatic brain injury, as well as physical wounds.

"I got shot five times, once while located in Fallujah," Richard said as he spent a weekday morning working on commands with Charlie.

Once home, Richard spent time at the Wounded Warrior Battalion West at Camp Pendleton. Because of his symptoms, Richard knew he needed help. He began a strict training regimen with Charlie, while also spending time with another service dog named Jobie. When Richard was going through a difficult stretch and felt he could benefit from the companionship of a service dog, help was just a text message away. At the receiving end was Beth Russell, cofounder and lead trainer of Freedom Dogs, always at the ready with a service dog. "Beth texted me back with, 'I've got Jobie. Can he visit you today?' and she would deliver him to me."

On base at the Wounded Warrior Battalion West, Richard successfully completed the intensive training program he attended on weekday mornings with Charlie. Richard credits Charlie—or Charles, as he called him, a "more dignified name for the job he does," Richard explained—with helping his spirit heal as he prepared to leave the military and integrate back into civilian life. "I went through all the physical treatment and rehabilitation," he said, which meant that physically, he had recovered.

Mentally and emotionally, however, he was far from okay. Not long after they began training together, Charlie began having sleepovers with Richard to help him cope with his nightmares.

"I couldn't hold it in anymore. Everything hit me," Richard said. "I wanted to deploy again, but the doctor said, 'No.' I withdrew. I couldn't sleep. At night, it felt like the enemy was in my room as combat theater played in my head. One night, I was paralyzed with fear and couldn't move. I said, 'Charles, turn on the light.' That dog was there for me as I fought for a will to live. He stays strong for me."

Richard spent quality time with Charlie at the beach and gym, so he was not alone. He sometimes spent time hanging out with Jobie too. Richard eventually became a mentor at the Wounded Warrior Battalion West for Marines returning home from combat duty facing the same issues he was experiencing.

At a training session at Camp Pendleton, the connection between Charlie and Richard was evident when Richard sat down on a concrete berm and Charlie pressed his side against Richard to let him know he was there for him.

What came from those training sessions was good news: Richard Gonzalez no longer needed a service dog. "If a Freedom Dogs program participant decides that they want a dog on a permanent basis," said Ace Hoyt, a board member with the organization, "then we give them one at no charge. But the great success is that the healing they receive during our program has about 90 percent of the warriors deciding they have received the benefit from the dog's support during their recovery and they do not need a dog. The others, like Carlos Cruz and Melissa Jaramillo Ramirez, decide to keep a dog and get on with their lives as well."

Navy petty officer second class Melissa Jaramillo Ramirez did indeed discover that a service dog could give her the help she needed. After returning from overseas, she lived on the Camp Pendleton Marine Corps Base in Southern California. She found that she needed help in dealing with the stress of leaving her barracks.

Melissa had bravely served two tours in Iraq and one in Afghanistan, only to return home a changed person, so introverted and frightened of her surroundings that she could not leave home. Some days, she didn't even want to get out of bed. She felt she had no other choice but to retire from the military. She hoped that a trained canine would be the answer to help her transition back into the civilian world.

Melissa's emotions at times went into a tailspin. When she became anxious, she would hesitate to speak, and then begin to stutter. From everything she had heard and read, she thought a dog might be the answer. But she didn't know how to go about getting one until she learned about Freedom Dogs from fellow wounded warrior Richard Gonzalez. He told her about their program, where she could start working with a service dog right away. She was also relieved to hear that the group would absorb the expenses, and there would be no cost to her.

She applied for and began working with Gunner, a black English Labrador retriever who was trained as a psychiatric service canine through Freedom Dogs. Several times a week, both indoors and outdoors, Melissa spent time with Gunner, learning what cues he responded to, and allowing Gunner to get to know her.

Eighteen months later, Gunner, her fearless protector and companion, moved in with Melissa to her barracks, accompanying her wherever she went—to the supermarket, to her doctors' appointments, to college classes she'd enrolled in, pursuing a degree in interior design, and to friends' homes—trips that had once been unthinkable after her deployment had ended.

Once Gunner's vest is on his back, a serious look comes across his face as he focuses on Melissa and her needs. He's sensitive to her moods and responds to the intermittent anxiety that can quickly escalate to fear as she goes about her daily routine.

When Melissa trained in 2011 for a triathlon, Gunner paced her in the swimming pool in the same lane, providing her with the sense of security she needed to move through the water.

"He's my buddy," said Melissa, as she and Gunner sat together in a grassy area, taking a break during an outdoor training session near the Wounded Warrior Battalion West headquarters on base. Gunner, despite the break from training, remained in working mode. He had a steely look of determination as he responded to Melissa's every move and gesture. When she leaned forward, Gunner shifted his weight, watched her face, and readied himself to react when she moved again.

It was clear that Gunner knew exactly what his job was: watching over Melissa.

When Melissa was medically discharged from the service in 2012 due to her PTSD, then-three-year-old Gunner remained with her. With Gunner always at her side, she now feels more comfortable venturing out in public. "I'm lucky we found each other," she said.

⸺◆⸺

Retired army veteran Larry Whitted can't say enough about his service dog. He is his protector. Most of all, he is his best friend. The Doberman–chocolate Labrador mix has helped Larry heal both physically and emotionally.

Larry, an eighteen-year army reservist and former member of the army pistol team, has seen more than his share of adversity. He's survived cancer. He's suffered from the crippling anxiety of post-traumatic stress. Then a car accident left him with a broken hip and blindness in one eye.

Through it all, Leo has been his best medicine.

Leo, whose ears when they crinkle are almost as expressive as his soft facial features, can sense when Larry's anxiety is building and he's getting upset. If Larry, for example, gets into an argument with someone, Leo pulls on Larry's pant leg or nudges his hand to calm him down and pull him out of it.

"Leo is the reason I don't have to take mental-health medications anymore," Larry said. "He gives me psychiatric therapy."

Larry left the service in 2000 after a diabetes diagnosis. Before his medical discharge, he served twice in Germany. He was trained in communications and as a cook. During Desert Storm, when troops deployed to the Middle East, he moved from reserve duty to active-duty status. "I was a replacement soldier, doing the job of troops who went to Desert Storm."

He stayed at the army barracks at Fort Belvoir Garrison in Virginia, near Washington, DC. "I'd go to the kitchen on base and help the cooks," he said. "There was a lot to do."

One of Larry's morning duties each day when he was stateside during Operation Desert Storm was to pick up a colonel at his hotel, drive him to the Pentagon, go to his own job, and then pick up the colonel from the Pentagon at the end the day.

"I had about five different jobs," Larry said. "During Desert Storm, we worked our butts off stateside."

Leo's job today is to manage Larry's life and to also serve as an ambassador for service dogs. Leo is so in tune with Larry that he can anticipate danger. In fact, Larry said, had he heeded Leo's warnings one winter day, he would not have broken his foot by slipping on his ice-covered driveway.

"I was in a rush to get to school," Larry explained. "Leo stopped, like he was saying, 'Do not take another step. You're going to fall.' I told him, 'Come on, Leo, let's go.' And again, 'Let's go,' but he wouldn't move."

Larry gave Leo the command to "follow," and his dog still would not budge.

"He knew it wasn't safe," Larry said.

But Larry didn't take Leo's warning seriously. Instead, he took another step, and the next thing he knew, he was flat on his back on his driveway. Leo licked his face as he lay there and then barked, but neighbors weren't at home to hear his pleas for help. It took a while, but Larry managed to pick himself up, stumble to the garage, and drive himself to the emergency room.

"Next time," he said, "I'll listen to Leo."

Leo's graduation from service training inspired Larry to return to school. Leo accompanies Larry to school, from which he'll soon be graduating with an associate of arts degree.

"When I was on the mental-health medication, I didn't go any-where," he said. But since Leo has been with him, Larry has been able to remain off of psychiatric medications and has found the strength to try new things. "Leo has helped me so much, you just don't know," Larry said. "I'm so relaxed and more calm now. I am a better person today because of Leo."

Larry isn't the only person who's been helped by Leo. Patients at a Veterans Affairs hospice ward look forward to Leo's visits three times a week. "When I take him there, they are so happy," Larry said. "Leo has public-access training. That means if I'm walking a patient in a wheelchair, Leo walks right beside my knee. He doesn't get out of step."

Leo extends his paw to patients and, if invited, jumps on their beds and lies down beside them. Mostly, Larry said, "All they want is to rub his head."

One patient in particular, Larry said, "was crazy about Leo." The feeling was mutual. "Once we got on that floor, Leo went straight to his room. Mr. Kato always had a big bag of treats for him." Leo would jump on Mr. Kato's bed, put his face next to his, and shower him with dog kisses. After Mr. Kato passed away, Leo still headed toward his room.

Leo might be a service dog, but life isn't all work and no play. Larry and Leo enjoy occasionally catching a movie at the local theater. Larry commented that Leo "sits right up in the theater with me and steals the show. People gather around us to ask about him."

Larry Whitted and Leo have come a long way since they first met. Leo had been abused by a previous owner before Larry's then-girlfriend rescued him three years earlier and gave him to Larry for his birthday. Larry had Leo with him for those three years before he heard about Veteran's Best Friend, while volunteering at the hospice ward. He applied to the program, Leo was accepted, and they began training with the group as a service dog team.

At first, he didn't think Leo was going to be accepted.

"The trainers didn't think he was going to make it. His tail was between his legs and he was timid," he said. "But not now."

The yearlong training wasn't just for Leo; it was also for Larry.

"I had to learn too," Larry said. "It was like doing homework. You can only train them for twenty minutes at a time because of their short attention span."

Leo did make it, and today, he and Larry have each emerged from their shells. It's as if they were meant to be together.

"I am so blessed to have Leo," Larry said. "He is the greatest gift I've ever received."

~~~

Vietnam veteran William "Buddy" Wachtstetter credits his service dog Hillary with making him feel less self-conscious about being in a wheelchair.

"People always see her," he said. "They don't see the guy in the chair."

Buddy, who lives in the San Diego area, had been in the US Air Force beginning in 1968, during the Vietnam War era. Two years later, while stationed on the island of Guam, he was injured while cliff-diving thirty feet, leaving him partially paralyzed. He's been in a wheelchair ever since.

"I wasn't in a dangerous part of the air force, but I managed to injure myself over a weekend," he said. "I dove off of a cliff and unfortunately dove too close to the edge from thirty feet up."

Buddy had obedience-trained a couple of Labrador retrievers over the years. Then, he learned about service dogs after he met a woman who raised and trained puppies for Canine Companions for Independence.

"I thought my dogs were pretty smart," he said, "but they would have been maybe seventh or eighth graders compared to Hillary. She's at college level. I trained exotic birds for Knott's Berry Farm, so I had a lot of training background. My Labs were amazing, but when I saw how dedicated service dogs are—they are at a whole different level."

Soon after, Buddy met Hillary, a Labrador retriever–golden retriever mix. She goes everywhere with Buddy, and the two are now inseparable. "She knows more than thirty commands. She's smart," he pointed out.

While he said he's used to the things Hillary does for him, the public is not.

"I was at a store and I was checking out. I swiped my credit card, and it went flying. I said, 'Hillary, get.' She picked it up off the concrete floor, brought it to me, and everybody around us started clapping. They'd never seen a dog do anything like that before."

At home in his front yard, they play fetch—just a man and his dog. But when Hillary's working, she pulls doors open, turns lights on and off, and opens the refrigerator.

"If I can't reach things, she gets them for me," he said. "She enjoys the tasks. She's always ready to help. Hillary does an awful lot for me, mentally as well as physically, keeping my spirits up. It's the look in her eye when she picks up something for me and pops it on my lap that says, 'Yes, I did what he needed.'"

He also appreciates the fact that when they're out in public, she removes the focus from Buddy to her, "because people with disabilities have a little bit of a self-conscious feeling that people are watching them, even if they're not."

After Buddy retired from his job at Knott's Berry Farm in Southern California, he became an ambassador for Canine Companions for Independence. He and Hillary travel the region, showing people what a service dog can do to help people with disabilities like him live independently.

He also became a photo editor for his wife Sherry's photo books. "Whatever book I'm working on, Hillary makes it into it," he said. "I take her on all the photo shoots. It's great to know she's so docile and always so well-behaved. She always brings out the best in everyone, even other people's dogs."

His advice to people with disabilities who are thinking about applying for service dogs: "Don't procrastinate as long as I did. Start the process. A dog will enrich your life. I'm never alone. When I go to a baseball game, I'm not by myself; I have a partner with me. I have a companion everyplace I go."

# CHAPTER 2

# Healing Heroes

Guide dogs, in addition to being trained and provided to German soldiers blinded in World War I, have also been used for military purposes in all wars since World War II. But the movement in the United States toward companion and helper dogs for war veterans really took root in the mid-1970s, when organizations known for providing assistance dogs to disabled children and adults began placing trained canines with service veterans.

There's growing support in the military and increasing knowledge among injured service members that trained canines are available to serve as part of their treatment regimen, including treatment for post-traumatic stress. Nonetheless, many military men and women, including officers who suspect they may suffer from mental injuries, still hesitate to go to the doctor for fear their diagnosis may be detrimental to their career.

Such was the case with Lieutenant Chet Frith, a navy officer diagnosed with PTSD. In fact, Chet was one of the higher-ups who, while in the service, had doubted the existence of the invisible post-traumatic stress injury. "I didn't believe PTSD was a real condition," he admitted. "Honestly, I thought people were making it up. I used to be part of the problem."

Chet was told he suffered from PTSD in 2011 after returning from a twelve-month deployment to Iraq as an "individual augmentee"—a roving replacement who filled in wherever he was needed.

According to the results of a RAND Corporation study released in 2013, nearly 20 percent of Iraq and Afghanistan veterans have described symptoms of major depression along with post-traumatic stress. This statistic, in addition to extensive records on treatment and follow-up with patients, proves that combat-related mental trauma is perhaps the best-documented psychological condition found in American service members returning from Iraq and Afghanistan.

Although it is now more widely understood and acknowledged, military-related post-traumatic stress is nothing new. History has revealed that PTSD, a mental condition that arises from exposure to life-threatening circumstances, dates as far back as World War I, when one result of trench warfare was termed "shell shock." In World War II, it was called "battle fatigue." And in Vietnam, it was referred to as the "thousand-yard stare."

Evidence from the RAND Corporation study suggests that these deployments—many involving prolonged exposure to combat-related stress over multiple overseas tours—take a significant psychological toll on soldiers. In fact, the mental and emotional impact may be disproportionately more damaging than the physical injuries of combat. The RAND study also reveals that slightly more than half of PTSD sufferers have sought help. Translated, it means that up to 170,000 active and retired military personnel silently endure the often-incapacitating symptoms of PTSD. Moreover, medical experts have acknowledged that the adrenaline rush from the fight-or-flight reaction to stressful situations can contribute to PTSD.

Chet Frith first noticed his symptoms about a month after the end of his deployment in Iraq. While at an aquarium park with his family, he felt overwhelmed by the crowds of people. He experienced nightmares and had difficulty relaxing at home.

Like Chet, marine veteran Nico Marcolongo also felt that his emotions were stifled after he returned home. "After spending a year in a combat zone, you can't return the same person," Nico said. "Your brain is wired differently. You experience so many close calls that you become emotionally numb." In combat, that numbness, along with demonstrating constant vigilance, made him "brave and strong." But when you return home in that mind-set, you're "considered abnormal," Nico said.

For Chet, who earlier had not believed in the diagnosis of an "emotional injury," it felt like his world was falling apart. He described his journey to staff at Navy Safe Harbor Public Affairs, noting that he found comfort in the presence of his service dog, also named Gunner, a golden retriever he adopted in November 2011.

Gunner entered his life during a time when Chet desperately needed support. Not only did Gunner help him to venture out in public and assist him when he interacted with people in social situations, including at parks, his dog also gave him hope. "Gunner reminds me every day that there's good in this world—that there's love. He shows me how to forgive and forget, and helps me relax in times of stress," he told Safe Harbor.

Chet now considers PTSD a treatable illness that should not end a career. If anything, he emphasized, it has made him a stronger person.

In April 2013, Chet shared on a national stage exactly how he felt about Gunner. He wrote, in a letter to his dog, that Gunner had entered his life when he desperately needed help, giving him the confidence he required to move forward. "You had my back and made me feel safe," he said in the letter that he read aloud on *The Jeff Probst Show*. "Most of all, you brought a ray of sunshine to me and my family."

———

Former Marine corporal Chris Lance, upon telling a higher-up that something was wrong, was told to get past whatever was bothering him—or else.

"My command told me I'd better stop faking it—that there was nothing wrong with me, and if I didn't snap out of whatever was going on with me and start being a Marine, they were going to court-martial me," Chris said. "Of course, I never snapped out of it, I never got court-martialed, and I never got disciplined."

Chris was a foster kid from an unstructured background. "When I was younger, my mother did drugs, so I lived with my father and my stepmother, and I ended up in a state custody battle. Everybody told me I'd never succeed in life."

To prove critics wrong, he joined the military. He wanted structure in his life and opportunities for a career. He came to this decision early on, after commercial airplanes hit the Twin Towers. "I knew right then and there that I wanted to join the military and get in front of that fight," he said. He was seventeen years old.

He eventually joined up in 2008, going to boot camp in California. After eight months of training, they stationed him in North Carolina. His first tour was in Japan, where he stayed for six months. He was then sent to North Korea where he went out on patrols.

After Korea, a tragic accident occurred before he went into combat while assigned to an amphibious assault vehicle stateside. It would wreak havoc on his life and cause his eventual medical discharge from the service.

"I worked on an Amphib craft," Chris explained. "It ended up sinking and I had to ride it down to the bottom of the ocean, and I was in charge of it." After helping people get out, he swam to the surface. "I thought I'd gotten everybody out," he said, "but I miscounted. There were still two people down there, and they ended up dying. I was in charge of them. I should have been the last one out. I thought I was. That affected me. I suffer every single night with nightmares."

Afterward, "about six months after I got back from North Korea," Chris said, "I ended up going to Afghanistan. I got ambushed while I was there; I got blown up. It created a mood disorder."

He was sent home, to Beulaville, North Carolina, where he was diagnosed with traumatic brain injury and post-traumatic stress.

"This is the ironic part," Chris said. "I came back and everything was fine and dandy, and the next thing I knew, I'm suffering from stuff."

A psychiatrist stepped into the picture. Right before Chris was to be medically discharged from the military, in 2011, he attempted suicide by overdosing on medication that put him in a coma for four days. He recovered and was discharged from the service.

"The way they medically retired me was, they drove me to the front gate of the base and dropped me off," Chris recalled. "I felt like everybody had turned their backs on me—people I fought with, people I didn't fight with, and people who were my friends."

"They say Marines stand by each other," he continued. "Well, they didn't stand by me."

His doctor eventually wrote him a letter that made him eligible for a service dog.

"I went through an agency that lost funding for me to have a service dog. I didn't know what to do, so I just waited." As is often the case, when one door closes, another one opens, and that's what happened for Chris. "My counselor said that in the best interest of my recovery and treatment, she recommended I get a service dog, and she suggested Canine Angels."

Chris recalled the first time he met Moses, his future service dog, at a park. It was in the spring of 2013. Rick Kaplan had a few other service dogs with him, including Ralphie, Diva, and Leroy. But they didn't pay any attention to Chris. Moses did.

"He leaned against me. I sat down at a picnic table and he laid his head on my shoulder. He and I were attached to each other immediately."

Moses was rescued from a home because his owner was going to prison. "He didn't want to give the dog to a family member because they were just as bad as he was. A veteran who lived across the street from Moses called Rick Kaplan with Canine Angels, and Rick picked him up from the owner."

"It feels very good having Moses," said the reserved Chris, who wears his light-brown hair high and tight in a standard Marine haircut. He's physically fit, which, at first glance, gives him the outward appearance of still being an active member of the armed services. Moses, a strikingly good-looking Australian shepherd with deep blue eyes and a fluffy black-and-brown coat, is intensely devoted to Chris.

"I respond better to people since I've had Moses," Chris said. "I've never felt this way about an animal. I have the same love for Moses that I have for my own children. I could not imagine being apart from Moses for even a couple minutes. I just couldn't do it. He goes with me everywhere I go. He has a place in my heart."

＊＊＊

Iraq War Marine veteran James McQuoid was desperate for help after returning stateside from a second tour of duty in Iraq. Even shopping for groceries was excruciating, sending him into a panic. The activity and noise levels were overwhelming, especially since any sudden sound could trigger his PTSD symptoms.

When he heard a child crying, he remembered kids screaming in Fallujah. Coins dropping in a cash-register drawer triggered a flashback to the sound of an ammo belt carried around the neck of a soldier. A can of food falling to the floor reminded him of a fifty-caliber casing hitting the ground. Turning into an aisle and seeing and hearing a stock clerk bending over boxes, stamping price tags, made him feel as if he were about to be shot.

"My mind is rapidly firing on all cylinders, trying to make sense of this weird new reality," James told CNN in June 2012. This is what happens in the mind of a war veteran who has PTSD, according to James. Without his service dog, Iggy, he said, "I would still be in my house; I would probably be divorced from my wife, and very estranged from my son."

James's PTSD symptoms continued until Iggy, a three-year-old shepherd mix, entered his life with the help of the Freedom Dogs organization. Now Iggy goes with him to the store. If James feels anxious, he drops to one knee and hugs his companion to feel her reassurance. If someone approaches him from behind in line, Iggy plants herself firmly behind James, giving him space. Thanks to Iggy, he has been able to move on with his life.

"I love this dog to death," he said. "She reminds me to have fun."

—◦—

Anger-management issues that damaged personal and professional relationships had plagued John Saathoff, a veteran of the Vietnam War, for years. He was prone to outbursts and flashbacks from his two-year combat tour as a paratrooper in Vietnam, starting in 1967. By 1982, with his life bottoming out, he sought help from a psychiatrist, who diagnosed him with post-traumatic stress. But John did not pursue treatment.

It was just two years after the American Psychiatric Association (APA) had published a standard diagnosis for people who became dysfunctional as a direct result of a traumatic experience. The VA did not accept the APA's *Diagnostic and Statistical Manual of Mental Disorders* for psychiatric service-related disabilities until 1986. Before then, military physicians diagnosed service personnel and veterans who exhibited signs of stress from trauma as having personality or obsessive-compulsive disorders, paranoia, or schizophrenia.

John suffered from the effects of PTSD for the next two decades. Then, in 2001, the VA granted him full disability. That was when he got his service dog, Jake. The large mixed-breed canine changed his life. They became inseparable companions, and John began to heal.

John is not alone in his wait for PTSD treatment. *Stars and Stripes* reported in 2012 that studies indicated the average military person with PTSD waits twelve years before being treated.

Now, veterans like John use psychiatric-service dogs to help them perform everyday tasks, from putting laundry in a front-loading washing machine to retrieving a newspaper from a front porch. For John, Jake has been instrumental in providing moral support to get him out of the house. Since his dog has been with him, he said he now feels independent enough to go out to dinner or to get-togethers at friends' homes. His is a remarkable recovery from a condition that had incapacitated this war veteran for nearly thirty-five years.

An example of support by the military is the presence of Erica inside the acute psychiatric ward at the Veterans Affairs Hospital in Fresno, California. Erica is the first facilities dog allowed into an acute psych ward, through the pilot program—a big step in acknowledging that service dogs do, in fact, help to heal the wounded.

Canine Companions for Independence bred Erica to become a service dog. At eight weeks old, she went to live for eighteen months with volunteer puppy raisers, Kathy and Mike Bennett, to socialize her with people and other animals, and to learn basic commands. "That's the biggest thing," Mike said, "to socialize them."

Wherever the Bennetts went, Erica went with them, including to their civilian jobs at the Space and Naval Warfare Systems Command, better known as SPAWAR, which is a military facility.

At the end of her socialization, Erica left the Bennetts for advanced training at CCI's training center in Oceanside, California. She was matched with David Balentine, a nurse at the Fresno VA hospital, to become a facilities dog assigned to the psych ward. She graduated as a psychiatric service dog in May 2012 and goes to work with David for four-day work weeks in twelve-hour shifts.

"Erica's on the inpatient psych ward and does amazing things," said Jack Shantz, a nurse and psychologist at the hospital. "She seeks out veterans. Her training is to soothe, comfort, and love them. It diminishes their anxiety."

It is unusual to have a facilities dog on the job as part of the regular workday. "I've been told she's the first and only service dog who goes regularly into a locked psychiatric unit," Shantz noted.

Another dog, Vivi, goes to work every day at the Fresno VA hospital too, but as a pet. Because she was diagnosed with diabetes insipidus, Vivi did not get to finish her advanced training. Instead, Jack helped match Vivi with Dr. Paulette Ginier, an endocrinologist at the Veterans Affairs Central California Health Care System, in the extended-care facility. Now, instead of working, Vivi has become Paulette's pet. In addition, after getting special permission, Vivi goes to work each day at the hospital with Paulette.

As for Erica and her job at the VA as a facilities dog, it has gone so well that Jack said he'd like to have five or six more facilities dogs working at the VA.

"I haven't done research with Erica," he said, "but the emotional and behavioral aspect is huge. We have some very psychotic patients at times, and most of the time she's out with the patients. The comfort level she brings is noticeable."

The Bennetts, who raised Erica, could not be happier about her success. "We are very proud of her," Kathy said. "We were so pleased when we were told she was going to the VA. Erica helping veterans is especially gratifying. Having worked for the military for over thirty years, I feel a bond with our military personnel. It feels like we're giving a little back to the veterans."

Kathy Bennett, who's worked for the military at SPAWAR as a civilian for more than thirty years, said she couldn't be happier that Erica is doing well helping veterans. Dogs like Erica are exactly why she and her husband, Mike, have been raising puppies for several years, letting them go when it's time for advanced training to start.

"Having Erica helping veterans is especially gratifying," Kathy said. "It's exciting to know she is part of a pilot program, the first service dog the VA has placed in an acute psychiatric ward. I hear she is doing great, and the veterans are responding well."

Kathy's hope is that Erica's placement at the Fresno hospital will lead to more facilities dogs being placed in VA hospitals so that "more veterans get the help they need and deserve."

"All eight of the dogs I have raised were raised at SPAWAR," she continued. "I wouldn't have been able to do this without the support of my command. Having Erica at the VA hospital allows me to show them that by allowing me to bring my dogs to work all these years, the military is getting something back for their support."

According to David Balentine, Erica's official handler, the dog is giving a lot back to the veterans. "She's a big comfort to them," he said.

The psychiatric ward doesn't have long-term patients. The average stay is three to four days, during which patients receive psychiatric care in a homelike atmosphere rather than a sterile hospital environment. Even having Erica lying on the floor in the dayroom as they watch TV adds to the patients' comfort, David said.

One morning in the dayroom, a patient sat with his head in his hands, his eyes closed, and his hands over his ears. "Erica went up to him, sat down, and within a few minutes he was petting her and I was having a conversation with him."

She's hard to resist.

"She looks up at the patients with those big brown eyes, and the patients calm down," David said. "It's fantastic. To watch this happen is the best job in Fresno."

And moments like this make David glad he switched careers midstream to become a nurse.

"I get a huge sense of purpose out of this job," he said. "That's why I went to school and became a nurse—to get a greater purpose in my life—and Erica is an extension of that. There is good in this world, and I get to see it. All Erica knows is people are nice to her, and she likes the connection."

David had heard talk that a facilities dog might be going to the veterans' hospital as a working canine. The idea of Erica as his teammate first came up when he discussed a patient's care with the head nurse of the ward, and she said to him, "Maybe you'd be good with a dog."

They were looking for someone at work to be Erica's full-time teammate. David had previously owned a black Lab mix named Beacon who died after spending thirteen years with him.

Having a dog accompany him to work was nothing new to David. Beacon had gone to work with him each day at the small auto shop he owned, before he finished school to become a nurse.

"I was having dog withdrawal," he said. "But no one at work knew about my dog. I named him Beacon because he had a little white tip on his tail, like a beacon in the night. He passed away in 2005. There was a seven-year gap, and here I am with a dog again."

Today, David said, "I work twelve-hour days, and so does Erica." A typical day as a facilities canine begins around six a.m., when Erica gets up and eats breakfast. She and David then go into the backyard so Erica can run around and play for a few minutes, and then David gets them both ready for work.

"Once I put the vest on her and my backpack is out, she knows we're going to work. When we get there, she walks around the nurses' station and says good morning to everyone. Erica likes other dogs, but she really loves people."

Once David reads the ward's morning report, they head down the hallway for the dayroom. As soon as patients see David, they ask, "Where's Erica?" Even though the typical stay in the psych ward is between three and four days, repeat patients get to know Erica.

"At first, they're amazed there's a dog on the ward. When Erica walks in, they say, 'Wow, look at her.' She's this beautiful honey-colored dog with a good disposition. I go around and talk to the people individually. She stays on the leash at all times, and I make sure that each person has an opportunity to interact with her. Some fall on their knees and start hugging her." When Erica attends group sessions, she walks around the room to each person so they can pet her.

"The military experience—and certainly combat—is profound," David noted. "It's a rough business. It can be traumatic. Just having Erica there is a comfort. She's like the family dog at the VA. She's making a difference."

He used the analogy of a mechanic's toolbox to describe Erica's usefulness. "I have a whole box of tools, but I don't use all of my tools all of the time. Erica offers a lot of tools, and one of them is comfort. The comfort she gives is always there."

It's not all work and no play for Erica at the hospital. She takes breaks outside, including playtime with Dr. Ginier's dog Vivi. "They've got a nice closed-in area, and they love each other. They run around and chase each other," he said.

Then it's back to work for both David and Erica. It's David's job to introduce new patients to the ward, and that's when the veterans first meet Erica. She sits in a crate, just in case a patient isn't used to dogs. "I say, 'I'm David. I'm your nurse,' and then I ask, 'Do you like dogs?'"

Everything within the ward is meant to soothe, including the soft interior wall colors, all geared toward easing the veterans' discomfort. "When people have anxiety to the point of distraction, Erica comes along and soothes them," said David. "She's a significant part of this overall environment on the ward, what we refer to as *milieu*. I watch her work with them and say, 'I couldn't have done that.'"

"All the king's horses and all the king's men, couldn't put Humpty Dumpty together again," he continued. "But Erica can get a patient happy and smiling."

# CHAPTER 3

# "Someone to Watch Over Me"

First Class Sergeant Connie Rendon was gravely injured in October 2004 during Operation Iraqi Freedom when, despite the odds, she survived an explosion. Riding shotgun in the seat next to her during the blast that hit her truck was a nineteen-year-old soldier Connie referred to as a "best buddy."

"I was much older," she said, "but we got to know each other like best friends. Age didn't matter. He told me about his girlfriend. We talked a lot. I felt as if he was looking out for me," she said.

Now, someone else—her service dog, Blaze, a standard black poodle who was raised in a prison—is watching over Connie.

"Connie is an amazing woman," said Lori Stevens, founder and executive director of Patriot PAWS Service Dogs, where prison inmates train the animals using positive-reinforcement techniques so the dogs will respond to voice and visual commands. In other words, the organization trains inmates to train dogs, including Connie's service dog Blaze.

Connie's story is one of survival in the face of life-threatening injuries and extreme circumstances. She looked death in the face, and she survived.

The tragic bombing happened after a US Army Reserve transport unit called her up in 2003 to deploy to Iraq as a transport driver. At the time, she was a physical education teacher. Soon, she was stationed at Camp Anaconda, sixty miles north of Baghdad in the Sunni Triangle.

They were on their way back to camp after delivering supplies to Taji, a rural district north of the city of Baghdad. They'd lost sight of their convoy.

"I was injured when IEDs went off. The blast fractured the right side of my face. My jaw—my mandible—was fractured." As Connie described it, a portion of her face was gone, and her hand was dangling and barely attached. "I'm still being treated for that. They were going to amputate my hand, but I asked them to try and save it, and they did."

Seven days later, she awakened to see her husband Hector and her father standing next to her bed.

"My husband told me I had just arrived from Germany," said Connie, an army reservist since 1988. "I had breathing and feeding tubes through my nose. My left lung collapsed because I'd broken my rib." That was the least of her injuries that occurred the night of September 8, 2004.

She has vivid memories of the accident. "I remember everything from when it happened until I was airlifted by Medevac." Then, she was out cold for the next seven days. "The next thing I recall is waking up at Walter Reed Medical Center."

Quietly, and in detail, Connie described the bombing.

"I was a truck driver on a night mission," she said. Halfway through that mission, she and her fellow soldier switched seats. "I noticed he was falling asleep, and I asked him if he wanted me to drive. He was tired, and we were waiting to get the okay to go back to our company. But we didn't have a radio. Nothing."

The explosion happened in the middle of the night while in a convoy with other trucks. "Maybe twenty-five to thirty minutes after we were on the road, we were driving alone, because we couldn't catch up with the truck in front of us."

Right before their truck ran over six explosive devices in the road, Connie glanced at her soldier friend beside her. "He looked so peaceful," she said. "I saw a glow around him just before the IED went off. He looked beautiful."

In a flash, she was pinned and gravely injured. The first thing she did was turn to look at her buddy.

He was gone.

Changing seats had proved to be a life-and-death decision.

"He got killed and I didn't," Connie said. "I was a squad leader, and he was in my squad. That made it harder. But I look at it like he was my guardian angel. He gave me the opportunity to come back to my family."

She knew she had to get out of the truck, but she was trapped.

"Because it was so dark and quiet, I could hear something dripping, and I thought it was fuel. I thought, 'The truck is going to blow up. Get the heck out of the truck before it blows.' My left hand was broken and my right hand was dangling. I was trying to hold my hand to my chest to keep the blood from flowing, to elevate it, because I wasn't able to put a tourniquet on my arm. I thought my hand was going to fall off. That's how bad it was.

"Here I was, stuck in the truck with my hand dangling and my face feeling like it had split wide open. I was all alone with no one to help me."

When she saw that the side window behind the driver's seat was missing, she somehow managed to wriggle her way out of the front seat. "I remember pushing myself all the way to the back. I slid out the window and climbed out of the truck. I hit the ground hard. But I was still holding on to my hand," she said.

Suddenly, help arrived, which felt surreal to Connie.

"Just like in the movies, out of nowhere, a truck pulled up and a soldier ran to me. It was pitch dark." The soldier hollered out for a medic, who jumped out of the truck and ran to her.

"It must have been the medic's first time seeing an injured soldier," she said. "I remember he started to panic. That's when my right arm started to really hurt. I remember the medic putting my hand on my chest. I remember my chin, because I had really bad damage to my face. I kept saying, 'Please, Lord, don't let me die.' I felt a big relief, like a hundred pounds had just lifted off my body, and that everything was going to be okay. I told myself, 'I've done my job here. I want to go back to work, I can do therapy.' That's what was running through my head. I kept saying that. I felt like God listened and a weight was lifted."

Medevac's Black Hawk helicopter arrived to airlift her out of the area.

"I was thinking, as I looked out of the side of the helicopter, 'It's time for me to go home and get my right hand back to working.' I knew I wasn't going to die and everything was okay. My job was done there," she said.

Her job before she left for Iraq, besides being in the US Army Reserve, was as a civilian employee for the navy. She was able to keep her job. "I'm a parts and tool-room attendant," she said. "I used to be a plane attendant. I worked on the flight line. I was a plane captain. But I can't do that anymore. My job was to marshal the aircraft in and out. You need two hands when they come in after a two-and-a-half- to three-hour flight. You have to guide them as they park, and you need both hands to do that. I was pretty blessed that they gave me something else and I kept my pay."

When she was back in San Antonio, Texas, with her husband and two sons, surgeons relocated arteries and tendons from one of her legs to reconstruct her hand. "They've labeled it a 'claw hand.' Half my arm is still numb. My hand looks messed up. But from what it was before, it's much better. It's amazing what technology can do. I had a good hand doctor. They sewed and attached my hand to my body and moved skin over it. It's called a flap." She added, with a laugh, "If you look at my wrist, there are stretch marks from when I was pregnant. And I used to be right-handed. Now I'm left-handed. I had no choice. I've learned to type with one hand."

By October 2006, Connie had been medically discharged from the army. Toward the end of her rehabilitation, following surgeries to repair her hand and jaw and therapy to deal with her PTSD, she heard about service dogs for veterans.

"Blaze picked me," Connie said of the standard black poodle trained by a prison inmate as a potential service dog. She and her husband went to the Patriot PAWS facility in Rockwall, Texas, to be matched with a dog. "My husband fell in love with him the first time he saw him," she explained. "He said, 'Pick the poodle, pick the poodle.' I told him, 'Honey, the dogs choose. I don't know if he'll pick me.' Sure enough, he chose me."

Two other candidates who were hoping to be matched with dogs joined Connie in a gym, and "they let the dogs loose to see who they'd go to," Connie said. "If another dog came near me, Blaze nudged them away. Each morning, Blaze looked for me. He'd wait to go to someone until I arrived, and then he'd come to me. Right off, we started working together. We clicked."

After she completed her training at the center and Blaze was officially matched with Connie, it was time to take him home. "The day I left with him, the inmates cried. Even the warden got emotional," she said. "A lot of the girls told me, 'We've done wrong, but we want to give back to the community.' It's therapy for them also."

When she left the prison with Blaze, "he was so happy. He didn't turn back and look. He was glad to be going home with me."

Today, in her job as a tool-room attendant for the navy, Blaze accompanies her to work. "If I drop a pen, I say 'Uh-oh,' and he picks it up." Also, paperwork needs to reach mechanics, and it's a hike for Connie to get there. "Sometimes I'll give Blaze a paper to take to a mechanic. I say, 'Go to Ron,' and Blaze takes it to him. I'm on light-duty work. I have restrictions. I can't walk everywhere."

When the smoke alarm system is tested at work and the alarm goes off, "we have to get out of the building," she said. "I have hearing loss, so I wear hearing aids. Blaze can hear the alarm and he's like, 'Let's go.' I can't hear it in my office. He looks at me like, 'It's time to leave. What are you waiting for?'"

She still has anxious and sometimes sad moments, because of the PTSD, traumatic brain injury, and all that she's been through. "All of a sudden, I'll start crying and someone will ask, 'What's wrong?' and I say, 'I don't know.'

"I'm in a lot of pain. Sometimes pain triggers the emotions. Blaze helps me and I start thinking differently when I start petting him."

Once home in the evenings, "the second I take off the vest, Blaze starts jumping up and down. He jumps so high. He's so happy to be home."

Blaze helps her off the job too. "I have sleep apnea," she said. "My husband works nights. One night, Blaze hit me on my chest to wake me up. I must have hesitated in my breathing."

Blaze is so popular at work that the union made him an honorary member, as mascot of the International Association of Machinists and Aerospace Workers, Local 2916. "The union brothers and sisters all voted him in as a member," she said.

In addition to assisting her up and down stairs—Blaze is tall, so Connie doesn't have to bend down to reach him for balance—Blaze has also helped her to regain her confidence.

"I used to not want people to see me, because of the way I looked," said Connie, referring to her disfiguring facial and hand injuries. Today, when Connie interacts with people, she is poised and self-assured.

"If you have a disfigurement, you're not used to it," she said. "By having a service dog, people look at Blaze instead of looking at me. I feel like I'm prettier now than when I was younger."

Retired army sergeant Major Jesse Acosta also had a catastrophic injury to his face and lost his sight with it during a mortar attack in a combat zone in Iraq. That was January 16, 2006. Forty surgeries and a service dog later, his face has been reconstructed and his life is intact.

Jesse said he gets more compliments now about his looks than he did before the attack. "People say to me, 'Gee, Sergeant Major, it took a bomb to make you good-looking.'"

The journey getting there was long. But as with Connie Rendon, his previous employer came through for him too. Jesse had been working for Southern California Gas Co. for twenty years when, as an army reservist, he was called to active duty and deployed to Iraq in November 2005 with the 63rd Regional Readiness Command headquartered out of Los Alamito. His unit was based at Camp Anaconda near Balad,

Iraq, which, he said, troops had nicknamed Mortarville, and where he supervised soldiers in his battalion.

Two months later, he was injured. The last thing he said he remembered was hollering, "Get down!"

Once he returned home, because of the extent of his injuries and the length of his rehabilitation, he was unable to continue working.

His circumstances began to improve significantly, however, when a surgeon, Captain Kevin Flynn at the Navy's Balboa Hospital in San Diego, made his face whole again. "My eyes were blown away," he said. "They had to reconstruct my sockets. They had to rearrange my nose. I was disfigured. There was nothing in my mouth because my teeth were knocked out. I can't taste or smell anything. Bone grafting was done."

After completing his treatments and therapy, "I didn't know what I was going to do or how I was going to do it," Jesse said in a telephone conversation from his Santa Fe Springs home in Southern California, where he lives with his wife, Connie Acosta. "I made it through all my surgeries, rehab, and therapy. I had to get back on my feet."

Then Jesse met a blind man who had a service dog. He recommended Jesse get one too. But the VA would not endorse his getting a dog. They told him, he said, that he was mentally challenged because his sentences were backward and his cognitive thinking was off.

He persisted, and at his new friend's urging, Jesse enrolled at a private school for the blind. "I went through my orientation and mobility class and passed," he said. The organization, based in Morristown, New Jersey, set him up with a service dog, and in November 2007 "I came home with my dog, Charlie Boy," a 125-pound German shepherd guide dog.

Once he began training with Charlie Boy, he said, "it was like night and day." With a dog for the blind assisting him, he was determined to participate in the world around him. He contacted his former employer, Southern California Gas Co., and they rehired him as a customer service field analyst. One of his job duties is to help the company improve its services for blind and vision-impaired customers.

He's grateful to be given a second chance after suffering such severe war injuries. "The gas company made it possible for me to get back on my feet," Jesse said.

And Charlie Boy keeps him physically on his feet. Because of balance issues from the brain injury, Jesse said his left leg doesn't work well. That is where Charlie Boy's skills come into play. "He guides me where I need to go," he said. "Charlie Boy doesn't let me run into things. My equilibrium is all jacked up. He keeps me upright, and I rely on him to keep me in a straight line."

Jesse gives his guide dog credit for a lot more than keeping him balanced. "Charlie Boy changed my world. He is my friend in total darkness."

Thanks to a couple of loyal service dogs that watch over him, retired army sergeant Clay Rankin has retained one of the most important elements of his life: his independence.

Clay, who sports a military crew cut, although it's now salt-and-pepper, served a quarter of a century in the military as a squad leader, combat military officer, and sergeant. He first joined the National Guard as a military police officer. While deployed during the Gulf War, he was exposed to sarin, a nerve agent used in chemical warfare, which caused him to lose his ability to sense hunger. "The more pain I'm in, the more it affects my liver." Despite the illness and injuries, Clay says, "I love my country. It's a side effect to combat. You never come back the same."

Statistics bear this out. From 1995 to 2005, combat veterans experienced the onset of new chronic diseases, such as what Clay has experienced because of his exposure to sarin gas. The illnesses, according to a report by the Iraq and Afghanistan Veterans of America, can cause functional impairment, chronic fatigue syndrome, and post-traumatic stress. Iraq and Afghanistan veterans may also suffer from Gulf War syndrome, a chronic multisymptom disorder caused by factors ranging from exposure to sarin gas and depleted uranium and smoke from burning oil wells to vaccinations and combat-related stress.

Clay served in Iraq in the early 1990s, and again in 2003, landing at Camp Udairi in northern Kuwait at the Iraqi border just as the ground war began. It was during the second deployment that his back was broken when he fell off a truck in Iraq. Undiagnosed, he stayed in-country.

"It's amazing I was able to continue in Iraq an additional eight months even though my back was broken. You have responsibilities to the people you're with," he said. He was examined before the military allowed him to stay on. "They didn't do all the tests to see if my spine was injured. They weren't concerned about the vertigo and the massive migraine headaches. The military's only philosophy at the time was simply identifying whether or not I could continue to go into combat. It's different today."

Throughout his career, he served in combat missions.

"You can only sustain those types of events for so long before it impacts you," he said. "Each time you're deployed to a combat zone, it changes you. It makes you a different person. I have a brain injury as well."

Clay received a Bronze Star with Valor for his actions at Camp Udairi, where he was credited with saving three hundred lives in a terrorist attack.

"I did what I did for twenty-five years, because I love my country. What happened to me is because I did what I loved to do. I came home [with injuries], and I'm okay with that."

Clay's physical condition continued to deteriorate after he returned home. Doctors gave him the bad news that he'd spend the rest of his days in a wheelchair. It was a medical prognosis he refused to accept. Little did he know at the time that it would be a service dog that would get him back on his feet again.

"Once they switched me over to the VA, I ran into some smart people in physical therapy who got me to the point where I started improving. Before that, it was downhill for a long time. I had a fall in the driveway; my wife was gone at the time, and we lived in the country. I was outside for six hours before I could drag myself inside." A therapist eventually helped Clay learn how to walk again.

While in physical therapy, Clay said, "I realized I was going to have to have a dog if I was ever going to be independent. My wife and I have been married almost thirty years now, and I was dependent on her. Doctors told me this is what is going on, and this is what you're going to live with," he continued. "Nobody was doing service dogs for veterans at the time."

After the army retired him in 2004, Clay discovered Lori Stevens with Patriot PAWS, who trains her dogs for twelve to eighteen months after they have been trained by prison inmates for three to six months. The group donated his first service dog, Archie, a black Labrador retriever, who became his helper and constant companion in 2006.

Clay worked as a liaison with the Army Wounded Warrior Program at the time, speaking at training seminars around the country. Archie, voted the ASPCA Dog of the Year for 2009, went with him, including on planes. One day, upon returning from a trip, eight-year-old Archie wasn't himself. He became lethargic, so Clay took him to a veterinary clinic. The dog's heart gave out, and Archie died in October 2009.

"I blame myself quite a bit for Archie," Clay said. "I thought it might have been too much traveling on a plane that did it."

After Archie's death, Clay's wife Stephanie wrote a post for the AW2 Blog, the official blog of the Wounded Warrior Program, detailing the impact Archie had had on her husband's life: "Archie was more than a service dog. He was Clay's companion, his freedom from a wheelchair, his courage to get up every day and live. Archie was there when the pain got to be overwhelming, when the nightmares visited, and when scenes from the past came unexpectedly crowding in. Archie was Clay's anchor."

Clay not only grieved the loss of Archie, but he also felt a huge void in his life, without a service dog to assist him. Still, at first he wasn't sold on the idea of getting a second service dog.

"I wasn't going to get a dog after Archie," he said. "I was done. I was back in the wheelchair." Ultimately, he realized he had no choice. "It was a matter of getting another service dog or giving up on life," he said. "Without a dog I had no independence. Archie was my primary caregiver." So he said yes to another dog.

Enter Harley Davidson. Four months after losing Archie, Clay Rankin took in the yellow Lab as his second service canine through Patriot PAWS, where Clay later became a member of the board of directors. In this capacity he helps veterans realize that although they may be severely injured, their lives are not over; they can continue living full lives with the help of service dogs.

Harley provides independence not only for Clay, but also for his wife Stephanie.

"The independence my wife has is she doesn't have to worry about me," he explained. "I don't relish going to the grocery store. Without Harley, I don't like it. There's nothing there I need so badly that I have to go."

Before his service dog, "I didn't want to be around people. I didn't like my anxiety going up and being on alert. Harley takes all of that away. If someone walks toward me, he puts his body between me and the person."

As dangerous as it was in combat zones, Clay had his battle buddies by his side; he felt comfortable in that atmosphere. In addition, he felt he needed to be there so that others didn't have to go. "The only place I felt normal was in combat," Clay noted.

"Those of us who were created to be warriors," he continued, "who didn't care about the money, who walked away from civilian vocations making $150,000 a year to make $30,000 to $40,000 a year, so other people didn't have to go—we were willing to deal with combat so others didn't have to."

His service dog has eased the side effects that come from years of battle duty. Harley's balance-training skills keep Clay upright and mobile, so that he doesn't fall. Harley also alerts Clay when his blood sugar is low and he needs to eat.

"Harley's my primary caregiver. Without a dog, I would have no independence. Without him, my wife couldn't leave me here at the house. I'd be in a wheelchair and she'd have to stay home with me," Clay said from his home in Clarksburg, West Virginia.

With all he's been through, he still counts his blessings.

"It was amazing I was able to continue in Iraq an additional eight months, even though my back was broken," Clay said. "You have responsibilities to the people you're with. We were in combat. I wanted to be there."

Clay's combat time in Iraq took its toll. Not only did he have a serious back injury, but he was also diagnosed with post-traumatic stress and a brain injury, on top of his toxic gas injuries from the Gulf War.

Clay's relationship with Harley, now a middle-aged, devoted yellow Lab, isn't the same as the one he had with Archie. "Archie and I were very tight too. It's different with Harley. Harley is mine," Clay says. "If my wife walks out of the room, Harley stays with me. I'm always concerned when I go to the hospital for surgery. He can't be with me in the operating room. He frets from the time I leave to the time I get home. If I walk into the backyard without him, when I come back, Harley acts like I've been gone three months."

Harley does a great deal for Clay. He senses when he has a glucose problem or his liver is acting up, alerting him by punching him with his nose or a paw. "He's a hundred pounds," Clay says. "When he punches you with his nose, you know it." Harley turns lights on and off, and hands money to store clerks for Clay. He also calms him during flashbacks and rouses him from nightmares.

"He helps me into bed at night," Clay said, "and he helps me out of bed in the morning. I grab his collar and pull myself up. Whatever I need doing, he can do. Harley helps me live a more normal life."

While Clay recommends a service dog for others who need them, he also points out the responsibility that goes with having one.

"It's a huge responsibility," he said. "These dogs need to go to the vet on a regular basis. They constantly use their backs and hips more than other dogs. You have to make sure they have good dog food—not the cheap stuff. You have to make the decision that you're willing to do what it takes. The doctor is constantly monitoring my condition. It's the same with Harley. I need to know what's going on with him. If he gets sick and he's down, then I'm down. I make sure I'm doing everything I can to keep Harley as healthy as possible."

Clay has experienced firsthand that Harley is much more than a service dog. "He's my friend," he says. "I count my blessings every day."

———

Retired corporal airman Donovan Mack didn't intend for his new puppy to end up being his service dog, but that's how it worked out.

He wouldn't have it any other way.

He took in Midnight after his grandmother's dog had puppies and she needed to place them. The timing was perfect.

"I got him about two months after I got back from Iraq, but I didn't train him. He was just a dog," he said. Midnight was a black Labrador mix that grew to be medium-size.

Meanwhile, Donovan had begun to show signs of post-traumatic stress after returning home from his ten-month deployment in Kirkuk, a town north of Baghdad and south of Mosul, where he'd spent his eighteenth birthday in September 2008.

After he returned in October 2009, Donovan noticed he no longer enjoyed going places. "I'd start shaking," he said. "I felt like I was getting sick to my stomach. I couldn't control it, so I'd stay home." He'd gotten married not long after his return, and he tried to cope with his anxiety, but he didn't have a way to manage it.

If he did go out, it caused him to go into panic attacks. "My mind started working," Donovan said. "I'd think about the little things, like how many people would be there, if we were going to a restaurant. I tried to deal with it by not eating. I was afraid I'd lose control of my body and get sick, so I figured if I didn't eat, I wouldn't throw up. That helped, but I wasn't eating enough and I wasn't getting proper nutrition. My body would get cold and I'd get the shakes."

He went back to school, and, once in the classroom, he was fine. "But the second the class was over, I'd have to think about how to get to the next class," Donovan said. "The hallways were only three feet across. Just the thought of walking down the hall would send my body into chills and I'd feel sick. It would set things off because I wouldn't eat that day. I was too nervous."

When he did manage to go out, he took photos of people. He said it made him feel safer and more in control of his environment to document the outings with images.

"My grandfather thought I was crazy," Donovan said. "He'd ask me, 'Why are you taking pictures?' My mom tried to get me to talk to somebody. I started going to a therapist. My therapist asked, 'Why don't you try a therapy dog?' I told him, 'I don't want to get another puppy and step on the toes of my dog Midnight.'"

Then Donovan's wife found the Veteran's Best Friend program, and the couple learned that the group would train both Donovan and his own dog. He took Midnight to meet Lisa Slama, founder of the organization. "They worked with Midnight, and he was amazing. She'd tell him 'Down,' and he'd lay down. Lisa said he did well, so I should bring him back in and see how he'd do again." He and his wife returned the following Sunday.

Midnight started catching on. "He didn't listen like he does now," Donovan said, "but he knew what I was kind of expecting from him." He and Midnight began going to five classes a week, which Donovan said took him out of his comfort zone because he had to drive forty minutes each way. All the while, he said, Lisa Slama gently encouraged him to continue.

Soon, he said, "I felt comfortable because everyone was a fellow veteran."

"Had I not gotten Midnight, things would be different," Donovan said. "Regardless of what's going on—say I'm doing homework and I'm getting mad because I can't figure it out—he can be in the other room and he senses something's wrong. He comes in, nudges me, and takes my mind off of whatever's going on. He looks at me like he's saying, 'I love you just because you're you.' That in itself is therapy."

# CHAPTER 4

# Life with Tali

The flight attendant announced the presence of the black Labrador retriever mix. "Ladies and gentlemen, this is Tali, a service dog for a military veteran injured in Iraq. They are flying with us today." The passengers aboard the coast-to-coast flight applauded as the attendant walked Tali down the aisle. Children and their parents patted Tali's back and head and scratched behind her ears. All the while, the dog's tail never stopped wagging.

Six-year-old Tali, a trained working dog, had spent her entire life—about forty-two dog years—in service to others. In 2008, more than a year after returning from his second tour of duty in Iraq, marine veteran Nico Marcolongo took Tali in as his assistance dog. Their hard work had just begun.

From all outward appearances, Nico does not appear injured. He is still muscular and looks just as fit as when he first joined the Corps. However, the career marine who achieved the rank of major is suffering from the mental affliction that has become all too common for US service members.

The injury became evident toward the end of Nico's second year in war-torn Iraq. Looking back, Nico never saw it coming. After his first tour in 2005, he returned to Iraq the following year and joined a reconnaissance unit near Baghdad, where the insurgency was especially active. It was the height of the Iraq War, with regular—and deadly—militia attacks against US forces and the transitional Iraqi government.

Nico described 2006 and 2007 as "bloody," with his learning curve "steep." He spent the first few weeks catching up on the progress of the war, yet as commander, he was simultaneously responsible for keeping the infantry of Marines in his charge safe in a geographical area the size of South Carolina. He tracked intelligence about insurgents from Syria through the south, Rahl to the north, and to the remote Camp Korean Village in the southwest, near the Syria-Iraq border.

Nico's unit shared information with other Marine units, as well as with the army. All the while, the troops under his command continued their intensive training, preparing for the worst.

With the gathered intelligence, Nico knew that some sort of event was going to happen; he just didn't know the exact day or time when the next suicide bomber would appear, or when the next IED would go off. What he *did* know was that people were going to die, and he had no way of stopping it. That was the toughest part for Nico: He was powerless to prevent the next attack. Over time, this anticipation—coupled with an average four hours' sleep each night—started to take its toll. The effect would be far greater than he could know.

While in the battle zone, Nico desperately missed his family. As his second tour neared its end, he was overwhelmed with excitement about reuniting with his wife Lisa and son Rocco.

Once on American soil, however, life was not at all what he had envisioned.

Along with other wives and family members waiting at the US Marine Corps Air Ground Combat Center at Twentynine Palms in California's Mojave Desert, Lisa Marcolongo watched the roadway for the military bus carrying her husband. The moment she saw him step off the bus, she recognized the changes. She noticed the faraway look in his eyes, the wariness in his demeanor, and a disconnection she had never seen before. While his fellow Marines hugged and kissed their loved ones, Lisa just got a quick pat on the back from her husband. Nico tried to smile, but he couldn't.

Lisa was hit hard by her husband's underwhelming reaction upon seeing her, especially after being apart for nearly a year. Nico kept his guard up as though it were a protective military armor. He could not bring himself to force a feeling of joy when he felt none.

Once back in the States, Nico did not feel at home. Since it was his second time returning from Iraq, the new feeling—or, rather, the lack of feeling—took him completely by surprise. He couldn't quite put his finger on it. Had he become a war junkie, needing that adrenaline rush of deadly bombs and gunfire to feel alive? He had returned home a different person from the man he'd been before Iraq, but he didn't know how to bridge the gap. He seemed a mere shell of the man Lisa had married: cut off from his family, fearful, distant, consumed by a war within.

"I don't think the problem caught up with me until the end of the deployment," he explains. "They told me I had depression anxiety, and I didn't know what it was."

It was post-traumatic stress disorder, or what Nico calls post-traumatic stress *injury*. Unlike many of the physical wounds of war, PTSD conditions are often invisible—not only to society as a whole, but also to other service personnel, friends, family members, and even parents and spouses. These mood- and behavior-changing scars of war often go unrecognized, unacknowledged, and untreated.

What Nico experienced was a shock in two very big ways. The first consisted of his confusion and helplessness. The second was the threat to the well-being of his family.

He arrived home feeling no love for his wife or son—not even the barest connection to the two people he had missed so dearly while in Iraq. Worse still was that he was unable to accept the love that had sustained him through his war years.

Nico was sad. At the same time, he was angry and suspicious. Worst of all, he was devoid of joy. And he couldn't figure out why.

Lisa stood by her husband as he fought against the demons of combat. But she also knew how difficult the adjustment was for their son Rocco, who was barely four years old at the time. When Rocco hugged or kissed his father, Nico froze. He was completely numb. It was as if he knew that if he opened himself, his heart, even a bit, he would be immediately engulfed in profound, devastating emotions. It was safer to feel nothing.

Rocco was too young to understand, but old enough to feel hurt and rejected. The father he had missed so much was now unresponsive to him. Once, not long after Nico returned home, Rocco told his mother, "Daddy's still in Iraq." The young boy perceived that his father was present in body, but not in spirit. He realized instinctively that in many ways, his father was indeed still in the combat zone.

As far back as he could remember, all Nico Marcolongo had ever wanted was to be a marine—not a member of just any of the armed services, but an elite Semper Fi warrior. The reason never changed; to him, they were the toughest. At six years old, he was glued to the film *Sands of Iwo Jima*, starring John Wayne. At eight, his father took him to Camp Pendleton, the Corps' largest training facility on the West Coast, to watch live-fire artillery training exercises from a distance. He was hooked. Instead of playing cowboys and Indians with his friends, he pretended he was a member of a battalion in combat. He wanted to be a hero, the biggest and bravest. As a teenager, he continued his quest by learning all he could about the history of the Corps.

He never thought of doing anything else—except football. After college, he played professional football in France. In 1994, he joined the US Marine Corps as a second lieutenant. He met Lisa through family friends on New Year's Eve, 1998. Aware of his dedication, she embraced the military way of life.

Later, in 2007, when Nico returned from Iraq the second time, he tried to reintegrate into the life he'd left behind, despite his feelings of detachment. But Nico couldn't readjust. The disconnection propelled him into a post-traumatic-stress purgatory that left him feeling completely alien, not only in society, but even in his own body. Socializing was nearly impossible. Mundane tasks like going to the supermarket seemed like a life-and-death struggle with which he, along with many fellow veterans with PTSD, couldn't cope.

Nico now waged his war mostly from within. Vivid flashbacks of the horrors he'd experienced in Iraq invaded his mind, suddenly making him aware that all the discipline of his military training couldn't protect him from the haunting images that typically arise in the consciousness of PTSD sufferers. The memories were often accompanied by intense anger, fear, and guilt, along with phobias, panic attacks, nightmares, or a generalized sense of dread.

Nico's experience, though intense, was typical. Post-traumatic stress sufferers try to avoid situations that might trigger their symptoms, withdrawing into a protective cocoon in an attempt to shut out the memories and feelings. They feel empty, lonely, and misunderstood; their anxiety gives rise to mistrust and deadened senses. They can be moody, jumpy, and distracted, as well as easily startled, and they may overreact to common stresses. They often neglect personal hygiene. Many wind up homeless. And an increasing number of PTSD sufferers consider suicide as a way out of their having to live in perpetual distress.

Nico's major symptom was a feeling of detachment from everyone around him. His way of coping was to avoid at all costs social settings, especially parties and crowded stores and shopping malls. Ironically, his military training had focused on being where the action was, but the ethic of discipline and bravery of a Marine in battle did not equate with the uncontrolled horrors of recall that had their way with him now that he was far away from combat. In the war zone, the ethic had its place. Back home, it wreaked havoc on his mind, with no way, as far as Nico knew, to turn it off.

Now, the memories of that combat action manifested in living nightmares. As an example, soon after Nico arrived home and drove his car for the first time, he ran over a pothole in the road and instinctively ducked. He was conditioned for combat, for what the military calls "condition orange" (on alert) and "condition red" (ready for battle). The automatic response from that one short drive was so emotionally draining that he was disinclined to venture out again. He spent most of his time at home, inside, a virtual recluse.

His final tour had been much more stressful than he had realized. And as a Marine, he had not been trained to ask for help for what he initially perceived to be an admission of weakness.

He knew intuitively that he needed to be evaluated to see exactly what was wrong. He was wounded—the direct result, he later learned, of the deep psychological rifts of war that needed to heal. Worst of all, because of his debilitating depression and anxiety attacks, he was unable to deploy again. On February 15, 2008, after fourteen years of service and a year after returning from war, Major Nico Marcolongo was given an honorable discharge from his beloved Marine Corps. He could no longer avoid the fact that treatment was imperative.

Treatment for Nico ultimately came in many forms: support groups, counseling, therapy—and a service dog named Tali.

Tali was born on August 3, 2006, at the headquarters of the nonprofit Canine Companions for Independence in Santa Rosa, California, with the purpose of becoming a service dog. She was taken to Colorado to stay eighteen months with a puppy raiser to learn basic skills. In early 2008, a grown-up and well-behaved Tali arrived at the CCI facility in Oceanside, California, for several additional months of training with instructors and behaviorists.

At the end of that stint, Tali passed her tests and became a full-fledged service dog. She became one of the elite; only 45 percent graduate to become service dogs. Those who don't become K-9 working dogs are placed with law enforcement or as therapy dogs. Some go back to their puppy raisers to live as their pets.

Tali was ready to be placed upon graduation, but she was particularly special and needed to be paired with that perfect human partner who needed her specific skills.

That same year, during an open house for veterans at the facility, Nico learned about service canines. It was there that he saw Tali. After they were introduced, Nico discovered what he calls "the healing power of dogs." When Nico and Tali met for the first time, it was an instant connection and a life-changing moment. He could see that not only was Tali not bothered by loud noises and quick movements, but she could also be a companion to his wife and son—a family dog in addition to a service dog. Nico and Tali began training together so Nico could learn how to handle her and she could get used to working with him.

As an example, Tali was conditioned to run interference while they were in stores together. She would plant herself on the floor behind Nico, between Nico and any approaching shoppers. At a restaurant, she would sit under his chair, ready to assist him while also making him feel more secure. She would become a surrogate replacement for Nico's battle buddies. With Tali by his side, he gradually regained his self-confidence and a personal sense of security. The trust and affection soon flowed both ways between the dog and her handler as they looked out for each other.

Once he acknowledged that he had PTSD, Nico Marcolongo made a commitment to help himself first, and then others. He wanted to ease the suffering and encourage the healing process for those going through what he had experienced firsthand, to do something, he said, "that matters." He landed a full-time position overseeing Operation Rebound. This program, which he manages through the Challenged Athletes Foundation, provides post-rehabilitation support via involvement in sports for American troops who have suffered physical, mental, and emotional injuries in recent conflicts. Sports activities, he found, re-create the teamwork and military-like camaraderie the vets sorely miss in their lives and provide a healing effect. Tali became part of that sports world, including hanging out at the beach with veterans who enjoy surfing.

Nico began to feel whole again, comfortable in his own skin. With treatment, caring love, rewarding work, and training with Tali, his feelings for his wife and son began to return, and he slowly emerged from his shell.

Then came the day for Tali to move in with the Marcolongos. It was September 2, 2008, a Tuesday. The weather was sunny, the sky blue. Nico was about to officially adopt Tali.

He pulled into CCI's campus parking lot, stepped out of his car into the sunlight, surrounded by trees and grass in a wooded area of the coastal town, and made his way to the front door. He knew that Tali was inside, waiting. As soon as he saw her, he recognized that he was one step closer to gaining back the sense of security he had lost in Iraq. It gave him a sense of peace.

The homecoming was made even more special because it was his son Rocco's fifth birthday. On that day, Tali not only became Nico's constant companion, but she also became a member of the Marcolongo family.

Once she had settled in with the Marcolongos, Tali began accompanying Nico to the Operation Rebound center each day, offering the same unconditional love and support to veterans that she gives to Nico. Like other service dogs, she isn't intimidating; once her blue service dog vest is on her back and snapped around her chest, Tali is in uniform, in working mode. Nico too, wears an Operation Rebound uniform as he speaks to people and goes about his work at the center. For him, it's a shared experience. He and Tali are teammates.

Surfing is one of the sports offered through Operation Rebound, in concert with the Naval Medical Center at Balboa Hospital. At a surf clinic, held once a week at a Del Mar, California, beach, Tali accepts that Nico gets busy instructing, and that she can't stay by his side the entire time. "We have an understanding of each other's needs and moods. She knows what her mission is. She knows when I'm working and what her role is," Nico said.

That means comforting not only Nico, but others too. At the beach, Nico might give a veteran a brief lesson in dog training cues—sit, stay, down, come. Then the vet is welcome to take Tali for a walk down the beach while Nico instructs surfers at the water's edge. "They're not alone because they have a dog with them," Nico pointed out. "There's immediate trust. A dog forces them to look outside themselves."

Nico and volunteer surf buddies work mostly with amputees, those with spinal cord injuries, and active-duty service members. With her tail wagging nonstop, Tali appeared very much at home with everyone she met during the surf clinic.

On an overcast Thursday morning at the Del Mar beach, Nico chatted with Dave Rayder, a Vietnam vet who wears a prosthetic in place of the leg he lost fighting the Vietcong in the 1960s. As they talked, Tali sat at Dave's side, lapping up the attention. Dave, a former sergeant in the 101st Airborne Division, served on the front lines in Vietnam.

"I was barely six months there before I got zipped," he said as his prosthetic knee bent and he knelt beside Tali to pet her. He counts himself lucky, he said quietly, as he continued petting Tali. "I have friends who never came home."

Dave spent the next ten months at Letterman Army Hospital in San Francisco. Today, he works with a Wounded Warrior Battalion in San Diego.

Also on the beach with Dave that day was volunteer Bob Bishop. They were standing on the sand, watching two spotters with a veteran who'd lost an arm and two legs in combat. The vet was about to surf on his belly using his one hand to ride a specially made, extra-wide surfboard. The veteran held the board with his remaining arm while a spotter in the shallow seawater ran beside him. The vet caught a wave and rode it to shore, and then the spotter turn him around so they could head into the ocean to catch another wave. All the while, everyone on the beach that morning had smiles on their faces.

"There are no sad people here," Bob noted as he watched the scene play out in front of him. "You look around here and there are nothing but happy faces."

Nico agreed as he stood on the beach watching another injured active-duty service member, this one a woman, paddle, catch a wave, and then stand up on the board without falling. Excitedly, Bob said, "She's up on the board. That's the first time." Seeing the accomplishment firsthand nearly brought him to tears. "It's moments like these that we strive for—that they can do anything they desire. The first step to getting better is they have to want to get better," he said.

In that same vein, as supporters for veterans, once a week Tali and Nico head to the San Diego Naval Medical Center where they meet injured service members, many fresh off the battlefield, who are missing limbs. There to provide comfort for them, Tali, if invited, jumps up on their beds to cuddle. Many of the patients eventually move on to the surf clinic. On weekends, Tali and Nico participate with physically challenged veteran athletes in other sports activities, including triathlons, road races, and flag football.

For Nico, one of the biggest benefits of having Tali is her calming effect. "She grounds me, and I'm never alone," Nico explained.

The steadfastness of his wife Lisa also helped to bring Nico back from the emotional abyss. "I wanted so badly to get that happy side back," Nico said. Seeing his son's "smiling face every day" helped in this regard. And Tali's presence and confident demeanor served as a safety net, assisting his reintegration back into civilian life by breaking through the barriers he'd erected between himself and the outside world. Had this not happened, Nico admitted, "I might still be stuck in the house."

It took Nico several months to admit that he needed help for post-traumatic stress. At the same time, his diagnosis ended his military career prematurely, putting him out of a job.

But that was then, and this is now. Today, Nico is no longer emotionally shut down. He can feel again. "That's the most precious thing," his wife Lisa noted. And while he's not "cured," because the invisible wounds of war will always be with him, the symptoms are not nearly as severe as they once were.

Since they've been together, Nico and his dog Tali have rarely been apart. Tali makes sure to keep him in her sights. At home, if Nico goes upstairs, Tali follows him. On the rare occasion he leaves the house without her, upon his return, she runs to the door to greet him. At night, she sleeps in a crate next to Nico's side of the bed. To relax, connect, and let Tali have downtime from working, Nico plays with Tali and Rocco in their backyard, tossing balls for her to chase.

During a recent game of toss, Lisa watched contentedly, and then said, "Nico and Tali are spiritually connected. They're at home with each other."

# CHAPTER 5

# "From the Front Line to the Finish Line"

Retired army staff sergeant Sam Cila joined the New York National Guard when America was still reeling from the aftershocks of September 11, 2001. His father, a Marine, and his grandfather, a World War II army veteran, inspired him to enlist. "It was a no-brainer for me," Sam commented.

At twenty-seven years old, he was not a typical enlistee. "I thought, 'Why is it okay for an eighteen-year-old to join and not for a twenty-seven-year-old?' I was physically fit, and I joined because I felt it was right."

Sam's decision to enlist and fight terrorism overseas was not always easy for his wife, Anna. "It was hard, definitely hard, him being gone," she said in an interview for a military website. "I remember our son Sammy saying that his dad was going to get the bad guy." Their grade-school son, in the same interview, said, "Every night I'd always say a prayer for him and say, 'Dad, I hope you come home. I hope you don't get hurt.'"

Sam did not anticipate being injured, especially with Anna and their two children Evan and Sammy waiting anxiously for his safe return. All he'd wanted to do was fight for his country.

He joined the army and eventually became an active-duty guard and a trained sniper. In October 2004, three years after enlisting, his unit, the Fighting 69th Infantry Regiment's 1st Battalion out of New York City, deployed to Iraq for a yearlong combat tour.

His tour was cut short by a few months when, on Independence Day 2005, he and a handful of soldiers went on patrol in an area of

Baghdad just outside the Green Zone, considered a hot spot for IEDs and car bombs. "We had seen a suspicious object," Sam said, so he and his captain got out of their vehicle and walked next to it to try and see where the triggerman might be hiding. "We must have come right up on him, and he detonated it."

The blast blew out much of his left side, including his brachial artery, most of his left arm, bicep, and tricep. The quick action of a medic with a tourniquet saved his life.

At Walter Reed Army Medical Center in Washington, DC, he underwent more than forty surgeries to repair the damage. The wounds left him with limited mobility in his left arm and no use of his left hand. By 2008, after trying nearly three years to save his hand, doctors amputated it because of irreparable nerve damage. When a visitor one day said to him that he was sorry, Sam gave him his standard answer, "It's okay. It was part of the job."

He believes that wholeheartedly. He took the risk, and was recognized for his combat service when the military awarded him the Purple Heart. Injured and unable to remain in the service, he had difficulty leaving the military that had become so much a part of his life.

"In the beginning at Walter Reed," Sam explained, "I was separated from my team, my uniform, the war, and suddenly I'm in a hospital bed in my hospital gown, with nothing around me that I was used to." Most of all, he said, "I was without my teammates."

The transition took a lot out of him. "I built up an addiction to my medication. I lost about a year and a half of my life just being miserable, depressed, and addicted to painkillers," he said.

Nothing his wife did could help him get past what he faced each day. "I knew something was wrong with me inside," Sam said, "but I didn't know how to deal with it."

After fourteen months as an inpatient and outpatient, he left Walter Reed for his home in New York. "That sudden change from combat to a hospital, and then from a hospital to full-on civilian life with no one to talk to, was difficult," he noted.

It was during a trip he took to San Diego in 2008 that his friend Nico Marcolongo introduced him to sports through Operation Rebound. Soon after, he began racing bicycles and competing in triathlons.

Nico also introduced him to his service dog Tali.

"I watched how Tali interacted with other people and how she interacted with kids. That started the ball rolling in my mind to get a service dog of my own," Sam said.

By 2010, Canine Companions for Independence's northeast center, in Medford, New York, had matched Sam with Gillian. Since then, he and Gillian have visited patients in veterans' hospitals, including Walter Reed Army Medical Center, where Sam spent so many months recovering from his own injuries.

Sam cited a particular visit as an example of the impact Gillian and other service dogs have on wounded warriors. It was a day when he and Gillian, a large, black Labrador retriever, were at Walter Reed with CCI executives Debbi Duarte and Corey Hudson, visiting troops inside the hospital. Afterward, they cut across the grounds and happened upon an army private first class, practicing on his new below-the-knee prosthetic while using two canes for balance. When the soldier saw Gillian, he asked if he could pet her.

"The next thing we knew," Sam said, "the soldier got down on the grass and wrestled with her. Once he was up, he took her on a twenty-minute walk, without his canes. He forgot about them and just started walking a dog. It was the natural order of things. It shows that dogs make you more active and more physical."

For Sam, it was a seminal moment. He knew then that Gillian could help even more veterans. He wanted to volunteer as an ambassador for CCI, to let others know by example how much of a difference a service canine can make in their lives. "She's helped me live a productive, positive, active life. She can help other vets live that way too," he said. "I've seen firsthand the power of how service dogs change lives for the better—the emotional and physical peace they give. Gillian was trained as my service dog, but she also gets used as a facility dog because of the outreach I do."

Sam is now a retired staff sergeant who competes with fellow wounded warriors through the Challenged Athletes Foundation and its Operation Rebound program. As a spokesperson for the group, he volunteers at and participates in events for injured veterans, and has reached the status of an elite-level athlete.

One elite event he participated in was a three-day, 100-kilometer mountain-bike ride hosted by former president George W. Bush. It took place in April 2012, in the remote Texas desert. Bush bicycled the three days with fourteen men and women who had been seriously wounded in Iraq and Afghanistan while serving in the US military.

"I spent one-on-one time with President Bush and his staff," Sam said. "We went to his ranch. It was a great experience. Gillian was with me. I continually try to help men and women of all services and wars. We grow mentally and physically when we step outside of our comfort zone. If I continue to do that, I'm hitting the mark."

His service canine has helped him to reach the goals he's set for himself.

"Gillian has been a huge part of helping me grow," Sam said. "She took what I was doing in a new direction and helped me branch out. I use my right hand for everything, and my right shoulder, and if she can take a small percentage of that workload, it helps a lot. I can do things, but I may have Gillian hold the door open for me. It's just different. It's powerful for me, day in and day out. She's helped my family. I could never have scripted it the way it's happened. If one of my kids drops something as I'm getting them out of the car, Gillian picks it up. She's a tremendous help."

While it hasn't always been easy, Sam knew things could only get better, and that is what he shares with veterans who are where he once was. "I wake up in the morning and think, 'If I can help someone's life—because I know there's someone lying in a hospital bed who needs help—then I will.' I tell them, 'You can do the same things you used to, only differently, but still at a high level. It's worth it.' It really comes down to an individual choice of accepting what is different. It's not easy. It doesn't happen overnight. They have to accept it and figure it out. A service dog is a great way to figure out how to do things in a new way."

With Gillian by his side, Sam, who maintains the physique of an Ironman competitor despite his injuries, looks toward the future and doesn't look back. The Paralympic Games are on his horizon. He's also a two-time member of the USA Paratriathlon National Team, an Ironman World Championship finisher, and a high-altitude mountaineer.

Also on his mind is encouraging more service members to participate in life and be active. "I'm a big believer that a dog can bridge the gap to living a healthier lifestyle. I don't care what service dog agency it is or what path the dog comes from," Sam said. "From the front line to the finish line—that's Operation Rebound's slogan—taking men and women from the hospital room out into the physical life. It's had an impact on me. I live by that motto."

Like other loyal wounded veterans, he would not change a thing if he had it all to do over again. "Joining the service was a good decision," Sam said. "Getting injured wasn't in the plan, but I don't regret it. It's made me a better man. It's made me physically stronger. Gillian has been a huge part of it. She's been a powerful piece of my life."

"I don't see Gillian as a service dog," Sam continued. "She's a teammate. She does all the same things a teammate does. She comforts me in stressful situations. She's my battle buddy."

❧

A service dog named Gabe means just as much to former army sergeant Justin Lansford. An amputee veteran from the war in Afghanistan, Justin is an ex-high-school football player with an athletic build. "I owe everything to Gabe," he said. "I would jump in front of a bus for him."

On an April day in 2012, Justin was working as a turret gunner with the 82nd Airborne Division's 2nd Battalion, 504th Parachute Infantry Regiment, on a recovery mission to assist a unit with a broken-down vehicle. On the way, their vehicle hit a roadside bomb, flipping the truck on its back. Justin was pinned under the top of the mine-resistant, ambush-protected vehicle.

Because a firefight had broken out, and along with it, total chaos, Justin couldn't be freed from under the truck right away. It would be hours before they could remove him from the situation.

It was bad enough that ground combat prevented him from being rescued, but then the truck pinning Justin caught fire just as mechanics arrived at the attack site and medics began treating him. The fire was extinguished, and heavy equipment was used to lift the wreckage high enough off the ground to pull Justin out.

He was in grave condition and was airlifted from the battlefield to an air base hospital before being flown to Germany's Landstuhl Regional Medical Center, where the majority of injured American soldiers were transferred from the Middle East. The explosion had destroyed much of Justin's left leg, and doctors had to amputate above the knee. He also lost his spleen. On top of that, the blast had crushed his right ankle, fractured both femurs, damaged his back, lacerated his liver, punctured both lungs, cracked multiple ribs, and fractured his nose.

It didn't look good. During surgery, his heart stopped and doctors had to resuscitate him. He was placed on a ventilator because of the lung and chest injuries, and he was in a coma. Back home, Justin's parents understood the severity of his injuries all too well. His mother Kimberly worked as a trauma nurse, and his father Rick had retired after twenty-five years as a paramedic.

Against all odds, Justin survived.

His recovery, much of which took place at Walter Reed Army Medical Center, was helped by regular contact with his company commander, who called him often while the company was still deployed. "They worry about you, and you worry about them," Justin said at the time. "It's important for everyone to keep in touch."

On November 3, 2013, twenty months after the roadside bomb turned Justin's world upside down, the Maryland-based nonprofit Warrior Canine Connection graduated its first class of service dogs matched with veterans. Included were Justin and his striking orange Irish setter Gabe.

The bond between Justin and Gabe was evident during the graduation ceremony. Gabe stood on the stage with his trainer, anxiously watching and wagging his tail as Justin walked across the space to greet them. It was a special moment when the trainer handed the leash to Justin, officially giving the soldier his new service dog.

Even though Justin was well on his way to a physical recovery, he still faced challenges.

"It was really hard to go back into public places," said Justin. Once he had Gabe, however, he ventured out more, even finding new places to go. Justin is reassured by the fact that when Gabe is wearing his vest—inscribed with the words "Do Not Pet"—he is in full working mode. "I ended up going with Gabe on the Metro. We went to a grocery store. I can lean on him as a brace. He can open doors. He can do anything I need."

# CHAPTER 6

# MST: Healing the Wounds

A stress disorder related to—but not as widely known as—post-traumatic stress is military sexual trauma (MST), a form of sexual assault ranging from unwanted sexual contact to rape that occurs while a person is in the military.

Michelle Covert, who lives in Mansfield, Ohio, was in the army from 1980 to 1984, during which time she was sexually assaulted but did not immediately report it. As a result, she suffered from PTSD for twenty-four years before she realized it had a name.

According to the Department of Defense, 86.5 percent of violent sexual assaults are unreported. A 2013 794-page study revealed that military officials must do more to prevent these attacks. Mandated by the 2008 National Defense Authorization Act, the Institute of Medicine's study describes what troops faced upon their deployment to Iraq and Afghanistan. More than 21 percent of female soldiers reported military sexual trauma (MST), compared to fewer than 2 percent of men. The research suggests that as many as 45 percent of female troops experience some form of MST during their military career.

The report recommends a zero-tolerance policy toward MST be strongly enforced by using current rules of conduct, developing new policies and standards, and ensuring that effective handling of sexual assault complaints is a mandatory part of performance reviews and promotion guidelines.

The military sexual assault against Michelle Covert happened the night before she was to graduate from the service's advanced individual training program, when a drill sergeant raped her. Confused and distraught after the attack, she kept silent. She moved on to a civilian career, eventually going to work for a veterans' hospital. She tried to put it behind her, but she was unable to shake the cloud of gloom that shrouded her life.

Years later, a fellow veteran, at the hospital for treatment of his PTSD, noticed that Michelle broke into tears after a routine interaction with a patient, having what appeared to him to be a panic attack. The veteran said, "I've been watching you. You've got what I've got."

Not long thereafter, Michelle had a severe meltdown. This, along with the veteran's observation, convinced her to seek help.

Only then did she begin to understand that the rape—now termed *military sexual trauma* by the VA—was the cause of her long struggle with post-traumatic stress. At the same time, she accepted that the attack had not been her fault. In addition to psychotherapy, Michelle looked into getting a service dog. Several months into her treatment, she adopted Flower, a young Labrador retriever.

Flower was specifically trained to sense anxiety in Michelle before it turned into full-blown panic. The dog also learned to recognize when Michelle was in the midst of an anxiety attack.

Michelle is quick to sing Flower's praises. As an example, she described an event that occurred in the middle of the holidays—peak shopping season. Michelle and Flower were at the mall, and Michelle started to tense up because of the crowds. Flower immediately recognized it, nudged Michelle, and led her away from the people to an empty corner of the shopping center. After a few minutes, Michelle began to relax and the anxiety passed.

Flower is also trained to enter the house before Michelle to check and make sure no one is inside. Once they arrive home together, Michelle opens the door and lets Flower in. Michelle waits outside until Flower uses her nose to turn on the interior lights, a signal to Michelle that the coast is clear and she can safely enter.

Michelle's story is echoed by a growing number of women as well as men who have returned from Iraq and Afghanistan with both combat and sexual assault trauma. The behavior is acknowledged by higher-ups, often with just a letter of reprimand in the attacker's file. In military parlance, it is known as "rape by rank."

The reporting process has improved, however. In 2005, the Department of Defense introduced "restricted reporting," allowing a victim of sexual assault to make a confidential report and bypass the chain of command. While it allows the victim to get help, investigating the allegation does not automatically occur. The number of women veterans asking for help via the Veterans Health Administration doubled in a decade, growing from nearly 160,000 female patients nationwide in 2000 to 310,000 by 2010, along with increasing PTSD diagnoses directly related to sexual trauma, according to the Department of Veterans Affairs website. Also according to the VA, about one in 5 women and one in 500 men screened by the VA have reported experiencing MST during their military service. *Newsweek* reported in 2011 that women in the armed forces were "more likely to be assaulted by a fellow soldier than killed in combat." At the same time, investigations into the allegations have increased.

---

Dr. Chard, director of the PTSD and Anxiety Disorders Division at the VA Medical Center in Fort Thomas, Kentucky, explained treatment for PTSD on the Department of Veterans Affairs site:

*Cognitive processing therapy is an evidence-based treatment, designed specifically to treat PTSD and related symptoms such as depression and anger.*

*The treatment is typically twelve sessions long. The veteran works with the therapist to examine the impact of the trauma, especially related to the veteran's beliefs about safety, trust, power/control, esteem, and intimacy. Through practice assignments, the veteran is able to form a more realistic and balanced view of self, others, and the world, and to realize that they do not have to be controlled by the trauma any longer.*

According to the VA's website, Veterans Health Administration hospitals have designated contact people for MST-related issues to help veterans access VA services and programs.

As part of her seven-week PTSD inpatient program, Michelle Covert, a mother and grandmother, has been on a personal mission to help fellow veterans cope with PTSD. She shares her experience so other victims will not feel alone. At one speaking engagement, according to the Department of Veterans Affairs, she addressed about three hundred senior commanders from the Ohio National Guard and Air Guard, where the Guard presented her with an Eagle Award.

After completing an inpatient program with Dr. Chard, Michelle spoke to the staff at the VA Ambulatory Care Center in Columbus about her military experiences. Addressing her peers wasn't easy, she explained in an article on the Veterans Affairs website.

"This was the hardest briefing I have ever given in my life," she said in the article. "Standing up in front of all your coworkers and letting them know that you were raped in service, you suffer with PTSD, and had to attend an inpatient program, is not easy."

Michelle emphasized in the VA article that she does not want to "sit around talking about how bad PTSD is. I want to be a voice of hope." Michelle graduated in 2009 with a business management degree from Indiana Institute of Technology, and said she hoped to one day run her own business and write a book about living with PTSD, with the aid of a service dog. For now, she is a photographer with the VA public affairs office.

"I want to let other veterans know they should get help as soon as possible," Michelle says in the article. "I want to tell them, 'Believe in yourself.'"

Navy commander Theresa Everest, a nurse practitioner, became a voice within the military for those suffering from military sexual trauma. She was tasked with commanding a mission to Afghanistan to look into military sexual assaults and to study why they were prevalent there.

Before Theresa left for Afghanistan, her friend Helen Fidler, whom Theresa had met early in her navy career, told her about a beagle she was fostering. He was a rescued dog who was being treated for a variety of illnesses but would eventually be available for adoption. Helen knew that Theresa and her husband, Eric Everest, now retired from the navy, were beagle lovers, and already had two at home as pets.

Theresa was being sent to Afghanistan, however, and taking in another dog was the furthest thing from her mind.

But then everything changed.

Ten days before Theresa was due to leave for Afghanistan to oversee the study on military sexual assaults, she was brutally attacked. It happened at Camp Arifjan, in Kuwait, where she was the women's health practitioner and assistant director of five branch clinics. She was slammed into an I-beam, beaten, rendered unconscious, raped, and abandoned on gravelly dirt and sand between large shipping containers.

"I had two black eyes and an open-scalp injury," Theresa recalled. "It was like I was punched. I fell forward and hit my head on a steel I-beam that holds shipping containers off the ground."

Once she came to after about six hours, she was disoriented.

"I was covered in blood," said Theresa quietly as she recalled the details. "My clothing was half off of me. My legs and elbows were skinned up. I was a mess."

And she was alone. Somehow, she managed to pick herself up, get to a restroom, and clean herself up.

"The thing I thought about the most was whether I would be able to close the wound on my head myself," she said. "I thought, 'I can take care of this myself. I'm a nurse practitioner. I see patients on my own. Maybe I can suture it back. Maybe I can staple it.'"

Theresa also decided to cover up the truth, saying that her injuries came from a fall.

"If I had reported the rape and attack, I don't think they would have let me go to Afghanistan," Theresa said. "That was a big thing for me. I believed then—and still believe now—in what I was doing. I felt I needed to go and do that mission. It was important."

The doctor, a corpsman, along with the team who examined and treated Theresa, asked her how she was hurt. After she offered her explanation, the corpsman told her, "There's no way you got all of this from a fall."

A physician at the expeditionary medical facility sutured the open head wound. When asked by the medical team if she had lost consciousness, she told them "No."

"If I had said, 'Yes,' there would have been an investigation," Theresa continued. "I know they questioned it; I know they were concerned. I don't blame them. If I had said something else happened—the attack and rape—they would have been all over it. 'How could this happen to one of our commanders?'"

She instead repeated that she'd been injured when she fell, and the medical team didn't press further.

Once in Afghanistan, "I had a hard time putting words to objects," she said. "I would ask, 'Staff Sergeant, could you hand me that?' Instead of coming up with the name of the object itself, I'd say, 'thingy.' I had this wonderful staff, and they'd laugh about it. They had no idea there was any kind of issue, that it was tied to my head injury ten days before."

While still overseas, she received a second brain injury, this one from nearby explosions.

"Our base was attacked by Taliban and insurgents, and I ended up with another head injury, because of the blast force. I couldn't stand up."

Another woman, a petty officer first class, in the room at the time with Theresa, couldn't stand up either.

"By the time we were able to get up and get our gear, there'd been three blasts," Theresa said. "We made it outside. We banged on doors in the building we were in. A neurologist in the room next to us couldn't get her gear on. We got her out and got downstairs together to the bunkers. There were no sirens. It was just bombs, rockets, and mortars. There were no sirens until we were out and in the bunkers."

Theresa described the blasts in detail.

"You can feel the bomb concussion," she said. "It's enough to knock you down. It goes right through your body, which is what gives you the brain injury. The thing that was most on my mind at that time was, 'Where are my people, and is everybody okay?' I needed a head count."

Once everyone was accounted for, Theresa relaxed. No one had been killed.

While still in-country, she was acutely aware that something was not right with her.

"I knew before I came home that something was wrong, because I was having really bad migraines."

As a nurse practitioner, she knew that she was experiencing severe symptoms of traumatic brain injury coupled with post-traumatic stress disorder. She couldn't remember people she once worked with. On top of long-term memory loss, she also suffered some short-term memory loss, vertigo, and achalasia.

"Not being able to remember people was really distressing," said Theresa, who at the time was senior nurse corps officer of the branch clinics in the Great Lakes. "When I first got back from overseas to my base, I would run into people I had known for seven years, and I could not remember why I knew them, how I knew them, or even remember their names. I'd say, 'I'm really sorry, but I can't remember you or where I know you from.' It hit me hard. I thought I was losing my mind. These are people I worked with, was on committees with, saw on a weekly basis, and I could not remember them."

In November 2011, she was officially diagnosed with TBI and PTSD.

She had returned from Afghanistan and Kuwait on November 15, 2011, after completing the MST study. The study discovered a lack of personnel security on military bases. "We were paying attention to base security, but we weren't paying attention to personnel safety," she said, failings of which included the women's restroom. When a woman went in to take a shower, the bathroom door didn't lock. "What kind of security is that?" Theresa asked. "There wasn't very much money available for simple things like locks on doors, and locks for buildings that couldn't be cut open with a knife. The study brought public attention to the problem."

As for not reporting her own rape, Theresa said she's certain she would not have been able to go to Afghanistan to study the very thing that she herself had experienced: military sexual assault. "I'm torn about it. I'm so proud of what I did in Afghanistan. I am super proud of the people I was with and the mission we accomplished. We made a difference."

Much of what was in Theresa's command's survey findings from the Afghanistan mission came out in Congress and before senior military people. "It was all because of my people and what we did there—members of the military getting together and talking about the big survey and assessment done in 2011. That was my unit, myself and thirteen other people, who traveled around from base to base. We did the interviews and the reports. I'm proud of that," she said.

In 2013, Theresa finally reported her own sexual assault and beating, after talking with her therapists about it. One thing that helped her was that she had been knocked out during the rape. She did not know who attacked her, and no investigation was launched, because the obstacles of time, distance, and her loss of memory hindered any investigation.

"I was rendered unconscious," she said. "Unlike a lot of victims who have to be awake and endure it, for me, it was a blessing that I was unconscious."

Also by 2013, US Congresswoman Niki Tsongas of Massachusetts was speaking plainly when discussing MST. "It has become painfully evident that saying the military has a cultural problem in regard to sexual assault and sexual misconduct, is a glaring understatement," she wrote in a statement. "At worst, this is a deep-rooted and widespread acceptance of unprofessional, inappropriate, and criminal behavior. At best, it is willful denial or head-turning on the part of too many military leaders." Representative Tsongas also noted that it is a "deep-rooted cultural problem."

This problem, the congresswoman has pointed out, is not isolated to just women in the military. In fact, one in one hundred men screened by the Veterans Administration say they experienced sexual harassment or assault during their service.

"This is not just a women's issue, as the sheer number of men who are sexually assaulted is higher than the number of women," Tsongas has said publicly.

It's all about power and control, Theresa explained: "It is a very victimizing control—a lot of senior personnel on junior personnel. It is a very victimizing power. It does mental damage."

And treating the damage from military sexual trauma, a form of PTSD, is where a service dog for Theresa comes in.

While Theresa was battling with her own recovery, the beagle her friend Helen had told her about had been going through his own. His saga had started in 2005 in Mississippi, when the dog was rescued in the weeks following Hurricane Rita after someone spotted teenagers shooting a .22 at him as he chased rabbits. Rescuers said the beagle was in survival mode, hunting for food at the time the teens used him for target practice.

A no-kill shelter in Louisville, Kentucky, took him in, named him Spring, and then Helen, Theresa's friend, started fostering him.

Theresa, meanwhile, had left for Afghanistan. Upon her return, her friend updated her on Spring's status, telling her that the dog had been diagnosed with heartworm and was about to undergo treatment. Theresa told her she wasn't in a position to adopt a dog, because she was dealing with the effects of TBI and PTSD and just starting therapy.

"I had just gotten back from Afghanistan," Theresa said. "I was really too busy with my own injuries to think about getting another dog."

On top of that, Theresa's husband had been diagnosed with cancer. Instinctively, their two beagles seemed to know just what to do to help.

It's been found that dogs' heightened sense of smell make them acutely aware that people have cancer. "Some dogs, such as bloodhounds, have as many as 300 million scent receptors, where humans have only five," according to *TechKnow*, a TV series on Al Jazeera America. "While humans use the same airway to smell and breathe, when air enters a dog's nose, it splits into two paths. Breathing and smelling become two separate functions, so dogs can actually filter scents to a degree that humans can't begin to comprehend."

Theresa's beagles, like their bloodhound cousins, appeared very much aware of her husband's illness. "Through his chemotherapy and radiation, these two were his bed companions," Theresa said. "They were so in tune with his health needs and problems that they were able to help him. By staying with him, they comforted him."

Helen persisted in urging Theresa to get a service dog, to help her through her own treatment and recovery. Finally, in March 2012, Theresa told Helen that if Spring pulled through the heartworm treatment and she started him in service dog training, Theresa would adopt him.

Spring survived, and Helen enrolled him in an intensive training program, keeping Theresa up to date on the dog's progress. "Helen knew me," Theresa said, "and she knew the dog. She knew that Spring would be a good fit." Theresa had also seen firsthand the benefits a dog could offer through her own beagles' support of her husband, so, in August of 2013, she adopted Spring.

Once Theresa and her husband had brought him home, she enrolled Spring in additional service dog training, from which he graduated.

"Spring is amazing," Theresa said. "He knows when I'm going into a spin. He comes and puts a paw on me. He calms me down. He's done as much for me as Helen has done for him."

This calming effect was evident during a weekday morning at a well-attended surf clinic for veterans on a Del Mar, California, beach when Theresa, with Spring on her lap, sat on the sand, staring out across the ocean as Theresa's red hair and Spring's long ears blew in the light wind. If a passerby had happened to glance their way, they would have seen what looked like an average person enjoying the day with her pet.

For Theresa and Spring, it was much more than that. Spending time with Spring at the beach helps to lessen Theresa's symptoms.

"Anyone with a brain injury has to work really hard to get the other noises out, to be closed off and separate from the task they're trying to do," Theresa explained. "Teaching at a university or giving a webinar makes me work overtime to focus on one thing instead of the three hundred things that are going on in my mind. Some people don't learn to live with traumatic brain injury and they take their own lives. It's an awful thing to live with."

Spring lives those symptoms with Theresa, staying by her side to comfort her as she finds a quiet space. "The sound of the water and the rhythm of the ocean drown out a lot of other noises," Theresa explained. "Sitting on the beach, doing an activity, being out on the water—the stimuli are taken away. There's only you and your dog. Everything is gone. It's another world. The water, the sand, and Spring connect me to all of that."

***

The power and control involved in many military sexual assaults and referenced by Congresswoman Tsongas and MST victim Theresa Everest became a reality for army combat veteran Joe Qualls, who served in Iraq.

"I'm an MST guy," Joe said matter-of-factly as he talked about his mental and physical injuries, which, besides PTSD and MST, also include traumatic brain injury, depression, and loss of hearing. Overall, he noted, "My body's just beat up," referring to the multiple cuts and abrasions he got from being near mortar attacks on a regular basis.

And while he said he's open to admitting he suffers from military sexual trauma, it was not easy getting to that point. "It's a lot of things," he explained. "I'm six-foot-six, and I've always been the tough guy. I kicked butt, and for me to be the guy with it, well . . ."

His voice trailed off.

Joe traded playing football on his college team for boot camp when he enlisted in the army to serve his country in the aftermath of 9/11. While overseas in the early years of the Iraq War, he ignored the warning signs and symptoms of post-traumatic stress and tried to stay strong.

"PTSD was the elephant in the room back then. I was in Iraq in 2004 and 2005," he said. "Any kid who couldn't handle it was treated badly. You didn't talk about it. You just wanted to get out."

Joe faced more than he'd bargained for after his injury resulted in a side effect: enormous weight gain. During his hospitalization at the Palo Alto VA hospital, his weight soared. He needed help with his continuing anxiety and stress. He later joined a PTSD inpatient program at the Menlo Park VA hospital in California. It was there that he learned about a Ride 2 Recovery, or R2R, cycling program. An organizer lent him a bicycle, and Joe, who weighed in at 387 pounds at the time, eventually shed a hundred pounds.

Once home in San Diego, he began working for a nonprofit, where a friend mentioned psychiatric dogs as being helpful to those with post-traumatic stress. "I told the person, 'It's not for me.'"

Then, he went to a veterans' family forum where Patricia Dibsie, with Love Heels Canine Partners, had brought along a puppy-in-training golden retriever named Hooligan to spread the word about service dogs. "I started working with the puppy almost instantly, and got to know him," Joe said. "He started doing some exercises with me, and Patricia decided I was part of Hooligan's training." In November 2012, two months after Joe completed PTSD therapy, Hooligan graduated from the training program and became his service dog.

Hooligan helps Joe with mobility issues caused by the traumatic brain injury. "I have balance problems, and Hooligan kept bumping into me when I walked," he said. "My wife, Kami, said, 'He's balancing you.' Hooligan saw I wasn't walking straight, was off-balance, and he was straightening me out."

It's just one example of what Joe refers to as Hooligan knowing almost automatically what to do for him. Another example, he said, happens at night. "He intuitively started waking me up from nightmares," he said. The negative feelings from the nightmares disappear when he's awakened by Hooligan. "It's kind of hard to be upset when you've got a cute dog in your face," Joe pointed out.

Today, Joe is fit and remains active, continuing to bicycle with Hooligan and his family, including wife Kami, son Noah, and daughter Annabelle. The only place Hooligan can't accompany him is to cycling competitions, which he participates in through the Ride 2 Recovery program and California Challenge. "I can't take him everywhere," he said. "Bikes and dogs don't mix."

A positive side effect to having a service dog has been that Hooligan has inadvertently forced Joe to be more sociable. "I go out in public," he said, "and I have this dog attached to me, and he's cute, so people look at him. It forces me to interact with people. I can't be unengaged."

⁓

Just as Joe Qualls recognized that something was seriously wrong with him, so did April Cook, a now-retired navy logistics specialist who joined the service in the aftermath of September 11 so she could serve her country. She met her husband, Todd Wilson, at combat training camp just before they each deployed overseas.

April too experienced the unthinkable: military sexual trauma. And it was perpetrated by one of her superiors.

With a strong, confident voice, April says, "I am a survivor of military sexual trauma." Unlike some victims who are hesitant to make a report, April notified the chain of command soon after the assault occurred. "Unfortunately," she noted, "where I was stationed at the time and the command I was with, I was basically told to keep my mouth shut."

So she did. It sent her into major psychological trauma. "I started to isolate myself a lot, and my temper started to get short with people," she said. "So I avoided people and things. And I started to drink. I knew something was significantly wrong."

Once she had returned home from overseas, she found herself unable to focus. "I was at the point where I wasn't taking care of basics. For dinner, if I needed to eat, I would go to the nearest convenience store and pick whatever was close to me. If potato chips were near the aisle, that would be dinner. I wasn't physically taking care of myself."

She also had suicidal thoughts, taking them as far as making plans to kill herself. "I was putting myself at risk and putting my guys at risk at work," she said. "I eventually went to the medical office in my command and told them, 'Here's what's going on. I'm having flashbacks. I'm having trouble staying focused when we're working in an aircraft, and there's a lot of equipment. I'm losing where I am, and it's not safe.'

"I told them," she continued, "'Here's what happened to me when I was overseas.'"

This time when she reported it, they listened, because her symptoms had become a safety issue not only for her, but also for her coworkers. It was the beginning of her medical board evaluation, when the military began assessing her. They soon realized she needed to get help.

April was diagnosed with war-related anxiety and the effects of post-traumatic stress, and was honorably discharged from active duty in 2008. She went from active duty back to reserve status. In the process of leaving the service, she received the assistance she so desperately needed to deal with flashbacks from the sexual assault.

A big piece of that help came when Claire, a pretty golden retriever who was trained as a psychiatric service dog, entered her life. April, with short brown hair and a pleasant smile, had been volunteering for paws4vets, a program within the paws4people foundation based in Wilmington, North Carolina. She learned that Claire, a golden retriever, was having a litter of future service dogs in training, so April volunteered to help care for the puppies. She had trained with a dog at the center but had not yet formed a bond with a potential service canine—until she met Claire.

Soon after April began helping with the puppies, Claire picked up on April's anxiety.

"She noticed I was nervous," said April, who smiles when talking about Claire. "She started pawing me. She tried to bathe me, just like she did her puppies. She licked my hands, and she'd get close to me and try to curl up. It was like she was saying, 'Hey, I like you. Let me help you out here.' I loved her instantly."

Claire had been selected to go to someone else, "But they saw how we worked together, and decided we needed to be together," she said.

That was in 2011. Fast-forward a few years, and Claire continues to read April's anxiety. "If my heart rate increases," April said, "she nudges my hand to tell me, 'I'm here. Pet me, look at me, settle down, and stay focused on the here and now.'"

Therapy became more effective when Claire attended sessions with April—so much so that April was able to suspend therapy, although she returns for occasional follow-up sessions.

"I knew something was significantly wrong, but I think, just like anyone else having to live with a chronic illness, it became a new normal," she explained. That new normal meant adapting to both military and civilian life while experiencing MST.

One way Claire helps to ease April's anxiety is simply by being with her. "I had a hard time going to the movies, being in a dark theater, but with her help I can do things like that now. Before Claire, I would maybe last fifteen minutes in a store. Now I can go in, use coupons, plan a meal, and stay an hour. Because she's there, she keeps me focused and keeps me from ramping up."

In some ways, April said she's a better person because of everything she's been through. "I have a lot more patience and a lot more compassion, not only for others, but also for myself. I tend not to stress out about the small things anymore."

And having Claire at her side has made her stronger.

"She's taught me to rely on her, to give her more love and attention than I've ever before given," she said. "I learned an important life lesson."

April still has flashbacks, which Claire helps her with. "The best way to describe a flashback is that your brain and mind go to a really bad place," she said. "You go there for a long time. When you have a service dog licking your ear, it's hard to stay there."

When she first started working with Claire, "I thought a dog would be cool, that a dog could be useful," she said. "I didn't realize *how* useful. I was amazed. I not only had to be trained on how to handle her, but I also had to be trained on how to handle myself with her. You have to learn how to get the dog to move, how to give commands. Our training also involved how to use the dog when you're feeling anxious. Focus on the dog. It's a process you have to learn."

Because a service dog has been so helpful for her, April, who has a master's degree in licensed professional counseling, went to work for the paws4vets program. She is a peer mentor on the primary medical evaluation team and works with kids who are aging out of the foster care system. These kids are able to go to the center and work with dogs. "I get to be the program director for that," April said.

Also, she noted, "Because of what Claire has done for me, I'm starting the Claire Bear Foundation for female veterans, to help sexual assault victims get quality service dogs, because of what these animals can do for them."

Life for Claire is not all work and no play. "She has a work mode and a play mode," April said. "She doesn't play or jump around or do anything silly or goofy when we're working. When the vest comes off, she rolls on the floor. Off vest, she gets to be a goofball. Claire definitely lives in the here and now."

The sexual assault against Nancy Lee Augsbach, a former yeoman third-class for the navy, happened at the barracks where she lived on the Naval Air Station in Jacksonville, Florida, around 1984.

Nancy was gang-raped by a group of six to eight higher-ranking personnel. It started in the community center and moved to the barracks. Living quarters for women were flanked by barracks for the men, with a community center between the buildings. "Somehow, I woke up in my barracks, unclothed and with bruises."

Nancy reported the assaults, but some of her memories remain foggy, including the day after the rapes.

She saw a navy doctor after she didn't feel well and learned that she was pregnant. She reported the rapes at that time and was interviewed by MPs. She provided the names of the men involved, but nothing ever came of it. Almost immediately, "I was kicked out of the barracks because they said, 'If you're pregnant, you can't live here.'" She found an apartment and lived alone until her baby girl was born.

Then, Nancy was told she was would be receiving deployment orders to ship out of the country. Because she was a single parent, she instead requested to leave the navy. In 1984, she was honorably discharged.

Six years after the attacks, she sought help. "I couldn't be around men, I was so afraid," she noted. Nancy was officially diagnosed with PTSD.

She married and relocated to Texas with her husband and eventually had a second child, this one a son. She worked as a police officer in Texas for fourteen years. Once her marriage ended, she moved to Mechanicsburg and enrolled at Pennsylvania State University to pursue a degree in psychology.

An old back injury from a car accident in Jacksonville had been aggravated by another auto accident in Texas, and she eventually became wheelchair-bound from degenerative disc disease.

Around 2010, she learned about Susquehanna Service Dogs, an organization that provides service dogs to wounded veterans. She was matched with Gnat, a yellow Labrador retriever.

At the center, when candidates for dogs were introduced to a few canines, "Gnat came to me and put his head in my lap. I knew then that he was mine," Nancy noted.

Nancy can't imagine life without him. "He's made my life worth living," she said. She used to have someone helping her twenty-four hours a day. Now she has Gnat.

Attending Gnat's graduation from advanced training were his puppy raisers, Karen and Tom Johnston. "I asked Karen," Nancy said, "'How can you and your husband raise a dog for eighteen months and give him up?' She told me, 'We are not losing a dog. We are gaining a sister.'"

It was true. The Johnstons became like family to Nancy. She and Gnat still spend several holidays a year with his puppy raisers.

Today, Nancy teaches art at a community center, a feat that was unfathomable before Gnat. "I wasn't even living a life," Nancy explained. "I withdrew and was pretty much a recluse."

But along came Gnat, and everything changed. "He helps me with my depression," she said. "When I'm feeling down, he'll walk over and comfort me. No human could have changed my life the way Gnat has. He's the best thing that's ever happened to me. Every day is a new journey with him."

To let her know he wants to go outside, "Gnat brings my socks— the ones I wear when I go out—and carries them to me. In the four years I've had him, he has yet to have an accident in the house."

Sitting in her wheelchair, she takes him on walks in the neighborhood. "If the battery in my chair gets low, he pulls my chair."

One day after one of their walks, once they were inside the house, Gnat barked at her and wouldn't stop. "He kept walking over to the door, then coming back to me, barking at me. I couldn't figure it out. I thought someone was outside, prowling." Nancy called the police, and when an officer knocked on her door and she answered it, he handed her keys over to her. "I had left my keys in the lock of the front door. When I'd closed the door, Gnat could hear that the keys were still in the lock and he barked at me to let me know." These moments exemplify the value of a service dog in her life, she says.

"I couldn't be here today without Gnat," Nancy says. "Getting Gnat was a new beginning. He's the reason I get up in the morning."

# CHAPTER 7

# Agent Orange and Southeast Asia

Larry McMahan, a former marine, left the jungles of Vietnam after two tours of duty as an infantry platoon sergeant. Once he turned fifty, while working as a deputy for the Cuyahoga County Sheriff's Department, his medical problems started to add up.

Larry had served in Southeast Asia in what became known as the Vietnam War, which the US government at the time viewed as a way to prevent a Communist takeover of South Vietnam. Meanwhile, as American military personnel were fighting overseas, an anti–Vietnam War movement developed. Returning service members were not welcomed home with ticker-tape parades as had happened after past wars. The negative response to their service to their country only heightened the painful wounds of war they suffered. Adding insult to injury was the military's use of Agent Orange and its long-term effects.

"We knew there was a chemical, but we didn't know what it was," Larry said. "All we knew was that it cleared the jungle, and it killed the vegetation."

It also damaged humans.

More than forty years after the last US troops left Vietnam, the aftereffects of Agent Orange still haunt veterans, including Larry, retired army sergeant James Cadieux, and former Army Ranger Denny McLaughlin.

They are three of more than 450,000 military veterans who served in Southeast Asia during the Vietnam War who are experiencing physical problems caused by the herbicide and defoliant Agent

Orange. It was sprayed from planes over vast areas to kill jungle vegetation that concealed North Vietnamese troops. Related illnesses from Agent Orange, so named for the orange-striped barrels in which it was shipped, range from cancer and heart ailments to Parkinson's disease, according to the Veterans Affairs Agent Orange Registry.

Despite being told he would never be able to hold down a job again, Larry was determined to make it back into the workforce.

"I learned how to use a one-handed computer keyboard," Larry said. "I took a training class for six months and I went back to work." In 2007, at his new office job in Cleveland, Ohio, Larry met his wife Piper Belanger, who was also his boss.

"We became close friends," Piper said. "I kept an urn of coffee in my office, and he came in for a fresh cup quite frequently. He often tells the story of one worker asking him if he knew who I was, because I was a manager, and Larry's reply was, 'She's the little gray-haired lady who makes my coffee.'"

After a year and a half, they moved from Cleveland to South Carolina's Grand Strand to be closer to Larry's two grandchildren.

It was there that Larry first considered getting a service canine. "One of our neighbors had this beautiful service dog," said Larry. The neighbor recommended that Larry contact Rick Kaplan, president and founder of Canine Angels Service Dogs. After several conversations and an application process, he and Rick decided that Larry would be a good candidate for a service dog.

Canine Angels rescues dogs from local shelters and places them with a foster family while they are trained to be of service to veterans. The dogs are provided free to eligible veterans and first responders (firefighters, police, and paramedics).

In January 2011, Larry and his wife Piper met Abby for the first time.

"Abby adopted me," Larry said. "There were two golden retrievers at the kennels who couldn't have cared less about me." Abby, a pit bull mix, lingered precariously at the North Myrtle Beach Humane Society shelter after being saved from euthanasia several times by a staff member after being bypassed by the public for adoption. Described as a "wild woman" at the shelter, Abby was rescued by Rick. While she was trained and fostered for eighteen months by Canine Angels volunteers Ray and Arlette Van Arsdale, Rick worked with her as well. Then, once she and Larry were matched, the two went through an additional six months of team training.

"Abby has a purpose, and she knows it," noted Larry, who also has an aging beagle and a seven-year-old Walker hound as pets. "Abby goes from pet to service dog instantaneously. It's funny to see her change in attitude. We watch our granddaughters Monday through Friday," he continued, "and she is their dog during the day. But when I put her vest on, she becomes my service dog. When I take her vest off, she becomes a pet."

Abby is also goal-oriented. "She can actually open a cooler and get a beer," Larry said. "Anything I drop, she picks up. She jumps onto my lap with it, stands up, and hands it to me. She also picks my cane up and hands that to me. She will block me from falling. She'll lean on me to make sure I'm balanced."

Once stateside, Larry worked as a writer before leaving the US Marine Corps after nearly six years. As time went on, symptoms of Agent Orange poisoning along with post-traumatic stress were evident. After five heart attacks, paralysis on his right side, and kidney disease, Larry was put on 100 percent disability. In 2001, he was given just three years to live.

He's beaten the odds. By 2014, thirteen years after his three-year life-expectancy prognosis, Larry is still going strong.

A big contributor to that has been help from his service dog Abby, who was specially trained to help war veterans cope with PTSD.

Abby's twenty-four-hour presence with Larry allows his wife Piper to be at ease leaving her husband alone. Abby will lean on McMahan to make sure he is stable on his feet, picking up his cane and other dropped items, allowing him to lead a more independent life.

"The biggest thing for me is the comfort I feel when Larry goes out in public without me," Piper said, "because, with Abby at his side,

I feel that he is much less vulnerable to the perils of the world. She turns what could be a negative situation into a positive. She gives him so much comfort around the clock, so even though she is a physical aid—if he drops his cane, she picks it up, and she steadies him—she is also an enormous source of purpose, pride, and overall well-being."

On top of that, Abby is devoted to Larry. "She is as loving and gentle as can be. You will not find a more loyal friend than this," said Piper.

Larry takes Abby with him everywhere. On Abby's first trip to the VA Hospital, accompanying Larry as he visited a friend, "She did the most impressive thing I've seen so far," he said.

It happened as he waited for his friend in the PTSD clinic. "A veteran sat with his head in his hands, crying. Abby walked over, put her head on his lap, and waited for him to lift his head. It was like she was saying, 'Hey, it's okay. I understand.' He eventually stopped crying and started petting her. They stayed there for a good twenty-five minutes."

Abby's nurturing side helps Larry to sustain his positive outlook on a day-to-day basis. And while Larry lives with the effects of Agent Orange poisoning and a dire prognosis on top of his other injuries, he hasn't given up.

"I honestly think he is about the same physically as he was in 2007—maybe a little less mobile, but every bit as determined," Piper said.

"Until Abby licked my face," Larry admitted, "I was leery of pit bulls." On trips to the beach Larry, his wife, and Abby play together on the shore. They've also taken longer trips with Abby, including to two family weddings in Cleveland, which involved a twelve-hour drive each time. The invitations were addressed to Larry, his wife, and Abby, "She's a good traveler," Piper said, "and she's quiet in hotels."

Abby was the right choice of service dog for Larry, although he insists he had nothing to do with it. Upon first meeting Abby, he recalled, "Abby looked at me, jumped up on my lap, and licked my face. She definitely picked me."

It's been no different for Vietnam army sergeant James Cadieux. Walks on the beach with his service dog Cruiser have done more for his psyche than any drug ever could, he says.

Cruiser, a large, dark-brown, handsome chocolate Labrador mix, is equally devoted to James. While he wears his camouflage service dog vest, he's in working mode, and there's a calmness about him as he sticks like glue to James's side. Take the vest off while at the beach, however, and Cruiser runs around playing fetch on the sand just like any other active dog.

Cruiser has even contributed to James's weight loss. "He's helped with my health issues, both mentally and physically," James said. "I'm down forty-two pounds now, and I'm just enjoying life."

Seven years in the service and three tours in Vietnam as a supply sergeant took their toll on James's health. "I saw a lot," James noted. As part of the 1st Cavalry Division, James was sent in 1968 to An Khê, where the division was based, and then on to the Khe Sanh Combat Base, located eighteen miles south of the Demilitarized Zone (DMZ). His unit supported the Marines during the first Tet Offensive, which was a large wave of campaigns by the Vietcong and North Vietnamese Army against the forces of South Vietnam, the United States, and their allies.

Once he'd returned stateside, he tried to reenter civilian life, without much success. He had lived through the horrors of war, and he found it tough to acclimate.

"I wasn't able to socialize," James said. "I got married, had a child, and it didn't work very well, because I wasn't sociable. I couldn't be close to anybody. It took a long time, after about twenty years of struggling, losing houses and losing jobs, not knowing what was going on, to find out what was wrong with me."

Then, in 1992, the symptoms he'd been experiencing for so long were given a name. "They figured out I had PTSD, and Agent Orange contributed, and more things started going wrong."

He had spent time on the front line in the jungles of Southeast Asia between 1967 and 1969. He was discharged from the service in 1970.

"The planes were dropping Agent Orange right on us," he said. "You take a toxin like that, and you don't know what's going to happen. It was pure waste material. It worked very well. It killed foliage and did what they wanted it to do."

It did damage to James as well.

In 1994, two years after he first went to the Veterans Administration seeking answers, James was deemed 100 percent disabled.

Before serving in Vietnam, he'd been active and athletic. "I was a good athlete. I went over there healthy. I came back alive. I was fortunate I didn't get banged up too bad. I did a good job, received a lot of awards, got an honorable discharge, and continued with my life. I got married when I was at the end of my service, and that's when I realized I wasn't getting close to people."

That all changed when Cruiser entered his life. James heard about Rick Kaplan and his Canine Angels organization. "I contacted Rick and filled out an application."

The first time he met Cruiser was at a holiday event. "Cruiser walked up to me, and we bonded right away," James said. "He was given up by a family who said they couldn't control him. I take him to the beach, and he walks side by side with other dogs. He doesn't bark. He just loves everyone."

Cruiser is trained to retrieve things for him and accompany him in public. Most of all, what his service dog does for him, James said, is to simply be with him. "When I don't feel well, he makes me feel good. I want to be around him. He gives me a purpose."

---

Former air force master sergeant Roddy Lewis doesn't pull any punches about his time overseas. "I went to Vietnam three times and went through two wives," he said.

Roddy was an aircraft mechanic, assigned each time he deployed to Tan Son Nhut, a Republic of Vietnam air force facility located near Saigon in Southern Vietnam. "We went through mortar and rocket attacks at the base," he said. "They were always trying to overrun the perimeter. We saw plane crashes. We lost planes. They'd take off and not come back. That plays on your mind. We'd listen on the radio and we could hear them as they went into battle. And then we wouldn't hear them anymore."

Married a third time, life for Roddy and his wife Lee has settled down as Roddy has adjusted to dealing with severe post-traumatic stress, with the help of a small service dog named Jack. "My wife Lee is the one who got me to go to the doctor to see what was wrong with me. I thought I was just an angry old guy."

Make no mistake: Roddy still has his bad days. But six months of PTSD classes and a service dog have helped him learn to live with PTSD.

Roddy cited an example of how Jack helps by alerting him when he gets anxious, including taking over being the vigilant one. "If I start getting jumpy and looking out the windows, he comes over to me and calms me down. He diverts my attention."

Besides PTSD, he also has sleep apnea. "You name it, I've got it. I've got so many growths on my body, my doctor says I'm like an old ship with barnacles."

Barnacles and all, it's fine with Jack.

"I don't get angry like I used to," Roddy said. "I don't know how he does it, but it works. I feel secure."

Roddy and Lee rescued Jack from people who abused him. "They were going to take him to the pound," Roddy said, explaining that they instead talked the people into giving Jack to them. "He looked like a crotchety dog you didn't want to get near," he said, adding that he was immediately taken by him.

After the couple met Rick with Canine Angels, he evaluated Jack and approved the two as candidates for his service dog program.

"This dog is a blessing," he said. "We help each other."

# CHAPTER 8

# A Career Change

Finding twenty-three names of brothers and sisters he'd lost in combat during his time in Vietnam was too much for former Army Ranger Denny McLaughlin. As he stood at at the Vietnam War Memorial in Washington, DC, a wave of sorrow washed over him. He was overcome with emotion as decades-old memories surfaced. He was no longer the fit young man who'd left American soil to fight a war many Americans had protested. Now, standing there with his graying goatee and balding hair, he was transported back to those endless days with his regiment, I Company 75th Ranger, doing reconnaissance in the jungles. He felt like a broken man.

Still, Denny located the names of all his fallen comrades, along with five more who had since died. Afterward, he walked to the Three Soldiers statue, a bronze representation of young uniformed American soldiers who fought in Vietnam. He stood quietly, lost in thought, as memories he'd suppressed since leaving Saigon in October 1969 came rushing back.

"I couldn't wrap my brain around it," Denny said quietly as he described his 2008 trip with his wife to the Vietnam War Memorial. "I lost control of my emotions for about a half-hour." Sitting on a bench next to the memorial, he talked to his wife for the first time about his experiences as a ranger, wearing camouflage fatigues and face paint, crawling through the jungle foliage.

During his tour of duty in Vietnam, which he described as mostly spent in the south-central area, about a hundred miles north of Saigon, helicopters would move them from place to place, which meant jumping into the jungle from a chopper positioned about four feet off the ground. On the way down on one of those jumps into the jungle, his elbow hit one of the helicopter skids, which meant surgery later to repair the damage.

Then, he lost some of his hearing in that same jungle during a firefight, when his team leader used his shoulder to balance his arm for aiming at the enemy. "He had a Colt AR-15 rifle—which is an M-16 with a shorter barrel and stock," Denny said. "We were in the middle of a gunfight." Also armed, Denny said, "I protected him and tried to protect myself."

Because Vietcong were equipped with machine guns and rockets, Denny and his team needed to escape. They continued firing to buy time until a helicopter gunship arrived to help in the fight. "About an hour later, we were able to get to a safe landing zone. A helicopter picked us up and took us to a night defensible position with an aid station."

At the aid station, a medic put medication in his ears. "I couldn't hear," Denny said. Eventually, his hearing returned intermittently. "There were only five of us on that team, and we all made it out," he noted.

Mentally and emotionally, "I knew something was wrong four months before I came home," he said. The emotional stress of losing teams during battle took its toll. "On occasion, a five-man team would get in trouble and we'd lose a whole team," Denny said.

After his visit to the capital, during a routine health checkup at the veterans' hospital in 2009, a nurse asked Denny how he was feeling that day. He reached out to her by being honest instead of offering his pat answer—that he was fine. "I told her something was off, that I didn't feel right," he said. "She asked if I wanted to see a counselor. I said, 'Yes.' I signed up for treatment. That's when my healing began."

In therapy at the VA, Denny slowly began talking about his experiences in combat. After visiting the war memorial, he had difficulty dealing with the newly unleashed emotions he'd bottled up for nearly four decades. He no longer had the desire to venture outside his home, preferring instead to stay in bed. In the meantime, his wife Sandra had become his full-time caregiver.

That began to change once his doctor suggested that he and his wife get another dog, after their older dog had passed away, as incentive for Denny to venture outside on walks. He took his therapist's suggestion and adopted a black Great Dane named Abbey.

A year later, also during a session, Denny's therapist gave him information about Operation Freedom Paws, a service dog group in the Northern California area founded and operated by former military dog trainer Mary Cortani. Denny and Sandra filled out an application to train Abbey through Mary's organization.

Soon, they heard from Mary, and she met with them and their dog Abbey. The next thing Denny knew, he was in training with his dog, alongside fellow vets. As Abbey learned more commands to be of service to Denny, "I started feeling my confidence come back. It's because of Operation Freedom Paws. I told Mary I would walk to Hanoi with a butter knife in my teeth for her," he said, citing a saying from his service days, meaning he would give his life for her.

A Texas State University researcher in April 2014 completed a small but significant study that found a 22 percent reduction in PTSD symptoms in those veterans who trained their own psychiatric service dogs using a recommended and accepted program.

Graduate student Jeff Nelson told the *Army Times* that participants in the study completed a self-assessment PTSD Checklist–Military Version, which reflected positive results. Nelson explained that the veterans who successfully completed the program scored about twelve points lower—which meant they had fewer symptoms—than those just entering the program.

Nelson called the study "a good first step," telling the *Army Times* that serious organizations "are not going to give money for more research or programs without evidence of it being effective, and, if it works, it hopefully will bring more people into the treatment."

Before Abbey, Denny was what he called "hypervigilant," constantly checking the windows if someone walked on the sidewalk past his house, and checking to make sure doors and windows were locked. Now, Abbey does that for him. "She barks and has me go to the front window to see someone walking by," he said. "She's taken over that hypervigilance."

He continues taking Abbey to class once a week to keep her refreshed in her asks and commands. The training center, he said, has become a second home. "I like being there," he said. "I've become part of the family. I enjoy being around other veterans, especially younger ones."

For veterans recently out of the service, "I let them know that it does get better," he said. "I always tell them that no matter what overseas campaign, what branch of the military, there's a common thread. We're all brothers and sisters. There's a sense of camaraderie. We look out for each other."

He also demonstrates the things that Abbey is able to do at the center. "I go to training to stay refreshed," Denny says, "and me being there with my dog helps incoming veterans feel more comfortable. Mary has me show them examples of commands."

Two years earlier when he first applied for the program, "Mary told me, 'This is a safe place. I have your six.'"—military jargon for "I've got your back."

<hr />

A veteran who has a second service dog from Operation Freedom Paws is Jeff Wilson. After fourteen years in the US Army Reserve and a tour in Iraq, he had trouble sleeping—that is, until a bouncy, goofy two-year-old yellow Lab with a puppy face entered his life.

"Selah sleeps in bed with me," Jeff commented. "She'll wake me up when I start tossing and turning. She'll get me out of whatever dream I'm in. She snuggles. The other night she slept upside down, laying against my chest with her head right on my neck the entire night, and didn't move. I sleep much better knowing she's there. I can relax."

Jeff was a tank-commander sergeant and helicopter flight engineer who deployed to Iraq in 2003. "I was in the reserves when 9/11 happened. I was given an involuntary extension and was deployed to Iraq," he explained. While running on base, he tore the medial collateral ligament, or MCL, toward the inside of his knee and went through surgery.

As with any venture in life, unfortunate hurdles sometimes present themselves. Such was the case with Jeff.

He and his wife Gwen Templeton are unusual in that she also has a service dog, a Doberman-Labrador mix named Ellie, from Operation Freedom Paws. The challenge they faced happened before Selah and Ellie became their service dogs.

Jeff's first assistance dog was Lobo, a Border collie mix. On crutches at the time because of his knee surgery, Jeff was in his driveway at his home in San Jose, California, putting Lobo in the car, when a loud sound spooked Lobo, who bolted and ran down the street. Jeff dropped his crutches and attempted to go after him, but Lobo had disappeared from sight.

For two days, Bay Area volunteers scoured the area in a frantic search for Lobo. He was found on a highway after apparently being hit by a car. He didn't make it.

"It's a big loss," Jeff said through tears in an interview with the *San Jose Mercury News.*

Mary had a solution to help ease his grief, as well as the loss of his helper. She had just taken in Selah, who hadn't graduated from a Southern California guide dog program because of her rambunctious personality.

The afternoon Lobo was found, Mary drove Selah to Jeff's house, where friends had gathered. "There was a big group at our house," Jeff said. "We were gearing up to leave to search for Lobo when the phone call came in that he'd been found."

When Mary walked in with Selah, the dog only had eyes for Jeff. She ran straight to him. "Mary said, 'You're fostering this one for a while.'" They've been inseparable ever since.

"Selah knew she was my dog the second she saw me," said Jeff. He describes Selah as the good that came out of losing Lobo. "It brought me Selah and a new chapter of my life," he said. "She means the world to me."

When asked what Selah does for him as his service dog, Jeff answered, "What *doesn't* she do?" Because she had been trained as a guide dog from the time she was a puppy, she'd learned skills that couldn't be applied when she was with Jeff, who described Selah's shift from guide dog to service dog less as a failure and more as "a career change."

"If I drop a water bottle or my keys or my cane," he said, "she picks them up and hands them to me." To train her to pick up the cane, he attached a teddy bear near the handle, so she could easily pick it up by the toy. "That's right," Jeff said jokingly, "I'm a six-foot-two big guy with a teddy bear on his cane."

When his wife, who suffers from chronic pain, got Ellie as her service dog, Ellie and Selah hit it off from the start. "They get along great," he said. "They sleep against each other and run around in the yard, chasing each other." But as soon as their vests go on their backs, "Their demeanors change. They stop playing. Selah focuses directly on me."

The playful Selah helped Jeff get past his grief as she stepped into the role Lobo once held. "Selah came to me when I was in a really, really bad place," Jeff said. "She brought me back."

Selah made him laugh, Mary Cortani noted. Most of all, she said, Selah made Jeff feel safe again.

Mary's first concern is for the veterans, so getting another rescued dog for Jeff was a given. "The dog is capable of bringing a veteran here, into the present moment. They're taught to focus on the dog, to read the dog's body language, not to worry about the environment."

It worked for Jeff. For him, getting Selah was less a happy ending than a continuation of all that Lobo had done for him. "She provides comfort," he said.

Former master sergeant Richard Mosley never saw it coming. "I didn't know what it was or what I had," he said. "I ended up losing my job and my military career. I lost my family. I lost everything."

And he nearly lost his life to suicide. But a police K-9 brought him back from the brink, and now his service dog helps keep him calm.

A member of the California Army National Guard, Richard suffered for a decade with post-traumatic stress before he learned how service dogs can help to manage the symptoms.

The end to his police career and nearly his life began at the police station as he tried to suppress his anxiety to keep up the calm exterior facade he'd created.

He was anything but calm.

While stationed in 2003 and 2004 for most of the yearlong tour at Camp Speicher in Tikrit, in northern Iraq, he was regularly in the line of fire. "The PTSD happened after being on several convoys and being hit by IEDs," Richard explained. "Our convoys were ambushed and we took small-arms fire."

At the end of his deployment, he returned to law enforcement in the Riverside, California, area. But it wasn't the same as before. His experiences in Iraq had changed him, and not for the better.

"One of my major assignments for the police department was working surveillance in the desert," Richard explained. "I found myself in the exact same world I had been in when I was in combat. I was working with young guys. I started having panic attacks when I'd put on my uniform and my gun belt. It felt like I was getting ready to go out on another convoy. It felt like I'd never left the war."

As a supervisor—a lieutenant and canine handler in charge of specialized teams—he said, "I had to keep everybody safe and keep everything organized. They were looking to me for leadership. I put on this great front. They didn't see the ulcers, the stomach problems. They were excited to go out in the field while I was secretly having major anxiety attacks. I had to be strong at work and strong in the military. I didn't even remember what it felt like to be normal anymore."

He was still a reservist in the Army National Guard, overseeing military exercises on weekends. "I was the chief of instruction at the military school, working with people getting ready to deploy. I was in a high-profile situation at the school. I led a double life."

He knew his PTSD was getting progressively worse, but he continued to put on a show. "I was having suicidal thoughts daily." Finally, Richard said, "I couldn't take it anymore. I snapped."

One night at work, a couple of officers were talking about some minor problems. "One wanted a day off to attend a birthday party. I don't remember what the other issue was. It was important to them, but to me, I thought, 'They don't know what a real problem is.' I told them I had to leave. I drove away and found a remote area. I had a patrol dog, Jango, with me. He was in his travel carrier in the backseat."

"I sat in the car with a gun in my mouth," he continued. "I was a few seconds away from becoming a statistic. I was all but gone."

Then Jango got restless, moving around in his carrier and barking at rabbits in the desert.

"I reached back in his kennel," Richard said. "I said good-bye to him. I realize now he was distracting me, and doing what my service dog Captain now does to calm me."

It worked. Jango took his thoughts elsewhere. Richard said he thought about homeless people. "I remembered talking to some homeless people who said they live for the moment. I thought of them and knew I couldn't do this job anymore, and I couldn't go home like this. I put the gun down. I took off my uniform shirt. I took off my gun belt. I unrolled the window, and opened the kennel door for Jango. I got out of the car and started walking. When someone says they walked away from their job, I literally did."

Richard passed out in a gutter about eight miles from his police car. "I woke up in an ambulance," he said. "I remember the lights. I must have said something about the military, because the ambulance took me to the VA. I was checked in as a John Doe."

In the meantime, when he didn't answer his cell phone or respond to his radio, his department began to worry. "The dog had water in the car. I knew he was in a safe place. They found the car, and Jango was fine."

A few months later, Richard was released by the VA to return to work. But back on the job at the police department, his PTSD got the best of him, and he was let go.

When it was time to go for his weekend at the National Guard, he told his commander he needed some time off to get some help.

"I didn't ask to get out. I told them I needed a couple of months to get myself some help. The commander told me I was faking it and I was just trying to get out of work," Richard said. "My twenty-year military career was spotless until then. I had applied for a service dog, and I needed some time to meet with dogs and get therapy. My commander said, 'Nope, I'm not going to approve it.' So, when I finally asked for help from the military, the military told me no. That made it worse for me. I had to go back on a weekend. But I was humiliated. I couldn't face them."

He checked himself into the VA hospital again. "I missed a weekend drill," he said. "I started getting letters that I was AWOL." It took a year until he got a letter in the mail telling him he'd been medically discharged from the service.

Some veterans are hesitant to get service dogs, because they feel someone else might be more in need, or there might be a stigma attached to having a dog. Such was the case with Richard.

"I thought if I walked around with a service dog," he said, "it would be like walking around with a billboard saying, 'I have problems.' Now I realize service dogs show people how others can get help. I hid my problems for years. I was tired of hiding."

He applied for a dog through Freedom Service Dogs, and the healing process began once Captain, a black Lab trained by Guide Dogs of the Desert, entered his life. Captain had been successful during guide dog training, but he'd torn a ligament in one of his legs. Because of the heavy harness required for guide dogs to wear, and the fact that a person would be hanging on to that harness, he was released from the guide dog program and given to Freedom Service Dogs while his leg was healing.

"He is very highly trained," Richard said. "I feel very fortunate to have him."

Through his service dog, Richard has worked hard at repairing his marriage with his wife Shauna. "Captain is my dog, but he's also our dog," he said. "He's helped our marriage quite a bit. He's a part of our lives."

While Richard continues to have sleeping problems, Captain is there for him. "When I finally fall asleep, the dreams start," he said. "Captain wakes me up."

Other times, if he becomes anxious, "Captain leans on me, or he puts his paw on my leg or his head on my lap. He alerts when I have the onset of a panic attack. When I recognize he's alerting me as I'm starting to go into a bad situation, I can pull myself back and calm myself down. He does a lot of physical things too. He does a 360 around me, standing on all sides to make sure people don't get too close."

As for his former K-9 police dog, Jango went home with Richard.

"Jango was a patrol dog, and I was the only one who could handle him. He was part of the family at home. He was fine with my wife Shauna and the kids. I took him home."

Today, he has a management job with a county office.

"I went from being a police lieutenant to unemployed to working in an office," Richard said. "I'm very fortunate. The office job pays the bills."

It also helps that after he got Captain, he went to work part-time as a mentor dog trainer for Freedom Service Dogs, working with veterans in Southern California. After spending nearly two decades as a law enforcement K-9 handler and trainer, it has helped him to heal, training dogs again.

"I'm in a much better place now, because I am getting help, and I have an opportunity to work with other vets," Richard said. "I understand how hard it is to go through the healing process. I see people who are hurting very badly and are reaching out for help. Without a doubt, what really helps me is working with wounded veterans and their service dogs."

# CHAPTER 9

# Operation Red Dawn and the Dirty Deuce Platoon

When Jamie Camacho, a former army sergeant first class, volunteered with the 4th Infantry Division's 1st Brigade Combat Team, he wasn't sure where or what the mission would be. After an all-night raid, he and the rest of the world were about to find out.

The operation was officially called Red Dawn, and the number-one target in military parlance was the Ace of Spades in a fifty-two-card deck of the most-wanted terrorists. In other words, his unit was charged with finding and capturing then Iraqi president Saddam Hussein. The fallen dictator had been on the run for nine months.

"Our unit got twenty-six out of fifty-two cards," Jamie said quietly as he showed visitors the medals and citations he received for his bravery.

Capturing the Ace of Spades was the icing on the cake, he said. It happened in the Iraqi farming town of ad-Dawr, near Tikrit, on December 13, 2003.

"It was done during an all-night raid," Jamie continued. "We did parameter security while the others in the unit raided the house. We'd raided that house before." Applying the term *house* to this structure would be a stretch for many people. These were tiny makeshift structures with no electricity and no running water, for workers who planted and tended the fields.

"The next time we went to the house," Jamie continued, "someone noticed a Styrofoam plastic block on the ground."

It stood out, because it had what looked like a plastic-coated electrical wire coming out of it, and none of the small houses had electricity. Soldiers, on high alert, cautiously lifted the Styrofoam block and discovered Saddam curled up in a six-foot hole in the ground, which has since been widely described as a "spider hole." The hideout was located just nine miles outside of Hussein's hometown of Tikrit.

The plastic tubing turned out to be a source of oxygen for the fallen leader as he hid out in the hole with a stash of $750,000 in cash. Hussein, armed with a handgun and an AK-47 assault rifle, did not resist capture.

It was tough duty, but Jamie said he is proud to have participated in such historic events. As he and his fellow service members secured the parameter, he recalled watching the helicopter land in the area and then leave. "When the helicopter left, we knew they'd gotten him. That was the goal, to capture Saddam Hussein, because of the awful things he did to his own people. We met our goal."

Despite Jamie's size—tall, thick, and muscular—there is a stillness about him. Soft-spoken and shy, he said he still grapples with anger and anxiety. Still, Jamie said, he would do it all over again if given the chance—this, despite the difficulty in transitioning from combat duty to civilian life.

"It was rough the first couple of years," Jamie admitted. "There was a lot of adjusting. I knew something wasn't right. The first six months, I went into a Veterans Administration residential treatment center in Temple, Texas, in a dormitory. I was one of the first combat vets to turn myself in at that center for mental issues. They labeled me with extreme acute anxiety disorder."

While at the treatment center, he learned breathing exercises to do during anxiety attacks. He can still be jumpy, as he puts it. This includes being on high alert while driving, because he associates every car he sees with a Humvee, just like he's still in the combat zone. Besides the mental-health diagnosis, he was also injured in combat, tearing a meniscus in one of his knees that still acts up. Eventually, he was medically discharged and determined to be 90 percent disabled.

Suffering from severe PTSD, by early 2014, Jamie was still accli-mating to life as a civilian. He moved into a studio apartment above a garage in a large home in Chula Vista, California, south of San Diego. The property owners, who live in an attached house, have two York-shire terriers. Jamie's lease agreement required that the dogs still have access in and out of the apartment through a dog door. That was fine with Jamie, whose family had dogs when he was growing up. One of the Yorkies, five-pound Ali, became attached to Jamie from the start.

On a weekday afternoon, as he walked through the gate into the yard, and then up the stairs to his studio apartment, his face lit up as Ali ran through the dog door and jumped up on his bed where Jamie was sitting.

"She's a happy little dog—a lover," he said as he picked her up. "She keeps me occupied and grounded. She's perfect."

Ali spends most of her days with Jamie when he's home. "I've always had dogs, and having Ali with me is like having a dog of my own."

While he remained in his apartment, Ali went back outside through the dog door. Later, when Jamie walked down the stairs to the backyard, Ali ran across the grass to greet him. "Just look at this little face," Jamie said as he bent down to pick her up. Ali immediately rested her head against his chest.

"You can't stay anxious or angry with this face," he continued. "I don't jump as much since she's been with me. She knows when I'm jacked-up and anxious or when I'm having a bad day. That's when she jumps up to me, gets on my chest and right up to my face. She calms me down."

Christopher Gibson, a former sergeant in the Dirty Deuce Platoon in the 1st Marine Expeditionary Unit—"the nation's ready force," Chris pointed out—has had a similar experience. After he joined up in 2004 in Florida, he deployed to Iraq. Then he went to Afghanistan for his final tour. He saw combat while in both theaters. As a result of being in combat and too close to explosions, he lost all hearing in his left ear. But he didn't leave his tour early because of his hearing loss. "I came back with my unit," he said proudly.

After he returned to the States in November 2010, Chris knew something was off other than just his hearing. He underwent tests and was diagnosed with both traumatic brain injury and post-traumatic stress. While getting treatment, he knew he needed something more in his life. "I needed someone to keep me company," he said.

First, he adopted Kodiak, a Great Dane puppy. "I wanted something of substance to take care of, to have a purpose," he explained. "I would do anything for Kodiak. He's always here for me."

Feeling secure and personally safe is a major concern for many returning service members. Kodiak has provided Chris with the security he was seeking. "He hears everything," Chris said. "I can't hear some things, because of my hearing loss. If someone tried to break in, he'd wake me up."

Tattooed on his upper chest are the words "Calm Chaos." Chris also wears a metal bracelet from his company with the heading "KIA," followed by a list of those from his company who were killed in action, inscribed in a tiny font. "It serves as a reminder of those who gave their all," he said solemnly.

For downtime Chris plays with Kodiak and Rolo, a puppy he adopted as a companion for Kodiak.

On a sunny weekday afternoon, he demonstrated playtime with Kodiak and Rolo. Because Kodiak is a companion and not a service dog, he can't take him to work with him or to a personal training facility, where he's training to become a certified personal-strength trainer. So he adopted Rolo, a wire terrier mix who's tiny compared to Kodiak's large size. As the two played, Rolo appeared oblivious to the stark difference in size.

"Where'd the ball go, boys?" Chris asked just before he produced a ball from behind his back and tossed it their way. Kodiak jumped first to grab it, missed, and Rolo jumped in the air and caught it on its way down, before it could hit the ground. A happy Rolo, practically preening, ran from Kodiak with the ball in his mouth as he dodged the Great Dane's attempt to get it from him. "Rolo's my comedy," Chris said as his face broke into a smile and he stood watching the pair. "Both of them are like kids."

Each morning before leaving for the training center, Chris takes "his boys," as he calls them, to the back of his condo for a thirty-minute game of fetch. Then, on weekends when he's free, "Kodiak pulls me on my bike," he said.

As Chris stood in the alley and signaled Kodiak to face him and put his paws on his shoulders—making Kodiak nearly his height—Chris said, "He's single-handedly saved my life when I've been unsure about things. He calms me."

—◦—

In the case of former army soldier Joel Rudnick and a pit bull named Wigwam, both have survived traumatic circumstances.

Wigwam once lived in squalor in an abandoned house with no electricity and no water. She was discovered by an undercover police detective who entered the house during a sting operation. Detectives were working to break up a dog-fighting business, revealed, in part, because of the telltale signs of blood on the walls. The officer, allowed into the house under the pretense that he was shopping for a dog, found Wigwam in a dark, dank room, off by herself.

Once removed from the house, Wigwam was collared, photographed, and confiscated as evidence. The suspect, in turn, was taken into custody and charged with felonies. In the past, dogs like Wigwam languished indefinitely as evidence in animal shelters until the criminal cases were resolved, their dubious fates left up to the operators of the crowded shelters.

Not so for Wigwam.

She was pulled from the shelter by Chicago Pit Stop Rescue, which then placed her into the Court Case Dog Program, founded by Safe Humane Chicago. This program provides a dog-friendly approach to canines that are confiscated by law enforcement and entered into the court system. Working in partnership with law enforcement, animal control, judges, and rescue groups, the Court Case Dog Program rescues dogs like Wigwam from shelters, places them in foster care, trains and rehabilitates them, and then offers them for adoption—a process that often includes placing the dogs' photos and information on Facebook.

It was a Facebook photo of Wigwam that grabbed the attention of former Army National Guard sergeant and squad leader Joel Rudnick. Just home from tours of duty in Iraq and Afghanistan, he was searching the Internet and spotted Wigwam on the social media site.

All it took was one look.

"I saw a picture of Wigwam online, and she absolutely melted my heart," Joel said. "I was having sleeping and anxiety issues. She's just been a godsend. It's probably one of the best decisions I've ever made, getting a dog. She definitely helped my transition coming home."

Joel, who suffers from traumatic brain injury and post-traumatic stress, arrived home from Iraq in 2009, but it took a few years to get diagnosed. "The VA told me it was a readjustment issue," Joel said. "I was showing anger and anxiety issues. It took me about nine months to get just four hours of sleep a night."

He knew what was bothering him. He just needed help dealing with it.

Then, he was deployed again, this time to Afghanistan. He returned home for good in 2012. "For some reason, that transition wasn't as tough."

When he thought about it, Joel realized the difference: He'd lost two friends while he was in Iraq, which was very difficult to live with.

Peter Bouckaert with Human Rights Watch points out that living with the horrors of war is more difficult at home than it is in combat. "After a while, war becomes a reality," said Peter in the documentary, *Which Way Is the Front Line from Here?* "And the hard part is not about going to war. It's about going back home."

Joel had other adjustment issues, so he knew that while he wanted a dog, the timing wasn't right. He needed more time. "Once some financial situations were cleared up," he said, "I started getting serious about adopting a dog. I saw Wigwam online. She had been a court-case dog, and I put in an application to get her."

Wigwam's initial night at home with Joel was the first time he was able to fall asleep without a problem. That hadn't happened since his return from Afghanistan.

It didn't come as a surprise to Cynthia Bathurst, who founded the court-case program that helped save Wigwam from an uncertain fate. Placing a pit bull from precarious living circumstances with a military veteran, she said, makes her job worthwhile.

"Wigwam was found in a back room in despicable conditions," Cynthia said. "Police went in purposefully to look at dogs that had been used for dog-fighting. She was saved by them."

"It means everything for Wigwam to have been seen by such a wonderful man as a US veteran who then took her in," Cynthia said. "Joel says they needed each other, and it's clear how much they're connected."

Joel now regularly volunteers as a photographer for Safe Humane Chicago, which is responsible for matching him with his court-case dog Wigwam.

This match was so successful that it prompted the nonprofit group to launch VALOR—Veterans Advancing Lives of Rescues—a program that connects five US veterans each year with court-case dogs while also providing an eight-week training regimen.

"Research shows that animals are an amazing source of physical, emotional, and social healing," Cynthia said. "And watching Joel's and Wiggy's bond grow stronger as they became a bigger part of the Safe Humane family has motivated the organization and me to make opportunities more available by pairing brave and valiant veterans and a very special group of brave and resilient shelter dogs, our Court Case dogs." The end result, Cynthia said, is that the match provides the dogs with a purpose in an environment that's healing, leading to renewal for both.

That source of comfort and healing has been evident in Joel's well-being since he adopted Wigwam. When Joel went to army training in the summer of 2014, Cynthia set up boarding arrangements for Wigwam, and staff members spent time with her each day. "Watching Joel say 'I'll be back' to her before their first separation was touching," Cynthia said. "She was so good when we visited with her while he was gone. But the strong bond they share was obvious when he returned. It's palpable."

Joel agreed with Cynthia that the two are strongly connected, especially since they've each experienced tough times.

"I think Wigwam and I both know that we've helped each other," Joel explained. "I got her two and a half months after being home, and she's been a godsend. Adopting her was one of the best decisions I ever made in my life. She's definitely made a difference. She's helped my transition coming home."

"I've given her a good home," he continued, "and she, in turn, calms me down and makes me smile and laugh every day. We sort of rescued each other."

# CHAPTER 10

# TBI: From Surviving to Thriving

Getting a service dog for retired army sergeant Javier Negrete took him back to his roots in Mexico where he had once had a loyal dog by his side.

He survived an injury after an ambush while on patrol in an Iraqi market, only to visit his family in Mexico while on a two-week leave and experience a life-changing car accident that cracked vertebrae and caused additional trauma to his brain.

"I was a cavalry scout in the army. My job was to find the enemy and get information from them," he said from his home in Pearland, Texas, south of Houston. "We encountered direct fire almost every day."

His job was to perform reconnaissance, which can be just as dangerous as combat. Yet, his only injuries—each invisible to the naked eye—were traumatic brain injury caused from the concussion of rockets and post-traumatic stress from dealing with the chaos and loss of life around him. Still, he counts his blessings. "I was lucky I came back home alive," he said.

Now retired, Javier, sporting short black hair and a trimmed beard, has gone from being wheelchair-bound to walking short distances with the assistance of a cane and his service dog, Cash, who was placed with him through the Patriot PAWS program. He credits Cash with ending the loneliness he felt while spending much of his time at home alone.

One type of thing that can trigger anxiety is lightning, thunder, and fireworks. "I hate storms," Javier said. "They remind me of Iraq. Everyday situations remind me of it. I can't watch war movies, and

I can't play some video games. My PTSD," he added, "will never go away."

But through the companionship of a service dog, his circumstances have improved dramatically.

Several people had suggested to him that a service dog might help his day-to-day living. "I applied to several places. Patriot PAWS accepted me first," Javier said. During the introduction process, Cash chose him, as is typical with many groups where the dog's preference plays a big part in which dogs the veterans are matched with.

Javier was glad Cash chose him.

"Before I got Cash, I was depressed, because I lived alone," he said. "I got her and I wasn't alone anymore. She's glued to me. Besides helping me with everyday tasks—like picking up things I need and bringing them to me—she helps me with my depression. She makes my life a lot better."

While growing up in Guadalajara, Mexico, Javier had a pet dog named Russo. "He was so loyal," he said. "My father used to tell me I spent more time with Russo than with my family. To me, Russo was family too."

His mother died of cancer when he was nine, and his father, two years later. "My father missed my mom so much, he became an alcoholic. It killed him."

When he was eleven, his dog Russo was hit by a car and died. His family kept the truth from him, saying that Russo had run away, so he spent hours each day looking for him. They finally had to tell him that Russo had been hit by a car.

Later, an uncle moved Javier to America to live with family members. While he was in high school, at age seventeen, a recruiter approached Javier. "I enlisted in the army," he said.

Because of his injuries, Javier was discharged from the military in 2006. It took him until 2009 to get a service dog. All the while, he never forgot his boyhood dog Russo.

Now with another dog by his side, he is no longer self-conscious about his injuries. "I'm not the guy in the wheelchair anymore," he said. "I'm the guy with the cool dog."

Veteran Lance Weir pets Auggie.

Three-month-old Hallow at CCI's puppy kindergarten.

CCI puppy raiser Heidi Badger-Chrisman with Lois, Stanza, and Nira at the weekly playdate.

Veteran Calvin Smith with his service dog Chesney.

Veteran Buddy Wachtstetter with his service dog Hillary.

Marine staff sergeant Richard Gonzalez training service dog Charlie at Wounded Warrior Battalion West headquarters.

Puppy raiser Mike Bennett helps Meeko practice skills with a wall-jumping exercise.

Navy corpsman Melissa Jaramillo Ramirez training with Gunner at Wounded Warrior Battalion West headquarters.

Leo helps veteran Larry Whitted feel at ease in public places.

Service dog Moses has veteran Chris Lance's back.

Veteran Connie Rendon walking with her service dog Blaze.

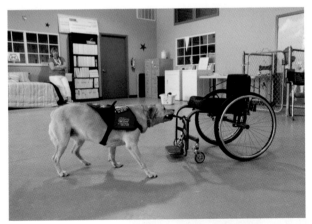

Lori Stevens watches as Jazz pulls a wheelchair during a training session.

Veteran Clay Rankin with his service dog Harley.

Veteran Donovan Mack with his service dog Midnight.

Veterans Nico Marcolongo and David Rayder with Tali at surf clinic.

Veteran Nico Marcolongo kisses Tali's face at veterans' surf clinic.

Veteran Justin Lansford plays fetch with his service dog Gabe.

Navy commander Theresa Everest relaxes on the beach with her service dog Spring.

Veteran Nancy Lee Augsbach shares a moment with her service dog Gnat.

Veteran James Cadieux walks Cruiser on the beach every day.

Veteran James Cadieux's service dog Cruiser.

Veteran Larry McMahan on a walk with service dog Abby.

Veteran Chris Gibson stands eye to eye with Kodiak.

Veteran Jamie Camacho shares a moment with Ali.

Veteran Javier Negrete hanging out with his service dog Cash.

Barrett, a "lean dog," helps veteran Joel Hunt keep his balance.

Opening the refrigerator is just one task Barrett does for veteran Joel Hunt.

Veteran James Van Thach and Liz.

Uno helps veteran
Douglas Knieriem while
out in public.

Veteran April Cook's service dog Claire gives her the courage to feel comfortable in public.

Wendy brings the phone to veteran Richard Heath.

Veteran
Roddy Lewis
and wife Lee
pet Roddy's
service dog
Jack.

Trainer Cindy
Kilgore hugs Keller
after training at a
home improvement
store.

Joel Hunt, an army specialist, also suffered traumatic brain injury along with paralysis on one side after being injured by an IED while on patrol as a demolitions specialist in Baqubah, Iraq. The details of that day are foggy.

"I don't think they can pinpoint when I was injured," he said. "I was in multiple explosions, including a roadside blast. I don't know the date. Most of my deployments, I don't remember. On my discharge record, it says I was in Iraq in 2003 and 2004." Because of the traumatic brain injury, Joel experiences what he calls "missed time."

Always with him, even nearby when he's skiing on the slopes, is his service dog Barrett, a golden retriever and Lab mix, matched with him by Freedom Service Dogs. Barrett, he said, brought meaning back into his life.

Joel left the army in 2007 and went into intense therapy. Confined to a wheelchair for a year, he felt helpless. His parents moved in with him to be his caregivers. The most difficult part of his homecoming was remembering his battle buddies.

"I couldn't get the memories of my dead buddies out of my head," he wrote on his blog. "I felt that I should have done more to keep them alive. I wished that I had died in Iraq rather than having to face the difficulties of my situation."

At the same time, his determination remained intact. He set a goal to walk again. He knew he couldn't do it alone, however; he needed help.

In the meantime, Joel's parents—"my biggest supporters at the time"—motivated him to leave his house and participate in life again. In late 2008, "My parents forced me to go to a ski camp for veterans with TBI."

He surprised himself by learning how to ski. He asked if he could compete, and a coach told him he was too old. On top of that, he didn't have the funds necessary to compete, to cover the expenses of travel and lodging. So, he turned to the Challenged Athletes Foundation

(CAF) and its Operation Rebound program for injured troops and first responders, which provided him with the equipment and funding to compete as a downhill ski racer.

In 2011, Joel put in his request for a service dog, and was ultimately matched with Barrett.

With his dog's help, not only did Joel walk again, but he also put on skis and competed, becoming a top-ranked Paralympics skier—the first ever with a traumatic brain injury. A sponsorship with the Japan-based Ogasaka Ski Company and training with the Paralympic Alpine Development Program in Aspen helped him to qualify for the 2014 US Paralympic Alpine Skiing Team. The Paralympics provide an opportunity for athletes with varying physical disabilities to compete at an elite level.

Joel competed in the Paralympics in Sochi, Russia. While Barrett traveled with Joel to most of his skiing events, he couldn't go on the slopes with him because he's not a certified search-and-rescue dog. Barrett always waited for Joel at the finish line. Joel retired as a skier with the Paralympics after the 2014 Games; he will still ski, just not at a competitive level.

Joel worked as an ordnance disposal technician, detonating roadside bombs along what he called "RPG Alley," a reference to rocket-propelled grenade attacks, making the road between Baghdad and the international airport a dangerous one. It was while he was on patrol in Baqubah, Iraq, that he was hit by an IED blast, causing his brain injury and paralysis on one side of his body.

As for Barrett, he arrived as a nine-month-old puppy at Freedom Service Dogs through the Intermountain Humane Society, along with his brother, Tex, who also graduated from the group's program to become a service dog. The two were pulled from a shelter, and Intermountain Humane Society identified them as possible service dog candidates.

"They tested unbelievably well at the shelter for me," said Sarah Keyes, who trained Barrett. "They went into a foster home for a few months before they started their service dog training. Barrett was a blast to work with—very smart, and he loves to please."

Dogs like Barrett and Tex, once homeless and rescued from shelters, are symbolic of dogs and veterans helping each other, said Sharan Wilson, executive director of Freedom Service Dogs, who paired Joel and Barrett. "I believe there's an affinity between these rescued dogs and the soldiers who feel like they've been abandoned," Sharan said. "They have a natural connection. These dogs have gone from no one wanting them to being with a veteran twenty-four hours a day. They're in heaven."

Air force airman first class David Rogers suffered a debilitating traumatic brain injury. The prognosis: He wouldn't make it. Along the path toward learning how to communicate, walk, and participate in life once again, he was paired with a skilled companion dog to help support him in his struggle.

David joined the air force in 2005, not long after graduating from high school. His first assignment was at Luke Air Force Base in Arizona, followed by a deployment to Korea. Then he shipped out for Germany.

While on active duty in 2009 at the NATO base in Spangdahlem, Germany, David was injured in a car accident. During a light rain, he lost control of his car and was broadsided by another vehicle. David was unresponsive at the scene, and was Life-Flighted to a trauma center in Trier, about twenty-five miles away.

David had a shattered pelvis, broken ribs, thoracic injuries, and internal-organ damage. Worst of all, he had suffered a traumatic brain injury that was so severe, it sent him into a coma. Doctors didn't expect him to live more than a couple of days.

Against all odds, David survived. After four months in a coma, he emerged with limited verbal ability. From that point on, it was up to David and how he responded to the therapies provided by a team of doctors and experts. After more than four months in Germany, David was transferred to the VA Polytrauma in Virginia. His family relocated to Chesterfield, Virginia, to be near the VA facilities so that David could continue the rehabilitation that he'd begun there.

Dr. Shane McNamee explained David's lengthy rehabilitation to BrainLineMilitary.org. "One of the concepts that we try to get people to understand is that things are going to be normal again someday. But it's going to be a new normal.

"Whatever happened to them and the current struggles they're having are not going to define their lives. There's going to be joy. There's going to be pain in their lives. But if we can help reawaken the person inside of them, I think we've done a tremendous job."

During his lengthy rehabilitation, David was matched with his skilled service dog, Jersey, through Canine Companions for Independence, at its facility on Long Island. According to David's mother, Lauri Rogers, Jersey has been a big factor in supporting what she calls David's "determination and faith."

David has learned to communicate via a laptop attached to his wheelchair. Through continued rehabilitation therapies, he has also learned to walk again and to dress himself. "David used his arms and strength and gained coordination as he brushed Jersey and dressed him in his vest and collars," Lauri recalled. "David got out of the house, and slowly his walks increased in frequency and length, so that he can now walk two miles with a walker, no longer using a wheelchair," she said. "Jersey also jumps on David's bed, on cue, to snuggle with David when he experiences severe headaches."

Jersey also serves as an icebreaker for David with strangers. "Jersey's calming effect as an unconditional friend," Lauri said, "has helped David through setbacks and crises, as well as sharing the joy of social events." When David was in the hospital for major neurosurgery, Jersey visited daily. Jersey has also "enjoyed licking the frosting off David's beard at his birthdays."

The amazing thing, Lauri Rogers said, is to watch the influence Jersey has over David's growing independence. "As David's mother, I sometimes succumb to my emotions while caring for him," she said. "Jersey is so much more unconditionally caring for David than I am. Much of the grief involved with caring for a brain-injured person is directly connected to dependence/independence issues."

It's David's job to care for Jersey and help see to his dog's needs, such as feeding and taking him outside. "Caring for Jersey, and interacting with him, has David trying to be independent and, over time, succeeding," his mother noted.

"The progress I have seen from David personally since the first time I met him is quite remarkable," said John Bentzinger, a public relations officer for Canine Companions for Independence. "Most people don't survive his type of injuries, and he has literally rewritten the book about TBI and rehabilitation. Many of the things doctors learned from his care have been adopted by the VA doctors and are being used to treat other combat-wounded veterans."

In May 2014, David and Jersey, along with his mother, joined a rally of about two hundred people asking lawmakers to pass regulations that would make it easier for veterans to acquire service dogs.

Without Jersey, Lauri Rogers said, her son may not have made such enormous strides. "I'm not sure he would have made such progress, from needing hands-on assistance in his activities, to achieving much more independence. Jersey has enabled David to recover."

Physicians are learning more about traumatic brain injury as it relates to combat, particularly that this type of injury can cause permanent physical afflictions, including immobilizing migraines and even seizures.

For former army staff sergeant Jason North, having a service dog in his life that can detect epileptic seizures before they happen has been a blessing not only for Jason, but also for his wife Maryjoy and daughter Hayley, who no longer have to be on the alert for the onset of a seizure. Jason's safety was at risk because he would often fall during a seizure. Now, Parole, a large, white Labrador retriever, is there to sense seizures before their onset and to bark for help when Jason is experiencing one. By Parole alerting Jason to an oncoming seizure, he has time to sit down and prepare for it.

In March 2012, Parole and Jason graduated from advanced training, and Parole went home to Killeen, Texas, with Jason and his family.

When Jason is about to have a seizure, "Parole will nudge me and try to wake me up, or he'll go and get help," said Jason, noting that he's installing a safety button in his home so that Parole can also call for an ambulance.

Jason's seizures were brought on by a traumatic brain injury he received in October 2008 during his second tour in Iraq, while attached to the 3rd Cavalry Regiment. When the Humvee he was riding in fell into a pit trap, after being lured there by several Iraqis on horseback, the impact slammed Jason's body into a fifty-caliber machine gun in front of him and a fifty-caliber ammunitions can behind him, leaving him with a fractured face, broken vertebra, and his first grand mal seizure.

Enter Parole, a dog specially trained to detect seizures and to comfort and protect the person during the event.

Parole has changed Jason's life.

"We do everything together. It makes a lot of things a lot easier," Jason said about the dog he received in March 2012, through a grant from the nonprofit organization, Dog Bless You.

"He always keeps me busy; he helps me pick up the house all the time, and he helps me with Hayley. He's like another part of the family," Jason said.

Parole is so named because he was raised at a women's correctional institution in Gatesville, Texas, by inmate trainers Valerie Fry, in prison for aggravated robbery, and AJ Blanchette, convicted of credit card abuse. Parole is an example of specially trained dogs—some rescued and some donated by breeders—that have successfully graduated from Patriot PAWS through a partnership with the Texas Department of Criminal Justice, said Lori Stevens, founder and executive director at Patriot PAWS. After two years in prison, Parole was matched with Jason.

"Our mission is to train and provide service dogs of the highest quality at no cost to disabled American veterans with mobility disabilities," Lori said.

But it goes deeper than that. Lori took her dedication to helping veterans a step further by hiring two inmates who voluntarily trained puppies for Patriot PAWS while they were in prison. Upon their respective releases, Parole's puppy trainers went to work full-time at Patriot PAWS. Valerie was hired as a trainer and rescue program coordinator, while AJ went to work for Lori as a trainer and puppy-raiser program coordinator.

Valerie served seven years and was released in May 2012. While she was still incarcerated, she told *WFAA News,* the Dallas, Texas, ABC affiliate, "Each and every day I wake up and put one hundred percent of myself into this program. My dad was a veteran, and that is why."

AJ, who lives in Terrell, Texas, and was an attorney who practiced law before she went to prison for credit-card abuse, wrote on LinkedIn about her work as a trainer. "Veterans of the armed services inspire me daily to do my very best in training these amazing four-legged creatures, which will one day be their forever partners in service work."

---

Douglas Knieriem is one of the many veterans diagnosed with combat-related traumatic brain injury. For him, a dog named Uno has helped him deal with the loss and injuries he suffered on the sands of Iraq.

Douglas, a captain with twenty-four years of service—eleven in the air force and thirteen with the army—was asked to escort the remains of his good friend, army captain Joshua McClimans, a fallen brother in arms, home to Jamestown, Pennsylvania. Joshua was an army head nurse of a Medevac unit that served with the 848th Forward Surgical Team, who died in April 2011 at the Forward Operating Base Salerno, Khost province, Afghanistan, when insurgents attacked with rocket fire. Joshua had been in Afghanistan just six weeks.

"I got the phone call that Josh was killed, and within twenty-four hours, I was given orders to be his military escort. I stayed behind and then was with him twenty-four hours a day."

Before he left to deliver Captain McClimans's flag-draped casket to his family and his final resting place, Douglas wrote in a public

Facebook post, "I will sleep beside him so he is not alone, and he will comfort me, for he loved me as I did him."

And so he did.

Once he arrived at the mortuary, Douglas stood guard. "I slept on the floor of the funeral parlor for a few nights," he said. "That was tough. It was a small town. They asked where I was going to stay, and I said, 'I'm going to stay right here.'"

As is military protocol, he remained next to the casket so that the captain's body was not alone. "I stayed there about five days. I stood at a position of attention for sixteen hours straight," he said. The duty of a military escort is not fulfilled until they meet with the mortuary director. He also delivered the personal effects.

As a nurse anesthetist, Douglas was used to taking care of people. He was one of two anesthesia providers in the Iraqi region and saw his share of combat injuries. "I saw a variety of things," he said. "I took care of Iraqi soldiers and children. I saw a kid who was shot in the eye. The guys who were suspected insurgents would attack us at night, then they'd get hurt, and they'd come to us during the day for help."

One night his unit got a call for Medevac to transport someone. When Douglas went on those calls, they would fly in the Black Hawk helicopter to the destination and then they'd fly him back. Douglas's job was to intubate the soldiers. On that night, Douglas flew with a new Black Hawk crew.

"We came up over the wall in Balad," he said, referring to the Shiite stronghold that was a vital supply hub fortified by the United States during the war. "They always flew with night vision, without the lights on, so we couldn't be seen. We came up over the wall and we were being shot at by an AK-47. The pilot had left the navigation lights on." No one was injured, but it left Douglas shell-shocked.

Douglas, who lives in Valley City, Ohio, began his service in the air force, stationed at Nellis Air Force Base in southern Nevada. After a stint there, he left the service and a year later joined the US Air Force Reserve for seven years, until 1997. Then in 2003 he joined the army. His unit eventually deployed to the Forward Operating Base

Delta, located in Al-Kūt, which lies along the Tigris River in eastern Iraq about a hundred miles southeast of Baghdad. Al-Kūt is where he received his traumatic brain injury after just two and a half weeks in-country. All told, "I was boots on the ground a total of four months at FOB Delta," he said.

"The night I experienced the TBI," Douglas explained, "I had been feeling better for a day or two after having a viral infection, and I went to a workout facility with Scott Henry, a cardiac surgeon." The workout center was set up in two tents and provided a place for military personnel to exercise during their downtime.

"Scott and I stuck together," he said. "We went to the gym together every day. My appetite—lost when I was sick—started to come back.

"'I'm hungry,' I told him. 'I'm going to get something to eat. Want to come?'

"'I'm going to finish working out,' Scott said. 'I'll catch you later at the unit.'"

To Douglas, everything on the FOB Delta felt like it was a mile away. The mess hall was no different.

"From the chow hall to the gym was about a mile," Douglas said. "You can walk on a hardened surface. But if we could find a trail that was a direct line, we'd use that and cut down the time. I took a trail in the dirt. I could see the lights of DFAC, the dining facility, which were hard-surface tents. All branches of service and contractors and foreign services ate there."

Scott called Douglas on the radio.

"Where are you on the trail?" Scott asked.

He told him the distance he'd walked.

"I changed my mind," Scott told him. "I'll catch up and eat with you."

"I stopped and waited for him," Douglas said.

It was pitch black that night. Suddenly, Douglas heard an incoming rocket and immediately recognized it as a 120-millimeter. "I could hear it coming," he said. "I could tell it was at a high rate of speed, because it went from a low sound to a high sound."

He could see just sixty or seventy millimeters ahead of him. He described what happened as similar to fireworks being set off.

"I could see the blast," Douglas said. "I'll be damned if that rocket didn't land on its tail about seventy meters ahead of me. It knocked me off my feet. My ears were ringing, and I couldn't hear for about ten minutes. It was like one of those bright-white flowering fireworks. If you put five of those together, that's how bright it was. I couldn't hear anything. I thought, *I'm going to die here*, because there was more than one rocket coming in."

Then, seemingly out of nowhere, a soldier grabbed him.

"All of a sudden, a guy picked me up by the back of my shirt and pulled me into a concrete bunker placed all over the place on base," he said. "A bunch of people were in there. They put flashlights on me, but I couldn't hear them. But after a while, I could hear."

The people in the bunker had watched as debris flew over Douglas's head and thought for sure he'd been injured. They all told him how surprised they were to see him unhurt.

In the meantime, Scott was on the trail, trying to catch up to Douglas.

"He could see my silhouette running when the rocket hit the ground. I knew Scott would think I got killed because he knew I was on the trail."

Douglas couldn't find his gear, and he lost his radio when the rockets hit. He had no way to communicate with his unit or with Scott. He left the bunker and started running toward his unit.

"The adrenaline was rushing," Douglas said. "I had to get back to my unit to let them know I was okay. As I got closer to my unit, I saw a silhouette running down the trail. It was Scott. I started yelling to get his attention."

Scott stopped in his tracks and the two greeted each other. "Scott started crying. He told me, 'I thought you were dead.'"

Douglas Knieriem hasn't forgotten what Scott did for him.

So, each November 3 at 7:40 p.m., Douglas telephones Scott Henry.

"I give him a call to say 'Thank you.' We're as close as brothers. If he hadn't radioed and asked me to wait for him, I would have been killed."

Also close as brothers are Douglas and his dog Uno. On top of the traumatic brain injury he suffered, Douglas also damaged a rotator cuff and has a herniated disc, in addition to some permanent hearing loss.

When he returned home from Iraq, he already had a dog, a Labrador named Harley.

"Harley was about thirteen when I went to Iraq," he said. "I didn't expect him to still be alive when I got home. We'd never been separated before. There was a good chance I wouldn't see him again. I was super excited he was still alive."

Nine months after Douglas returned home, Harley passed away. "He turned fifteen. He was getting confused at night. He paced and had a lot of pain. He couldn't sleep. I sat on the floor with him to comfort him."

On his last day, before he took Harley to the veterinarian, "we went to the park," Douglas said. "Then I took him to McDonald's and gave him as many cheeseburgers as he could eat. It was kind of like his perfect day. And then I took him to the vet and said good-bye."

Some time had passed when he noticed a sign advertising puppies for sale as he drove his daughter, Madelaine, to a piano lesson. He stopped on their way home to check out the pups.

"The puppies jumped up on my daughter," he said. "She asked, 'Daddy, can we have a puppy?'" After discussing it with his wife, he returned the next day to talk to the woman who owned the puppies. "She told me, 'Take one home and see how it works.' I took him home. I told my wife the dog was in the car and I wanted her to see our daughter's face when she saw the puppy. My wife opened the car door and the little puppy jumped out. My daughter was so excited."

They named the puppy Uno, who was nine weeks old at the time. At about fifteen weeks, Douglas started Uno in basic obedience classes.

Meanwhile, "I was still struggling with my buddy being killed and what happened over in Iraq," Douglas said. "I was looking for a support group online and came across Veteran's Best Friend."

Douglas read an online article about psychiatric service dogs provided to help with recovery. He called the contact number for Jesse Tanner, one of the mentors in the group, and Jesse invited him to visit the center.

"I went there to see the facility," Douglas said. "The next Sunday, I took Uno there. I didn't know this kind of training was available."

Douglas lived just twenty minutes away from Veteran's Best Friend. He and Uno were accepted into the program, and the two ultimately graduated as a service dog team.

While Douglas had a tight bond with his dog Harley, what he experiences with Uno is a first. "I've never had a relationship with a dog like I have with Uno," he said. "He just wants to love on me. He can actually give me a hug. He puts his head on my neck and leans into me. It's comforting."

Uno helps Douglas when he gets debilitating headaches by comforting him and taking his mind off of the pain. Douglas adds, "Uno is very supportive on the days when I can't get up and move like I usually can. He just stays with me. He knows when I'm stressed out or angry or sad. He picks up on that. Sometimes I don't want to talk. There's too much going on in my head, and then here comes this big dog and he wants to cozy up with me. He knows when I'm upset and he wants to help."

Finding Veteran's Best Friend was similar to finding a support group, he said.

"It was long overdue for me to start talking. I hadn't talked to anybody. I was looking for a support group, and Veteran's Best Friend became a support group. It's full of veterans. We don't sit around and tell war stories," he continued. "No one wants to talk about it. It's like an unspoken understanding. Many of us have the same stories, just different people in different places. It's all traumatic."

Uno is so connected to him that one day when Douglas went to the VA hospital without Uno, he walked past the information desk, just as he always does, but no one said hello to him. Douglas said, "Hi," and one of the employees looked surprised and then said, "Oh, my gosh, we didn't recognize you without your dog."

That's because, Douglas said, "He's become a part of me. He goes to counseling with me. He goes to restaurants. He's been to Cleveland Indians baseball games. He's been to country concerts. Last year we went to a Luke Bryan concert together, myself, Uno, and my wife."

While people comment on how well-behaved he is, Uno does have his moments.

"He's a really smart dog. He wants to learn. But he can be stubborn too. You can tell when he's being stubborn, because he'll moan. If I'm watching TV at night, he'll give me a long moan as if he's saying, 'Come on, dude, it's time to go to bed.' If I'm talking to someone and I'm in a long conversation, he'll moan because he wants to leave. He's got emotions too. Sometimes it's like having a toddler."

Around the house when his vest isn't on, Uno "is a regular dog," Douglas said. But when it's time to work, "He has my back and I have his. I'm really proud of my dog. It's a trust thing. I never have to worry about the trust being broken. It's a closeness I never thought I'd have with a dog. Uno not only takes the burden off of my wife, but he also takes that feeling of me being a burden to someone else off of me. Uno is more than an animal. He's more than a family dog. He's my teammate."

<hr />

It's the same for retired army captain James Van Thach, also diagnosed with TBI and PTSD, among other injuries. He refers to his dog Liz as "my lifesaver."

"Being in the military, my buddies were around all the time. My service dog Liz is here for me now, and she definitely has my back," he said.

At his home in Queens, New York, he proudly pointed out that Liz, a yellow Labrador retriever matched through Canine Companions for Independence's facility in Medford, Long Island, knows forty-five commands and tasks. "I can't bend down to pick up items because of my back injury," he said. "I need her to pick up my socks, my shoes, and my clothes." She also picks up individual medication capsules and pills and hands them to him. "I take medication several times a day—I take twenty pills a day to survive—and I sometimes drop the pills. She picks them up for me."

James—who wears an eye patch, including a white one with his white military uniform for full-dress occasions—was wounded twice in Iraq, once by an IED that exploded under his Humvee. Despite suffering a brain injury and other wounds, he asked to stay in-country. The second hit, in 2007, was from a Katyusha rocket fired into the base that exploded just twenty meters from James, landing him on his back. Again, despite his physical injuries, he asked and was granted permission to stay.

"I sat there in the hospital and I saw my fellow military brothers and sisters missing arms, missing legs, and then I looked at myself," he said when he and Liz appeared on the *Today* show in May 2014. "I had all my body parts. I felt so guilty. I thought it would be a dishonor to leave on the same airplane with them. I asked if there was any way I could stay in Iraq and assist, and it turned out that I could, but only on desk duty."

James has undergone medical treatments for a variety of physical injuries, including one to his back, loss of sight in his left eye, and sciatic nerve damage to his left leg, as well as treatment for short-term memory loss and post-traumatic stress. There are moments when "my body feels like a prison. It's trying at times," he said, adding that the emotional comfort and undying loyalty he receives from his service dog, who entered his life in 2012, has made all the difference.

"Liz is here to get me out of that deep, deep hole I'm in. She always lends a helping hand. She's my buddy, and I have to stay alive for her."

James had intended to join the service in some capacity, although not in combat. Military service was in his blood. His father retired as a lieutenant colonel in the US Army after serving in the Vietnam War, and then returned and became a New York Police Department officer. And his grandfather was a World War II veteran.

After high school, James attended St. John's University on an ROTC scholarship and enrolled at Touro Law Center. Then 9/11 changed everything for him. He finished law school, joined the service, and immediately volunteered for combat duty.

But instead of joining the service as a JAG advocate general—a military lawyer—he chose instead to be on the front line as an infantry soldier specifically trained to fight boots-on-the-ground, to engage the enemy face-to-face. He joined the 1st Battalion, 3rd Brigade, 6th Iraqi Army Division at Forward Operating Base Constitution in Baghdad, Iraq. While there, he served not only as an infantry officer in active combat, but also as a military advisor for twenty-four consecutive months. He also served as a vehicle driver on more than 150 combat missions, traveling along dangerous routes during daylight and night hours while avoiding IEDs, small arms and RPG fire, snipers, and indirect fire.

For his efforts, he was awarded the Bronze Star for his work as a military advisor to the Iraqi Army, plus the government of Iraq awarded him the rank of Honorary Staff Brigadier General in the Iraqi Army.

He retired from the US Army in 2013, but then returned to the war zone, this time as a civilian to Afghanistan on a humanitarian moral-welfare mission, shipping out in 2013. His doctor, who felt the field exercise would be therapeutic, approved the civilian duty.

Liz graduated from the Canine Companions for Independence program in December 2012. At the ceremony, James talked about the training and what having a service dog means to him. "It was a very long process, very challenging training," he said. "Not only did we have classroom instruction, but hands-on training. Me being matched with Liz is more as a team member, like in the military. And not only do we work together, but when it's time to relax and have fun, we relax and have fun."

James originally joined the service, in part, as a way to give back to his country, because, after his father met his future South Vietnamese bride while overseas and took her home to America on a fiancée visa, the US government helped his father bring nearly eighty members of his mother's family to America to free them from Communism. For that, he said, "I owed my country my service in the military."

That same sense of freedom his mother and her relatives felt at having been freed from a Communist country, James now feels he's gotten from his dog. "Liz gives me independence," he said.

———

A terrier named Major helped save a retired army soldier's life after he collapsed during an epileptic seizure. Retired Marine sergeant Terrance McGlade had known that Major was smart, but he was about to learn just how bright he really was.

Major, a terrier and Labrador retriever mix, was rescued from an animal-hoarding situation, taken in by animal control, rescued, and then trained by Stiggy's Dogs, a nonprofit organization that provides psychiatric-service canines to military veterans living with post-traumatic stress and traumatic brain injuries. Donna Fournier, the director of training at Stiggy's Dogs, had received a call about the hoarding situation from Detroit Bully Corps, a group that rescues and rehabilitates abused and unwanted American pit bull terriers, and rescued Major along with twenty other dogs.

The motto of Stiggy's Dogs is "rescue one to rescue another." And that's exactly what Major, a rescued dog, did after Terry McGlade collapsed outdoors with the onset of a grand mal seizure.

Terry suffers from severe PTSD and traumatic brain injury caused when a roadside bomb exploded in Afghanistan, after he'd served two tours of duty in Iraq and one in Afghanistan.

After Terry seized and fell outside his home, Major went into emergency mode, some of it instinctual and some of it learned, by pulling Terry's phone from his pocket, dropping it, and standing on the phone, which was programmed to automatically dial 911 when pressing the screen and holding it for several seconds. Major dialed the number multiple times, according to police reports. The operator grew suspicious when calls arrived from the same number and a muffled voice in the background could be heard that sounded like the person was confused. Police and paramedics were dispatched.

Ambulance personnel approaching the house spotted Major running to the sidewalk as he paced back and forth between Terry and the street, waiting for help to arrive. He led them to the backyard, where Terry lay unconscious on the ground where he had collapsed.

Jennifer Petre, who founded Stiggy's Dogs, and whose group had rescued Major, said part of the training calls for veterans to carry notes that ask for help, and, when possible, their dogs then hold the notes in their teeth and take them to the first person they see. The dogs are trained to bark and get someone to follow them back to the veterans.

Because Terry was semiconscious, "Major did the next best thing," Jennifer said. "He called 911 for help and ran back and forth and in a circle from the backyard to the front of the house until paramedics arrived and he could lead them to Terry."

Jennifer added that although the group trains dogs to dial telephones, "we can't train dogs to do what Major did. I can't fake a panic attack or a seizure. It comes from the close relationship between the handler and the dog. It's usually six months to a year before a dog figures out things like that. Major knew how to do it."

Terry was rushed to a hospital and observed overnight before returning home the next day. At home, after he was asked by *The Coloradoan* newspaper in Fort Collins, Colorado, about taking in a rescued dog, Terry said, "I don't think I helped him. I think we helped each other. I have a reason to live because he forces me to go out and pushes me out of the depression."

Jennifer noted that the doctors said Major made all the difference.

Terry agreed. Before his seizure, he had been getting ready to take Major for a walk; when he woke up, he was in a police station. "Major saved my life," Terry told *The Coloradoan*.

Another task that all dogs from Stiggy's learn to do is to make security checks at night. After arriving home in the veterans' houses, they check to make sure doors are locked and lights are out. For Terry and other veterans, feeling safe is paramount.

All told, since Stiggy's began in 2010, "we've paired forty teams," Jennifer said. "They're all different breeds, all rescued, and training is done one-on-one." Two of the things she looks for are temperament and intelligence when deciding which dogs to pull for the program. Dogs who are in tune with people, who want to please, are prime candidates. "These veterans talk to their dogs more than they do their spouses," said Jennifer.

Before getting his service canine, Terry said he was in "a dark spot. I was almost one of those suicide statistics due to the PTSD being that severe. Major and I met each other and hit it off." The two have developed a close bond, Jennifer Petre said. "For two years out of his life, Major didn't live outside a crate," she said. Now, he's in a home and has a purpose, adding that Terry "doesn't have kids and he isn't married, so it's just him and his dog."

For Terry's part, he can't say enough good things about Major.

"He is an extension of me," Terry McGlade said. "I don't think I could operate in the everyday world without him right now."

# CHAPTER 11

# Good-byes and New Beginnings

"If Derek can't be here, then it's fitting that his dog Gabriel is with me."

Those are the words of former army lieutenant Jake Murphy about his comrade in arms, army sergeant Derek McConnell.

Jake and Derek's unit—2-87 Bravo Company, 34th Brigade, 10th Mountain Division out of Fort Drum—was stationed in Kandahar, the second-largest city in Afghanistan.

Jake was out on a foot patrol with his unit in the Zhari District in July 2011 when an IED took both of his legs. Derek was one of the personnel who rushed to the scene to clear the ground for a landing zone so that a Medevac helicopter could safely land to pick up Jake and carry him to a hospital.

Once Jake was airlifted, Derek, who'd volunteered to lead his fellow soldiers on the mission, found himself in a small minefield, where death can come with one footstep. Derek's next step landed on the cap of an IED. The cap exploded, but the IED did not. He was okay.

Still, "it knocked him on his butt," explained Derek's mother, Siobhan Fuller-McConnell. Derek, who discussed the event in an October 2012 interview with *The Progress* in New Jersey, said he looked down to check his legs and was relieved to see they were still there. He even took a photo of them as proof. "The bombs were malfunctioning," he told the newspaper.

After Derek picked himself up, his squad leader gave him the option of standing down. Derek declined and opted instead to continue patrolling the area.

"Two steps later," Siobhan said, "Derek hit the IED that took him out."

He'd encountered two roadside bombs simultaneously, and lost his left leg at the hip and his right leg from the knee down. He also suffered a skull fracture and a devastating injury to his arm.

Despite the severity of their individual injuries, Derek and Jake each survived. But they were both in critical condition for weeks as they fought a new battle—this one on American soil—to survive.

Derek, in a medically induced coma, did not do well at first.

"They couldn't tell me whether he was going to live or die," said his mother, Siobhan. He went through seven months of rehabilitation. Doctors also tried to save one of his arms, which he was unable to use. Even so, Siobhan said, "He was doing really well."

Derek had been living in the barracks at Walter Reed. In his interview with *The Progress*, his positive attitude came across loud and clear. "There is nothing better than life," he said. "There's nothing better than living and breathing. You adapt quickly."

He'd also adapted well to military life after enlisting in the army in January 2009, following graduation from West Essex High School in North Caldwell, New Jersey.

"He wasn't exactly sure what he wanted to do with his life. He knew he didn't want to go to college right then," his mother said. "He needed the discipline, and he wanted to serve. His brother, Michael, was in the navy. Derek didn't want to be in the navy. He found something that suited him."

After finishing airborne training, Derek was assigned to the Catamount Bravo Company at Fort Drum and deployed to Afghanistan in 2011. That's when he was injured.

In early 2013, while he was looking to the future as he continued with rehab, learned to walk with prosthetic legs, and prepared to retire from the army, he searched online and spotted a German shepherd service canine named Gabriel. The dog was listed as available to an injured veteran from the 4 Paws for Ability nonprofit organization.

"Derek called me, all excited," Siobhan said. "He told me, 'Mom, you have to write this letter right now, today.' So I did."

He went through the application process at 4 Paws. Then his mother got another call from her son.

"I got Gabriel!" Derek told her.

"When he puts his mind to something, he wants it immediately," Siobhan explained. "He fell in love with Gabriel's face. He couldn't wait to get him."

Karen Shirk, who runs 4 Paws for Ability in Ohio, knew that Gabriel, who had successfully finished service dog training, would be a good fit for Derek. Gabriel was specially trained as a mobility canine, for balancing and preventing falls. Derek recognized that not only would he have Gabriel's companionship, but he'd also have more independence that only a service dog could provide.

"Derek was so excited about getting Gabriel," said Karen, named a CNN Hero in 2008 for her service dog work with autistic and special-needs children. "He texted me every day."

Karen knows all too well what dogs can do for people who require assistance. She found herself in a similar position years earlier, which is why she formed her own organization. After an illness sent her to the hospital, ventilator-dependent, and later confined her to a wheel-chair, her frustration at being turned down for a service dog by multiple organizations started her on a path toward forming her own nonprofit service organization. She felt for Derek, and knew that Gabriel, because of his advanced skills, would assist Derek and improve his life.

Derek and his high-school sweetheart Krystina planned to marry in January 2014 with a dream wedding, made possible after the pair won an engagement ring and formal wedding through an online con-test for a military couple, titled Operation: Tie the Knot. The ten best stories were chosen and then the public voted for the number-one couple: Derek and Krystina won with a landslide victory of close to 3,500 votes.

But before they got married, Derek wanted to go to the 4 Paws for Ability training center to work with Gabriel and take him home. He knew a service dog would help him better adapt to living outside the hospital barracks and, especially, assist him toward more independent living in his future role as a married man, giving Krystina more freedom. He also wanted the companionship of a dog.

"When he was home on leave, he got a lot of comfort from our cat," said Siobhan. "He knew that once he got Gabriel, he would be a companion for him, somebody to get him through the night. He was always around animals. They comforted him. He was really looking forward to getting him." Derek had even bookmarked items on online sites that he planned to buy for Gabriel, in preparation for taking him home.

Derek was in the midst of a lengthy military medical board—a full evaluation of his injuries—which was the final step before he officially retired from the service. He'd been fitted for prosthetics, and he was seeking special permission during the medical-board process to live off base, where Gabriel would be allowed to be with him, as dogs weren't allowed in the barracks. Everything was falling into place as planned.

To top it off, the daughter of a teacher who'd taught at Derek's high school had heard about his injury. Her mother had a wheelchair-accessible van and no longer used it, so they gave it to Derek's family. "When Derek was at the hospital, the van gave us the freedom to take him places, like to the park for the day," said his mother. Then, Help Our Military Heroes donated another van to Derek, this one fully outfitted for his needs. Although Derek didn't drive the van—Krystina did—it made him more mobile, because it was easier and quicker to get in and out of, and comfortable once he was inside.

Derek and Krystina decided to give their first van to another service member at Walter Reed.

"We've always paid it forward," Derek's mother said. It would be the first of several giving acts tied to her son.

Things were looking up for Derek, and his spirits were high. He'd met members of the Giants pro football team, as well as President Obama on two occasions. And the military had presented Derek with the Bronze Star medal with "V" device, its fourth-highest award of valor, for action in combat.

Derek McConnell's future looked bright.

While he had abandoned thoughts of one day working in law enforcement, he instead talked about becoming a writer and pursuing fiction. Most of all, he was equally excited about marrying Krystina and making Gabriel a part of his life by taking him home.

—◆—

The Murphys and McConnells got to know each other at Walter Reed.

"Derek's girlfriend and his mom were the first people I met," said Lisa Murphy, Jake's wife. "Jake's mom went to Germany and flew home with him. We were all in a room together, waiting for them. We didn't know the connection then—that they were in the same unit. Jake and Derek weren't aware either, because the first few weeks in the hospital, they weren't able to interact with each other. They both were in comas."

The families, she said, got to know each other as they stood vigil at the bedsides of Derek and Jake. Once both came out of their comas, Derek's family members got to know Jake's, and vice versa. What Lisa recalled about Derek was his generosity.

"I remember talking to Derek and Krystina one day," she said, "sitting there with them at the hospital, saying in passing that my Kindle was broken and I needed to get it fixed. Derek told me, 'I just got a new one; I have an extra. Take mine.' He was a giving person, very polite. And he was looking forward to getting Gabriel."

Derek, who was from Parsippany, New Jersey, was scheduled to go to 4 Paws for Ability's Midwest training center in June 2013 to work with Gabriel, and then take him back to Bethesda, to his new apartment off base.

But on March 18, 2013, Derek, the second of five children, died unexpectedly in his sleep. The cause of death was undetermined. He was twenty-three.

After his death, his mom and fiancée paid it forward again, this time with the new handicapped-accessible van that had been donated to Derek. They presented it to army staff sergeant Sam Shockley of Ohio, who'd lost both legs in an IED blast the day before Derek died. Sam was admitted to the same Walter Reed hospital room as Derek.

Sam told the *Jersey Journal* that the van would help him regain independence. "I really wanted to be able to go for a car ride by myself, to go to the store by myself," he said. "It's really going to help me."

In the meantime, Karen Shirk had been preparing for Derek to travel to Ohio to work with Gabriel and train so he could take him home. She was saddened to hear of his family's loss. At the same time, she was faced with having to match Gabriel, who was specially trained to assist a double-amputee military member. So Karen sought help in spreading the word throughout the Walter Reed Army Medical Center, to let veterans know that she had a dog available with special skills. "Find me another Derek," she told a volunteer at Walter Reed.

They didn't have to look far. Lisa and Jake had been looking for a service dog. While working for a nonprofit group at Walter Reed, Lisa learned that a German shepherd service canine was available, so she contacted Karen at 4 Paws for Ability. Lisa and Jake didn't know that he was the same dog who'd been intended for Derek. Karen was unaware as well.

Karen learned soon enough when she called Derek's mother to let her know that Gabriel was being placed with another double-amputee veteran.

"Who is it?" asked Siobhan Fuller-McConnell.

"His name is Jake Murphy."

Siobhan had known Lisa and Jake since her son and Jake had arrived at Walter Reed on the same plane from Germany, on July 29, 2011.

Learning the news was bittersweet.

"I was thrilled I knew who was getting Gabriel," Siobhan explained. At the same time, "it hurt, because he was supposed to be ours." Still, she noted, "I'm glad I know where Gabriel is. I know they're a wonderful family."

For the Murphys, it was a stunning twist of circumstances.

"We knew Derek was getting a dog. He had put up pictures of this beautiful German shepherd. We took the news very seriously. It's bittersweet for us too," Lisa said. "I hope Derek's family knows that we love Gabriel and take very good care of him. He was such a good gift for us at a time when Jake needed a service dog."

Lisa doesn't worry about her husband when Gabriel is with him. He's trained as a mobility canine, to not only help stabilize Jake and prevent him from falling, but to also help him up should he fall.

In fact, that happened one day when Jake was home alone with Gabriel.

"Gabriel saw what happened. He came over to me," Jake said, adding that he noticed after he'd fallen that Gabriel's body language had changed from playful to serious. "He immediately knew what to do. He'd practiced it before. It was as if he was saying, 'This is what I was trained for—this moment.'"

With Jake on the floor and Gabriel standing next to him, "I positioned myself to push off of him," Jake said. He was in a 'strong' position so I could push off of his back."

Gabriel also helps Jake with smaller tasks. "A lot of times I drop my keys," Jake said. "One time, it was my phone. He waited for me to tell him what to do. I said, 'Take it,' and he picked it up and gave it to me."

At home in the evenings, Lisa said, "We break all the rules and let him get in bed with us. Gabriel is a comfort. He's very focused on Jake. He'll give us both a kiss good night, but he wants to be with Jake. He's knows that he's here for him."

When Jake looks at Gabriel, "he reminds me of Derek," he said. "I feel a connection with Derek. We were in the same unit and injured the same day. I make sure I'm appreciative of Gabriel and what he does for me, and what service dogs do for their owners, masters, and friends."

As it is for other veterans who are married, many with children, their service canines become members of the family.

"Gabriel has been a great asset to me, to get around physically and spiritually," he said. "Emotionally, he's a big help for both my wife and me. He brings us joy every day."

〜

Slate, a black Labrador, was just as devoted to his veteran. Slate emotionally expressed that commitment at a May 2014 ceremony for retired first sergeant Brian Coutch at Arlington National Cemetery.

After a color guard left the burial ceremony and many of the mourners had dispersed, Slate walked to the side of the coffin, took one final step closer, put his chin on the casket, and rested it there. Slate knew that inside the coffin was Brian's body, his constant companion for four years.

In death, as he had in life, Slate offered comfort to Brian.

Brian didn't die on the battlefield, but, as his family said in his obituary, "he died for his country just the same." Like so many service members who returned from combat, Brian experienced severe post-traumatic stress and traumatic brain injury.

To assist him with his symptoms, he was matched with his service dog, Slate, who became an integral part of Brian's life. Simply put, they were inseparable.

Slate was alone with Brian at his home in New Kensington, Pennsylvania, when Brian passed away on March 14, 2014, at the age of forty-seven.

As an injured veteran, rather than talk about his war experiences, Brian instead preferred to be an advocate and ambassador for service canines, spreading the word about the benefits they afford veterans, using his own positive experiences with Slate as proof positive.

Close proximity to explosions left Brian with a traumatic brain injury; in addition, one of his hands was injured from gunfire in battle. Once he returned from overseas, Brian experienced post-traumatic stress, which triggered anxiety, high blood pressure, and nightmares so severe that he needed to be roused from sleep because his heart raced dangerously fast during the nightmares. Slate was there, at his side, to bring him out of those night terrors.

Studies show that dogs are good for the heart, according to a 2013 report by the American Heart Association. Having a dog is associated with a reduced risk of heart disease.

Brian's blood pressure and PTSD-related stress and anxiety were the main reasons he was medically discharged and retired as a first sergeant in 2006, after serving twenty-two years. Afterward, Brian continued his dedication to the military by working with the Wounded Warrior Project and the Pennsylvania Hero Walk, helping to raise funds by walking each year in its annual event.

His brother, Robert Coutch, said it came as a surprise when, after graduating from Valley High School in 1984, Brian enlisted in the service. "I didn't know he even had an interest in joining," Robert said. Brian was assigned to an engineering unit and did construction work in Korea. Later, he shipped out to Saudi Arabia during Operation Desert Storm. Afterward, he spent a few years in Panama.

Brian then served five combat tours—three in Afghanistan and two in Iraq, which included military operations Desert Storm and Iraqi Freedom as an engineer, whose specialty was disabling roadside bombs. For his service, he earned the Bronze Star and more than thirty-five other medals.

Being promoted to first sergeant, Robert pointed out, was merely a formality; taking the lead was a part of Brian's persona. "My brother was never *not* a first sergeant. He was always the guy in charge."

But after he returned from his final combat tour, Brian was a changed man with psychological scars from combat. His wounds were not visible, but they were evident.

"There was a period where he never left his house," his brother Robert said.

"My family and I couldn't help him, because there was no way we could relate. He was in kind of a dark place. He wasn't open about things, and he rarely spoke about his service. He didn't like to call attention to himself. We'd do holidays together, but he didn't have the vigor for life."

All that changed after Brian's mother, Madeline Laurent, shared information she'd discovered about the Pennsylvania Hero Walk. Participating in the fund-raising event for veterans, walking from Philadelphia to Lower Burrell, started a chain reaction for the better, Robert said. Brian had started volunteering with fellow veterans, and along the way, a woman familiar with a service dog organization mentioned that she thought Brian would be a good candidate for a dog—especially to help him deal with his night terrors.

The organization was Susquehanna Service Dogs. Brian applied, was accepted, and the local Wounded Warrior Project covered the cost of putting Brian through the rigorous training with Slate, the service canine he was paired with.

Brian suffered from nightmares so severe they would raise his blood pressure. When his heart raced during his nightmares, Slate nudged him with his nose to wake him up. Waking Brian up from his nightmares and comforting him afterward were Slate's main tasks.

"I was shell-shocked, and it shows up when I am asleep," Brian told the *County News* in Washington, DC, in an August 2012 interview. "He can sense the changes in my blood when my pulse starts racing. It's one of those things dogs can smell that we can't."

After Slate entered Brian's life, "you could never get ahold of him," Robert said, "because he was always going somewhere. He was very mobile once he got Slate. My brother was a prime example of the difference a dog can make in a veteran's life. The big thing Slate did was wake him up from nightmares,"

Each year after getting Slate, Brian participated in the Pennsylvania Hero Walk. His life had turned around, and he wanted to help spread the word about the Wounded Warrior Project, raising awareness so that others would know it offered guidance and assistance for veterans just like him.

Robert pointed out that his brother was a prime example of the change for the better that a service dog offers. "The difference was amazing in how Brian changed after Slate came into his life. It was life-changing. He started opening up more, and we started getting closer the past couple of years," Robert said.

Even so, Brian wasn't one to routinely share his experiences in the service with his family. He confided in a couple of veteran pals, one of whom was Rainier Schroeder, a former Marine, army soldier, Seabee heavy-equipment operator, and air force engineer. The two met at the Susquehanna Service Dogs facility, where Rainier had trained for two weeks with his service canine Tundra, and Brian had worked with Slate.

The two became fast friends.

"We pretty much connected because we'd been through the same situations," Rainier said. "Brian had twenty-one years in the military. I had twenty-eight. We had a lot in common, and we bonded. We were in the same areas of Iraq and Afghanistan at the same time, but we were in different commands."

Rainier "Ray" Schroeder joined the US Marine Corps in 1979 as an engineer. After three years, he left the Corps and joined the US Army Reserve, first with an engineer unit, and then with the post cavalry in a tank battalion out of New York. After several years, he left the army and joined the Navy Seabees.

"I activated during Desert Storm," he said. "After my unit shut down in 1993, I joined the Air Force Reserve's 105th squadron out of Newberry, New York, and soon went to heavy-equipment operating school. I was a heavy-equipment operations engineer. In 2002, I got activated and I was sent overseas."

On May 7, 2002, Rainier suffered a traumatic brain injury when a nearby road-grader hit an improvised explosive device while he was overseeing an engineering project at the Bagram Air Force Base in Afghanistan. The IED detonated a few feet from him, knocking him unconscious for a half-hour. "I felt different, but I still had my legs and arms, so I figured I was okay."

Three years later, in March 2005, he was back in Iraq supervising the building of a runway at Camp Taji, a former airbase north of Baghdad, when insurgents bombarded the base with mortar shells. He suffered a fractured foot and a torn Achilles tendon. He also injured his hand. But he convinced the doctors to give him light duty, and he was allowed to remain in Iraq. "I was walking around with a broken foot, and I had a torn Achilles," he said. "I stayed an extra three and a half months. During that time, I limped badly and didn't get much sleep. I stayed, with my injury, and we accomplished what we needed to accomplish."

Once home in Carlisle, Pennsylvania, where he lives with his wife Anna Marie, Rainier underwent hand surgery to repair a crushed nerve. At the same time, he was diagnosed with TBI and PTSD. Eventually, he was deemed 100 percent disabled, unemployable, and retired as a noncommissioned officer in charge.

It took a few more years before he learned about service dogs and what they could do for him. He applied for a dog through Susquehanna Service Dogs and was accepted.

That's when he met Brian Coutch.

During the two weeks of service dog training with Brian, Rainier saw a change for the better in his friend. After they each graduated from training with their dogs, they stayed in touch. They periodically talked about their time in the service.

"Brian was a first sergeant in charge of something like a hundred people. Then when he came back to civilian life, like myself, it was difficult. He had a lot of issues adjusting to civilian life."

But once Slate entered his life, Brian became more comfortable and even "happy go-lucky," as Rainier pointed out. "Slate definitely had a huge impact on his life. He made all the difference," he said. "For the time Slate was with him, Brian was able to lead a more peaceful life."

Slate, whom Brian's brother Robert referred to as "my dogs' cousin," stayed at Brian's side, no matter what, to keep a watchful eye on him. Even during a camping trip with Robert and his dogs, Perseus, a golden retriever, and Odysseus, a chocolate Lab–German shorthaired pointer, when raccoons invaded their campsite, Slate ignored the raccoons and remained in working mode beside Brian.

The first time Brian and Slate met, it was in a room with other service dog candidates. Trainers walked half a dozen dogs to a large room to meet the candidates. "Slate laid right down next to Brian," Robert said. "They had that connection right away."

Slate picked up on medical issues with people other than Brian. One day he walked into a veterans' hall with Brian where a woman was selling T-shirts for the local Wounded Warrior Project. Slate ran up to the woman and nudged her. "Her heart was racing and he picked up on it. Slate started to comfort her," Robert said.

Another time, Slate started nudging a couple of people and wouldn't stop. "My brother told them they should have their blood pressure checked, because it was probably a problem. They did have it checked, and they had high blood pressure. They didn't know until Slate alerted them that they had a problem," Robert said.

Because of Slate, Brian's life improved, including his relationships with his family. So it was an enormous blow to the family when Brian died from what the doctors said was natural causes.

"When they called and told me he'd passed, I was shocked," Robert said. "He was doing well. He was happy."

Most of all, he had been happy having Slate in his life for three years.

Susan Makara, Slate's puppy raiser, wrote on Brian's obituary legacy page that "Brian always made us feel like we did not lose Slate, but gained a friend. We are proud to be a part of that which provided him with comfort and companionship."

In the summer of 2014, Slate was about to make a similar difference in another veteran's life. After Brian's death, Slate went back into advanced training at Susquehanna Service Dogs' facility in Harrisburg, Pennsylvania, said Kerry Wevodau, development director for the organization, and has been partnered with another veteran in need.

On May 28, 2014, retired first sergeant Brian Coutch was laid to rest in a full military ceremony at Arlington National Cemetery in Virginia. At the service, standing by his casket with dog trainers in a display of respect, were Slate and Uncle Brian, a puppy in training born in the days following Brian's death and named in honor of him. Slate stood stoically with his trainer during a twenty-one-gun salute to Brian.

At the end of the ceremony, one by one, Brian's friends, family, and fellow veterans, who were used to seeing Brian and Slate hanging out together at the local VFW, said their final good-byes, not only to Brian, but also to Slate.

Then Slate walked around Brian's casket, sniffing. Nearby, trainer Amanda Nicholson and Slate's puppy raiser Susan kept a watchful eye on him as he approached the casket.

That's when, as attendees milled about, Slate paused and rested his chin at the head of Brian's casket in the same way he'd rested his head on Brian's leg so many times before, which he was trained to do to offer comfort to his veteran. Then Slate walked away, but not before turning back for one last glimpse of the casket that held the remains of his beloved veteran, Brian. It was a poignant, quiet ending to the morning ceremony.

Kerry described the special relationship Brian's family and circle of friends had with his dog. "Slate had become part of Brian, and after his passing, he provided comfort to Brian's family and friends. It was like still having a piece of Brian with them. As hard as it was to send Slate back, the family very much wanted Slate to go on and make a difference in someone else's life."

"Having Slate at Arlington," Kerry continued, "hopefully brought a sense of peace for the family and some closure for Slate." And having the puppy named Uncle Brian there, she said, symbolized the continuation of both Brian and Slate's legacy. "The puppy," she noted, "will go on to make a difference for someone, just as Slate did for Brian."

# CHAPTER 12

# Moving Past Physical Wounds

Lying on a bed at Walter Reed Army Medical Center, discharged army sergeant Robert "Bob" Andrzejczak could not have imagined that in less than five years he would be a member of the New Jersey State Assembly and attending a barbecue at a US vice president's home, watching their dogs play together.

Doors have opened for him in large part, he acknowledged, because of his service dog, Madeline. "Without her, I would be a shut-in," said Bob matter-of-factly.

That portion of Bob's life began on a January day in 2009, when he was traveling on a road north of Baghdad, not far from the town of Baiji, Iraq. Bob was a rear gunner in the army's 11 Bravo Company of the 25th Infantry Division, on the front line, when his mine-resistant truck was hit during a grenade attack. Although he survived the attack, his left leg had to be removed.

He soon realized he would face new physical challenges and might need assistance.

"On my first day of therapy at Walter Reed, I saw service dogs. Trying to move around on my own again is when I considered getting a service dog," he said.

Canines are brought to this ward by a group called National Education for Assistance Dog Services (NEADS), which has worked with recovering veterans at Walter Reed since 2006. They train dogs specifically for individual veterans' needs, whether the veteran is in a wheelchair, has a prosthetic limb or hearing loss, or any number of other conditions. The dogs receive advanced training as puppies, as well as after they are matched with veterans, and are provided to veterans free of charge.

After being accepted to the program, Bob traveled to Massachusetts for two weeks of intensive training. There, he learned to train and work with Maddie, as he calls his yellow Labrador. "The group's dogs all have a set routine," he said. "At the same time, it gave me a purpose. On a certain day, we clean her teeth. On another day, we trim her nails. She's on a strict diet. NEADS is regimented with it." And so, in turn, is Bob, with how much food to give her, how often she is fed, and a weight range she should stay within. "Being in the military made it easy for me to stick to a regimen," he noted.

Caring for Maddie also includes going over her commands on a daily basis to keep her trained to the optimum. To open a refrigerator or turn lights on and off, the training is broken down into individual steps, so the dog can eventually perform any number of tasks. With the routine and continuous training, Bob said, "It's almost as if Maddie is in the military, the way our schedule is regimented. I take all of the requirements very seriously, for her health."

As for their nightly routine, "When I take my prosthetic leg off, rather than hop around the house, if I fall, Maddie helps me. I brace myself on her." Not only does she open and close doors for him, but after closing a door, she nudges it to make sure it's securely closed.

Even though Bob initially applied for a service dog to assist him physically, which Maddie readily stepped up to do, she has evolved into so much more.

"I got her for the physical stuff and what she can do, but, really, she's turned into an emotional companion more than anything," Bob said. "It's a bond with her I knew would happen. I just didn't realize how close we would be."

At first, Bob was nervous about leaving the house alone. "Going through the recovery stage at the hospital, going home and missing a leg, I had to not only become comfortable walking around with a prosthetic leg, but also come to terms with the fact that I'd lost a leg. I didn't want to go out and talk to anyone. I didn't want to meet anyone. Madeline changed that for me."

At the park, for example, it was just the two of them at first. That soon changed, he said, "because people gravitate toward dogs. They'd come over, we'd spark up conversations, and I'd meet them. It's almost therapeutic being able to share what I went through. Maddie brought me out of my shell."

Like many veterans, Bob had trouble finding his way through the system to get his full VA benefits. A phone call to State Senator Jeff Van Drew solved some of the issues. Soon, the senator was calling Bob for his opinion on other veterans' issues. Then one night Senator Van Drew called and asked if Bob would consider taking over the district from retiring assemblyman Matthew Milam.

"Taking that seat," Bob said, "was my way of continuing to serve—not on the level it was before, fighting for my country, but fighting for my district and the people in the state of New Jersey."

Soon after being sworn in as a state legislator, he had dinner with Jill Biden and a small group of people. Vice President Joe Biden stopped by after dinner, and then both Bidens spoke with Bob about Maddie. They told him about their dog, Champ, a then-eighteen-month-old German shepherd. The Bidens wanted the dogs to meet, so they invited Maddie and Bob to a barbecue at the vice president's home, at the Naval Observatory. Once there, Maddie and Champ played together on the grounds.

If he hadn't had Maddie early on in his recovery, while still undergoing physical therapy at Walter Reed, Bob points out, the state assembly position would not have been an option for him.

"Maddie has done a lot for me," he said. "Without her, I'd probably be a hermit right now, a shut-in. Even enjoyable things, I would not be out there doing. I have Maddie to thank for it all."

# CHAPTER 13

# "He Saved Me from Myself"

During one-on-one time to get acquainted, army veteran Joe Buzay went on a walk with a service dog named Frankie. That was all it took. Joe now describes his life in simple terms: "Before Frankie" and "After Frankie."

"I met three of the dogs, and then they brought in Frankie," explained Joe, who sports a blond-and-gray goatee and ponytail. "It was an instant bond right there—love at first sight." Joe was a military police officer in the US Army and served with the infantry's B Company on tours in Somalia during the military's Unified Task Force, which placed him in combat during the Battle of Mogadishu. Officially code-named Operation Restore Hope, the purpose was to secure the trade routes in Somalia so food could get to the people.

After the two got back from their walk and returned to the group area, Joe sat down and Frankie jumped on his lap. "Frankie looked around at everyone like he was saying, 'Yeah, he's mine.'"

Frankie, a friendly, short-haired, white-and-brown husky–pit bull mix with light-blue eyes, was about to change Joe's life for the better. Earlier, his prospects at leading a full life while dealing with post-traumatic stress were bleak.

"Before I met Frankie, it was hard to get up every day," said Joe from his home in Loman, Minnesota. "I might have left the house every three or four weeks to get groceries, and it was usually in the middle of the night. It was bad, and that's probably what drove my wife away."

He had isolated himself.

"I couldn't deal with people. I suffered from severe depressions and I had panic attacks. I got into these moods. I called them my black moods. I broke into sweats. I was way overmedicated. It takes a while to get the right mix of drugs.

"This was all before I met Frankie," he continued. "I had no hope for anything. It was like I was dead inside, and I was barely hanging on."

He was drinking a case of beer a day and experienced blackouts. In the fall of 2009, he said, "I took my girlfriend for a ride on my Harley and we put on two hundred miles. I didn't remember a thing, because I was so drunk. So I quit drinking and my life fell apart. I got out of the service and married my girlfriend. I thought that would help. It didn't."

He entered a seven-week course aimed at aiding veterans with PTSD, but nothing seemed to help. One day, it all got to be too much, and Joe decided to end his life. "I took all my pills—over a hundred muscle relaxants and some pain relievers. The doctor called my mom and said there was nothing they could do. He told her they didn't think I would recover. Eight days later, I woke up and I was fine."

A year after he quit drinking, around October 2010, "it was still rough going," Joe said, and he continued to struggle off and on with suicidal thoughts. His contact at the local veterans' services office told him about a new program they were offering for service members with PTSD and TBI, and asked if Joe was interested.

He was.

Together, they visited Patriot Assistance Dogs in Detroit Lakes, Minnesota, an organization that provides service dogs at no charge to veterans who are struggling with post-traumatic stress.

As soon as Joe met Frankie, his future service canine, he knew the dog was his one hope for a brighter future. "I was having so many problems dealing with life that I was reaching for anything. I'm great with dogs, so I jumped at the chance to have one."

Working with Frankie brought with it some frustration. Frankie couldn't go home with Joe right away because the two needed to continue their training together at the service dog center. The longer it took, the more difficult it became after each session for Joe to say good-bye to Frankie.

"I was going in there a lot for training," Joe explained. "I worked with him one or two times a week. I was ready to quit going, because I couldn't handle putting Frankie in his kennel and then having to walk away from him. I couldn't do it anymore. I decided not to go back."

That turned out to be the day that Linda Wiedewitsch, who cofounded Patriot Assistance Dogs in 2011, asked Joe an important question: "Do you want to take Frankie home?" It was just what Joe had been waiting to hear.

It was December 6, 2011, a day Joe will never forget. Frankie went home with Joe under a foster agreement with Patriot Assistance Dogs. "They weren't done yet," said Linda. "They still had to come back for more training," Linda said, adding that Joe could have decided to "choose another dog instead."

That didn't happen. Frankie was home to stay.

"When I got Frankie, he was like the part of me that had been missing. He gave me hope," Joe said. "When I got Frankie, I was so close to suicide, it was unreal. I mean, I was barely hanging on. Frankie rescued me."

Getting to that new life with Frankie was very different from what Joe had experienced in his earlier years. From 1983 to 1994, Joe served in the army as a military police officer. He saw his share of fierce fighting on the streets during his tours in Somalia, including in the middle of the Battle of Mogadishu in October 1993. The area wasn't safe for Somali civilians, let alone the US military police, and Buzay lost a few combat buddies in the process. "I was there when the rangers got shot down in a Black Hawk, which was what the movie *Black Hawk Down* was about. Crowds of people gathered on the streets and they had AK-47s," he said.

He left Somalia two weeks before his unit was to end its tour to be with his family and visit his grandmother before she died. "We got deployed every couple of years," he said. His unit returned to Somalia in December 1993 for a final stint. Joe qualified for a separation from the military and was honorably discharged in April 1994.

Almost immediately, he went to see a psychiatrist because he knew something was not right. "He told me to get to the VA as soon as possible," Joe said. "I went to the VA, and they told me I had post-traumatic stress. I never before believed people had PTSD until I got it. I thought it was a scapegoat to get out of the service. You can see a physical injury. You can't see PTSD."

He quit drinking in 2009, after he'd gotten up to a case of beer a day. He was also weaned off of most of his prescribed medications. At one dark point, he tried to commit suicide by taking more than a hundred muscle relaxants and pain relievers—what he described as "enough pills to drop a Clydesdale." In 2010, Joe entered the seven-week PTSD course sponsored by the VA—the path that would eventually lead him to Frankie.

Frankie's past life hadn't been easy either. A couple found him on a highway in Wadena, Minnesota, fifteen pounds underweight and wearing a too-tight choke chain that had grown into his neck. They took him to a veterinary clinic, where his skin was soaked to loosen the chain enough to remove it. "He still has slivers of metal in his neck," Joe said. "One of the guys who fostered Frankie said he was an escape artist." The man took Frankie to the Patriot Assistance Dogs center, where he was placed in their service dog program.

Joe's life has completely turned around because of Frankie.

"Twenty-two veterans kill themselves each day," he said. "I was almost one of them. I was at the lowest part of my life, and now it's like I'm at the best part of my life."

The vets who need help are the ones who are the toughest to find, Joe noted. "They're not in the public view. They're isolating themselves at home."

With Joe no longer in isolation, Linda Wiedewitsch helped Joe and Frankie transition together at his home. "Frankie is so charismatic," Linda said. "He attracts people." This is why she named the dog after Frank Sinatra. "Frankie is talented."

Linda, an ardent proponent of public access for service dogs under the Americans with Disabilities Act of 1990, makes sure that veterans know their rights when it comes to service dogs. Sometimes, because the canines in her organization are not all purebreds, businesses do not always comply with the law, since German shepherds, golden retrievers, and Labrador retrievers were typically the breeds of choice for service dogs in years past, which the general public had become accustomed to seeing. Today, with more service dog organizations forming, a variety of breeds and mixes are trained as service dogs. Under the ADA, privately owned businesses that serve the public, such as restaurants, hotels, retail stores, taxicabs, theaters, concert halls, and sports facilities, are prohibited from discriminating against individuals with disabilities. The ADA permits service animals to accompany people with disabilities in all areas where members of the public are allowed to go. In turn, the ADA defines service animals as dogs of any breed that are individually trained to do work or perform tasks for people with disabilities.

"If a veteran and a dog are refused access, they carry a lot of identification. They have a wallet card with their picture and their dog's picture, and all my information is on there. The dog wears a vest; the dog has an ID that corresponds with the number on the wallet card; and the ADA citation is on the back of the vest. And they're still sometimes refused access."

When a veteran is denied access, Linda, a former police officer, sends out a form letter informing the business owner and the town's police department of the federal violation that occurred, while also reminding them of the federal law. "I don't care what their city ordinances say. We are dealing with federal law that trumps any city or county law. They need to understand that this dog has been issued to that person and has been recommended by their health-care professional. The dogs have been prescribed to them."

She tells veterans that if they're denied access to an establishment because of their dogs, to give her names, including any police officers and business owners.

"I tell the veterans, 'This is not your battle. Let us and the organization take it from here.' It's not worth the hassle of getting their blood pressure up."

Reputable breeders donate about 25 percent of the dogs to her organization, and 75 percent come from rescue groups or animal shelters. She got involved with the program by being a puppy raiser. Also, as a trainer of psychiatric assistance dogs, she used to receive a lot of requests for dogs. As far as she knew, no one was doing that in Minnesota at the time, so she founded her own group.

Joe and Frankie were the first certified graduates of Patriot Assistance Dogs. The goal for the end of 2014 was to have finished certifying thirty teams of veterans and service dogs. She is also working with prison inmates, helping them train young dogs for the program.

"I had success with Frankie from the get-go," Linda noted, adding that the group takes in rescued dogs that are just twelve to fourteen months old. "We're taking dogs off the street, out of pounds, and out of rescue. I can take those dogs who are killed in our nation every day and place them."

With saving rescued dogs, having some of them trained in prison, and by placing them with veterans, "it's a triple benefit," Linda said, "helping a dog, helping a prisoner, and helping a veteran. It's extremely gratifying."

For some veterans like Joe, talking about his dog is easier than talking about himself. Joe's face lights up when he tells stories about Frankie and the difference he's made in his life.

"When Frankie first came home, I was having night terrors," he said. "I was hardly getting any sleep. The first night with Frankie, I woke up from a night terror and Frankie was on top of me, licking my face, and he didn't get up until I'd calmed down."

It was like that from the first day. "He started training immediately, on his own. It just clicked. It's like he was training his whole life for this. He knew what to do instinctively."

Having Frankie as his service dog is what Joe Buzay was looking for to move on with his life.

"I began working with Frankie and my whole life started working," he said. "I'm on half the drugs I was on before. He made my life complete. When I look at Frankie, why would I ever consider suicide? He gave me an anchor to hang on to," he continued. "It was like I was adrift in a sea of darkness and Frankie was the only thing there. He saved me from myself."

# CHAPTER 14

# A Purposeful Life with Auggie

Once Lance Weir could see clearly, it became his lifetime goal to not let a boating accident that had left him partially paralyzed keep him down. He found a purpose.

But it would take a decade and a dog to truly turn his life around.

Lance grew up in Walnut Ridge, Arkansas, where as a child he spent halcyon days on his grandparents' hundred-acre farm every chance he got. He played Little League baseball for six years, beginning in grade school. In high school, he lettered in football, basketball, track, and tennis. The summer before his senior year, he worked as an assistant director and coach for the local Little League program.

After graduating from high school in 1990, he joined the US Marine Corps Reserves. He completed a three-month boot camp at the Marine Corps Depot on the bay in San Diego, and then went on to Marine combat training, as well as military police training.

After his reservist training was finished, he returned home and went to work for the Arkansas Department of Corrections as a drill instructor at a boot-camp program for first-time offenders sentenced to ten years or less. He soon realized that working at a prison facility was not for him. After a few months, he left his job and enrolled in college at Arkansas State University.

In late 1992, he went out for the football team as a walk-on player. Everyone told him it was impossible, because there was no such thing as a walk-on in November. Not one to take no for an answer, by December of that year Lance had talked a coach into adding him, and he officially joined the team. Still in a reserve unit, he drilled one week-end a month and the rest of the time took college courses.

Everything changed for Lance during a canoeing trip on August 8, 1993, in the Spring River rapids.

Lance had just pulled his canoe out of the water and onto the rocks. He was standing in a rocky area of the river, next to what he thought was a deep pool. He had tossed his baseball cap in the water and then, to cool off from the summer heat, he dove in to retrieve it. He realized afterward that he'd misjudged the depth of the water. What he thought was a pool turned out to be river rocks. Lance's head hit the rocks and he shattered his fifth vertebra.

In an instant, he was paralyzed.

Lance was Life-Flighted to a hospital in West Plains, Missouri. Once he was there, doctors recognized that the severity of Lance's injury was more than their facility could handle, and Life Flight again transported him, this time to the Elvis Presley Trauma Center in Memphis, Tennessee.

Lance has vague memories while he was in Memphis of a service dog being mentioned as a way to assist him. Even a trained monkey was suggested. "The concept of a service dog was new," Lance said. "It went in one ear and out the other. I could not see how a service dog or a monkey could help me. I could not picture the concept. And I didn't really care. I was trying to get my head right."

Lance was in Memphis for a few weeks before he was moved to the Baptist Rehabilitation Institute in Little Rock, Arkansas, where he stayed for six months.

Lance, physically fit and tall at six feet, went from being healthy to having a C5 cervical spinal injury resulting in quadriplegia from just below his shoulder blades down. The accident left him without the use of his legs and with partial use of his arms. On top of that, he suffered two concussions.

He was twenty-one years old.

The accident halted Lance's attendance at Arkansas U and, with it, his upcoming football season. The aftermath proved to be the biggest challenge of his life, as his circumstances had drastically changed.

After the catastrophic accident, Lance moved into his childhood home in northeast Arkansas with his family. He was discharged from the military in 1994. "He spent most of his time watching television," said Lance's mother, Gail Weir.

Lance agreed that finding his way back to his earlier active lifestyle was no small task. In one instant, his life had flipped upside down, from sports, college, and the military reserves, to confinement in a wheelchair and little hope.

"I was living in Arkansas with my family and just existing," he said. "From 1993 to 1997, I sat in a recliner watching TV." He was watching the world go by, which was uncharacteristic of his life before the accident. He was far from his old self and not close to getting his "head right."

"Those first few years were the worst," his mother Gail said. "We couldn't get him to do anything. He was depressed."

Lance summed up his feelings during that dark period: "I was angry, bitter, and felt like I was dead, but somehow I was living. I'm from a small rural town, so when I left the hospital and went home, there were no resources or opportunities for me at that time. There was no light at the end of the tunnel. I just existed, like there wasn't any purpose to my life. There were times when I would self-medicate."

Eventually, he found help and resources in other cities. The first was in 1997, four years after the accident, when he spent time in rehabilitation at Craig Hospital in Colorado, which specializes in treatment of spinal cord injuries. He met other people with similar injuries who were not only thriving but also had positive attitudes. It was at Craig Hospital that he learned how to drive an adapted van. He described the experience as "eye-opening." He also met service dogs and, for the first time, a puppy raiser—a woman who socialized puppies one at a time for a service canine group. "When I saw a dog with a puppy raiser, it clicked for me. It also left an impression—how professional the puppy and the woman were as a team."

Lance returned home to northeast Arkansas with a fresh outlook on life. He enrolled in school and got his associate's degree from Black River Technical College.

While his life had improved, he still did not know what the future held. "Going back to school was just a way to show I was doing something," he said. "College was a safety net. I didn't want to sit at home. At the same time, I didn't know what I wanted to do."

Something was missing.

For the next few years, he thought off and on about the people he'd met in Colorado, especially the puppy raiser and her service dog in training. Lance decided in 2004 to take the leap and apply for a dog through Canine Companions for Independence in California. "When I filled out an application, I wanted a companion to maybe pick things up for me," Lance said. He spent two weeks at the group's training facilities in Oceanside, north of San Diego.

He was matched with Satine, a black Labrador retriever, provided by CCI at no cost.

Traveling cross-country to see if Satine would be a good match for him, he received a lot more than a canine companion and helper. Satine forever broadened Lance's horizons.

"Satine changed my life," Lance said about receiving his first service dog. "She gave me my independence." As an example, he said, "If something is on the floor, there's no way I can get it." His dog was trained to pick it up and hand it to him. "Before I had Satine, if I dropped something, I would have to call someone and ask them to come over to get it for me or just do without it."

The independence she gave Lance went deeper than performing daily tasks. "Satine," he explained, "gave me the confidence to attempt to live on my own." The idea of living alone as a quadriplegic with his dog as his only helper seemed out of reach. But Lance was determined. He was even driven. It became his dream.

At that point, Lance had three semesters left to complete his bachelor's degree, so he returned home with Satine and enrolled at Williams Baptist College—this time with Satine in the classroom by his side.

Satine did much more than help him at school, Lance's mother Gail said. One day, while he was outside with Satine, it rained and he couldn't get from the backyard to the house. No one was home but Lance and Satine. At that point, Lance still had a hand-operated wheelchair and not a motorized one, making it more difficult for him to maneuver.

He told Satine, "Speak," and she barked—loud and clear—as an alert that Lance needed assistance.

"The neighbors all knew that Lance's dog didn't bark unless he was in trouble," Gail explained.

A neighbor a block away happened to be out walking on Lance's street, heard Satine's barks for help, and went to the house, where he found Lance and his wheelchair stuck in the mud.

It happened a second time when Lance and Satine were traveling with his mother and nephew. Their evening flight from San Diego to Arkansas had been canceled, and another flight wasn't available until the next morning, so the airline had put them up in a nearby hotel.

The next day, before dawn, while his mother and nephew Will checked out of the hotel, Lance wheeled himself outside to take Satine for her morning walk.

"My grandson and I were in the lobby and heard a dog bark," Gail explained. "My grandson looked at me and said, 'That's Satine.' The wheel of Lance's chair had gotten wedged in the sidewalk crack when he'd turned a corner. He was stuck outside in the dark."

Those instances cemented for Lance just how invaluable Satine was to his day-to-day living. Besides independence and security, Satine also gave him a new sense of direction. He could go places on his own without having friends or family help him. She had his back.

In May 2005, Lance graduated with a bachelor's degree in psychology, making him the first person in his family to complete college. That same year, Arkansas Rehabilitation Services and the Governor's Commission on People with Disabilities recognized Lance's achievements by presenting him with the Arkansas Ability Award. Upon graduating from college, Lance applied for a job at CCI as a volunteer coordinator. They hired him.

In 2006, he packed up his belongings, drove cross-country in his hand-operated van, and relocated to Carlsbad, California, on the Pacific coast. For the first time in more than a decade, Lance was independent once again, this time with Satine as his teammate.

"I wandered for ten or eleven years, not knowing what I wanted to do," he said, until he was exposed to CCI and the work they do for the disabled. "I knew the first week in team training that this was what I wanted to do. I wanted to help change other people's lives like Satine had changed mine. I wanted to be a part of that. CCI and Satine gave me the life I'm living today."

He's never looked back.

Lance's lifestyle is one that able-bodied people might have difficulty keeping up with. It's not for the faint of heart.

By 2011, Lance was an expert shooter in the Paralympics, with an eye toward competing in the 2016 Games. Every year, teams compete in the Warrior Games at the Paralympic Training Center in Colorado, and Lance is hoping to qualify.

The opportunity appeared when a fellow former marine told Lance about a shooting competition in 2011 and invited Lance to compete in the trial. It was at Camp Pendleton, where he had the opportunity to become part of a fifty-person team for the annual Warrior Games in Colorado Springs. At first Lance hesitated, because at that point he hadn't been active in sports for more than seventeen years, ever since his accident. He wasn't sure he could perform because of his injury. At the shooting range, however, an air rifle was adapted so he could compete. "It turned out it was something I was really good at," he said. He qualified for the team, and they won the competition at the Warrior Games.

Besides satisfying his competitive side, "It's given me the chance to be around my fellow Marines again, which is something I missed," he says. "It's opened up a lot of doors."

He also competes on an adapted, hand-operated tandem bicycle, riding with an able-bodied cyclist.

By his side, helping him before and after competitions, is his dog Satine. "There aren't enough hours in the day for what I want to do,"

Lance said. "I hate to imagine where I would be right now if I didn't have a service dog. I was an athlete in high school and college, and now I'm back involved in sports."

Now nine years old, Satine had slowed down and couldn't do the things she used to do for Lance. He was faced with not only getting another service dog, but also making the difficult decision to retire Satine. "It's not physically possible for me to take care of two dogs," Lance explained. While he is able to care for one service dog—feeding, grooming, and walking—having two wasn't possible. Satine needed a foster home.

"I was going to take Satine home with me," Gail said about her son's aging dog. "Then a foster home in San Diego became available."

But Satine didn't go to just anyone to live out the rest of her days. She went to Hall of Fame basketball player Bill Walton and his wife Lori. Lance visited Satine at the Waltons' San Diego home until Satine passed away in 2013. In the process of visits with his dog, the Waltons became two of Lance's closest friends.

Once Satine retired, Lance was matched with August II, a black Labrador retriever nicknamed Auggie, who has been at his side ever since.

"He's a pretty laid-back dog," Lance said, petting Auggie's neck while kicking back in a parklike area of Carlsbad on the Southern California coast, which he's called home since 2009. "When Auggie plays, there's a whole other side to him. He puts a big smile on my face," he said, adding, "I'm just along for the ride."

While Lance insists that "Auggie plays a lot more than he works," it's evident when watching the two of them together that Auggie is always on his game. When Lance's wheelchair hit a break and slight hill on a sidewalk that tipped his chair back, lifting the front wheels off the ground, Auggie quickly jumped behind the chair, ready to stop the fall if he had to. That didn't happen, as Lance quickly maneuvered it to get the front wheels back on solid ground. Auggie had done his job in a matter of seconds. Lance and Auggie were clearly in sync with each other.

Spend time with Lance and the fact that he's in a wheelchair is quickly forgotten. His quiet but friendly, easy manner and quick laugh are contagious. He likes people and animals, and it shows in the respectful way he interacts with both.

Daily life for a quadriplegic, Lance explained, "is a workout. It's a lot of hard work. Many people at my level of injury don't drive."

Lance's life thus far with his service dogs Satine and Auggie has been quite a ride.

Having a service dog like Auggie has eased his life in ways Lance has difficulty expressing.

"It's hard to put into words all the things that come with a dog like her," he said. "Satine passed the torch, in a sense, and Auggie's helping me to continue on my path, on my mission, to help educate people—not just those in wheelchairs, but also to educate people in general about service dogs and what can happen when they are paired together."

Lance is paying it forward with teenager Grant Pyle, a Magnolia, Arkansas, high-school senior who was paralyzed from the chest down in August 2013 in a car accident that occurred as the driver texted while behind the wheel.

Just as Satine passed the torch on to Auggie, Lance has passed his torch to Grant by helping him get a service dog, encouraging him to attend college, answering his questions, and letting him know about the opportunities available to him.

"Any type of injury like that is catastrophic," Lance explained. "The thing about a spinal-cord injury is, it's tough for a lot of guys and girls to deal with. All I can do is offer my support and let them know I am here for them. Once they realize they're not going to walk again, it gets easier."

During a vacation to Arkansas in spring 2014, Lance got together with Grant. "I saw a lot of myself in him," Lance said. "He's an athlete too—an all-star, all-state swimmer. He was the star of his team going into the season before his injury."

Grant asked Lance a lot of the same questions Lance said he had in those first years following his accident. "I want to give him hope," Lance noted, "and I want to be there for him."

One of the things Lance has done is to plant the seed in Grant about the possibility of getting his own service dog, as well as to offer moral support along the way.

In a telephone conversation Lance had with Grant's aunt, Michelle Paden, before Lance and Grant met, Michelle said Lance offered to assist Grant in getting into a rehabilitation center similar to the one Lance went to in Colorado.

"You mean you're going to help him?" Michelle said she asked Lance. "He said, 'Yes, I am. I'm going to help.' There have been so many decisions to be made, even about getting a service dog, and nowhere to turn," she said. "To know we have someone to turn to for knowledge and resources is reassuring. Lance gave me a new outlook to help Grant with whatever he needs."

Once he finishes rehabilitation, Michelle said, Grant has entertained the idea of attending college with the goal of one day becoming a swim coach. According to Michelle, connecting with Lance has been a highlight in her nephew's life. "Lance has been a godsend," she said during a telephone conversation. "He's an inspiration."

After Grant met with Lance, he was impressed. He called his aunt, excited about the get-together, saying, "Aunt Michelle, he's cool." Grant also spent time with Auggie and saw firsthand what a service dog does for Lance.

"Auggie knows about thirty-five commands," Lance said. "The one we use every single day is 'Get.' It used to be if I was at the grocery store or at the bank and dropped something, I'd have to ask for help. It got old." Satine first did those tasks for him, and now Auggie does.

He carries things for Lance, pushes doors open, opens and closes the refrigerator, and turns lights on and off. "It's endless the way these dogs help," Lance said, adding, "Auggie gives meaning to my life." As an added bonus, Lance noted, "He's a good icebreaker in conversations."

On a summer day in Carlsbad, Lance and Auggie's life together was about to get even better.

Lance had been searching in the coastal community for a retrofitted house that would accommodate a wheelchair. He talked to a neighbor who lived across the street from the house he was renting. This house was available to rent, and the owner was willing to give Lance a lifetime lease with a fixed rent.

Green Beach America, a nonprofit dedicated to providing sustainable housing for disabled veterans, paid for by donations, learned about Lance's need. With the blessing of the property owner, they raised the funds to retrofit the leased house from top to bottom, including a wheelchair ramp, a wheel-in shower, a refrigerator door accessible at Lance's level, a lowered sink, cupboards and light switches that Lance can reach, plus a backyard for Auggie. Having a wheelchair-accessible house is an even bigger help.

While Auggie has made it possible for Lance to live alone, he also has a part-time caregiver in the morning to help him get his day started and in the evening as the day ends. This caregiver has been needed, because the things people take for granted—getting water from a faucet, opening and closing window blinds, or getting into a shower stall—have been out of reach for Lance since he moved to California.

"He's a guy in a chair who gives back every day," said Peggy Mazzella, cofounder with her husband Dan of Green Beach, who learned about Lance's needs from her friend Lori Walton. "We're honored to be able to help Lance," Peggy said. "We're putting in a motion-sensor faucet he can use himself. The retrofit allows anyone in a chair access."

Now settled into his newly accessible home, specifically designed to fit his needs, life has gotten easier.

"Coming back after a catastrophic accident," Lance said, "is a tough place to be. It's even tougher to do it from a wheelchair, and even tougher still to do it as a quadriplegic." His new home eases many of the challenges he faces daily.

Despite those challenges, Lance says that he has no regrets. His life is full and, above all, he's happy. And so is his service dog Auggie.

"I had a few really rough years dealing with my injury. Now, I wouldn't change a thing," he said as he relaxed, with Auggie at his feet, at a local restaurant in the coastal Carlsbad he's called home since 2009. "I wouldn't trade the life I have now for anything. I wouldn't take anything back."

# CHAPTER 15

# To the Rescue

Sheri Williams knew she wanted to help people with disabilities after she found herself paralyzed, on her back, and in a rest home, with no diagnosis and no sign of help. Three years later, once she had regained her health with the aid of her service dog, she vowed to pay it forward by assisting others who found themselves in similar circumstances. More specifically, she wanted to help veterans.

So she started a service dog program of her own, where she will either train the veteran's own dog, or she'll take them to a municipal animal shelter to rescue a dog of the veteran's choosing, based on a variety of factors. Then Sheri works at training both the dogs and the veterans following the guidelines recommended by Assistance Dogs International (or ADI).

The illness that immobilized Sheri was eventually diagnosed as a staph infection. Doctors, after trying a variety of antibiotics, were initially unable to beat back the infection to put her on the road to recovery. During those dark days, as she sought help with seemingly no remedy, she was determined to fight her way back to good health.

A big piece of her recovery came through the invaluable assistance of her rescued dog, Debo. "My dog became my doctor and my healer," Sheri said from her home in Los Angeles. "I relied on Debo as a visual balance dog."

Sheri took in Debo, a Pomeranian, after someone she knew had dropped him off at a shelter. "His owner was getting ready to relinquish him, and I showed up and took him. My timing was perfect. I saved him. Then years later, he saved me."

Sheri's family members put her, a successful clothing model before she fell ill, in a nursing home. After three painful months with no improvement, she was admitted to a hospital where she was diagnosed with the staph infection. Following six months of hospitalization, she was released, but she was no further ahead physically than she had been at the time she was admitted. She was still wheelchair-bound with little energy because her illness had taxed her system.

To make matters worse, she'd lost everything she owned because of the cost of her hospital stay. "I had a lot of money in the bank and it was gone. I couldn't walk; I fell all the time." She lost her house, her business, her friends. And she lost her memory.

"I basically don't remember anything from 2008 to 2010," she said.

She was determined to feel good again. What the doctors could not do for her, help her gain strength physically, she did for herself—with the help of Debo. "I threw his toy and he'd bring it back," she said. Playing toss with Debo helped her to regain her strength.

Next, she worked on leaving her wheelchair behind. "I graduated to a walker, and then to two canes, to one cane, and then nothing," she said.

She had nerve damage, and depended on Debo for mobility, to prevent her from falling.

She taught her Pomeranian the command "Go ahead," which meant he was to walk in front of her. "My eyes watched his legs, which retrained my brain on how to move my legs," Sheri explained. "Since my eyes play such a big part in balancing me, just watching Debo balancing as he walked helped me learn how to balance on my own," adding that the cuteness factor of observing the small, fluffy dog she adores helped as well. "Seeing his cute little tail and how he pranced motivated me to want to walk again. It was the instant gratification of seeing my 'little monkey' walk that inspired me to keep trying."

The technique worked. Sheri's strength increased as she taught herself to walk again. "Therapy with my own dog made me think dogs could help veterans heal too," she said.

Sheri had read about the high instance of suicide with combat veterans. She knew firsthand the healing power of dogs. She wanted to help vets, to afford them the same comfort and assistance she'd found in her own dog Debo. Her work with Debo was the start of Animal T.A.I.L., which stands for Animal Therapists Assisting in Living.

Getting into Sheri Williams's Animal T.A.I.L. program provided a solution for the mental and physical issues former army corporal Darren Slotterbeck faced after injuring his knee in boot camp and suffering PTSD in the aftermath of combat duty. It came to a head for him after five and a half years and five deployments, including as a Marine infantryman, or, as he described his job, "a machine gunner."

In 2005, he was "boots on the ground" in Fallujah during his first Iraqi tour.

"Fallujah was pretty rough," he said. "I was a Humvee gunner. I did mounted and dismounted patrols. I was the gentleman outside of the truck, up in the turret, with the larger gun mounted on top, which would be a Mark 19 forty-millimeter grenade launcher and a fifty-caliber machine gun." Depending on the patrol, he also used an M240 Bravo fully automatic machine gun—heavy artillery for on-the-ground combat.

Since then, he's had what he and other veterans have termed "night terrors"—bad combat dreams that he can't control.

He left the US Marine Corps in January 2010, and by June of the same year, he'd joined the US Army Reserve.

While he was living with the effects of PTSD because of his combat duty, his mother became gravely ill, and the decision to leave her on life support—or not—was left up to him. "We medicated her and I made the decision," Darren said. "I stayed in the room and held her hand until she passed, and I still struggle with that decision."

"Losing a family member for me is more difficult than most of what I saw overseas," he continued. "I came back from Iraq in August of 2008. She passed in March of 2009."

Darren began treatment for post-traumatic stress in 2011. At home, he avoids driving on unpaved roads, and only drives during certain hours of the day in order to avoid too much traffic that might trigger anxiety. "In Fallujah, we had a lot of incidents on dirt roads and on shoulders of the road. I avoid driving on that type of surface," he explained.

Around the same time he went through PTSD treatment, friends found a dog named Mamas. They couldn't keep the dog and left her with Darren. Shortly after, Darren heard about Sheri Williams and her Animal T.A.I.L. program.

He and Mamas joined Sheri's first service dog training class. Initially, Mamas learned basic commands; after nearly a year, she moved on to more advanced skills and tasks. Mamas picked up some of her duties on her own.

"Mamas can tell when I'm having a bad day," Darren said. "She comes up to me and loves on me to make sure I'm not losing it. She mellows me out. She'll put her head on my chest to pull me out of wherever I am. She keeps me on my toes and keeps me mellow."

Mamas also picked up on a knee problem Darren has. "I messed it up when I was in boot camp, and over the years, it's sort of crumbled. I have a torn meniscus. If the need for mobility training comes along, then we can do that. She jumped on it once, saw me wince, and she avoids that knee entirely. She sleeps on the bed with me and doesn't go near that knee."

One of the funniest but most effective things that Mamas does for Darren is to wag her tail—but she does it directly against him. "She makes sure she has her hind end close to my body and wags her tail at an ungodly speed to let me know she's there. She'll do anything she can to get me to focus my attention on her."

Darren is grateful to be able to turn his own dog into a service canine. "Mamas and Animal T.A.I.L. are probably the biggest godsends

I've had in my life," he said. "With everything that went on before I got help, I was headed down a bad, life-ending path. I had drinking problems. I've been in fights. I got arrested for drinking and driving. Mamas is helping to keep me an active, helpful part of society instead of an angry, vengeful person."

———

Sam Hanson, a retired Marine lance corporal and Iraqi veteran, stumbled across his service dog when he rescued a puppy from a backyard breeder. He was in need of a service dog to help him with his post-traumatic stress after returning from overseas, but he didn't realize it at the time.

Sam was injured a month to the day after arriving in Iraq while on a military operation in Fallujah, in May 2008. For that, he received a medal and a medical discharge. The Marine Corps medal didn't change how he felt after arriving home.

"I went through a depression phase," Sam said. "I still had a lot of the 'Why wasn't it me instead of him?' guilt. I have a buddy who lost two limbs. I still deal with the guilt factor."

Sam, a mechanic who was laid off from his job in 2013, rescued his Siberian husky puppy from the breeder. "I saw the condition of the dogs. We went over there and talked to the guy. She was outside in the heat and on the dirt. I talked him into giving her to us. She was the last in the litter. I was kind of like, 'Dude, this isn't good.' He gave her to my girlfriend and me. We named her Brandy."

He learned about the Animal T.A.I.L. program by reading a flyer posted at a veterans' center. Nearly nine months into the program, "Brandy knows she's here for me." During a training session where the dogs were taught to ignore food, which is required in order for them to be allowed to enter restaurants or anywhere food is served, Brandy passed without a problem.

"Sheri dropped a filet mignon in front of Brandy's face and asked Brandy to 'leave it.' She didn't bat an eye at it. I take her to stores and she does very well. She's right next to me the whole time, by my side. When I stop, she sits."

Sam described the group of veterans in the Animal T.A.I.L. program as "a tight-knit group."

"There's a lot of help there. If one of us is messed up, we understand. It's like we're still in the military, but with each other. The dogs brought us together."

Sam is confident Brandy will continue improving until she is certified. As a result of her newfound role as his service dog in training, "I feel very secure with Brandy. Next to my girlfriend, Brandy's like my partner-in-crime type of deal, you know? She's here for me. Brandy gives me unconditional love and unconditional loyalty, and that's comforting."

"The last thing I thought would help me was a dog," said retired combat correspondent Matt Preston, who struggles with PTSD. "I'm a cat person." But "just the connection and the loyalty and the unconditional love that Gracie gives me is the biggest help."

That help—in the form of a service dog named Gracie, a terrier mix—has taken decades to reach him. And now that he's got her, he's not about to let her go. Gracie lived with him for two years in a Burbank, California, homeless shelter—where she was allowed to stay because Gracie was a service dog in training. In the summer of 2014, they traveled to Columbus, Ohio, to stay for a few months with friends.

A combat veteran in the 22nd Marine Expeditionary Unit, Matt served two tours in Afghanistan, left the service, and later voluntarily returned for a third stint in Afghanistan, but as a civilian working for a media marketing company.

"I had a rough time that third tour, both for physical- and mental-health reasons," he said.

When he came back to the States, he couldn't find work and ended up at the homeless shelter. "I had to move out of the apartment I was in," he said. "I have a lot of anger issues. Gracie keeps me grounded."

Until they left for Ohio, Matt took extension courses at the University of California, Los Angeles, and Gracie attended with him. "I'm very lucky compared to a lot of guys who came back. I have orthopedic issues. I can't run anymore. Bombing played a big role in my PTSD. I was right there with the line units doing patrol. Outgoing fire was the best thing we could hear—our guns going off. Incoming was the worst—enemy fire coming toward friendly positions.

"The thing about PTSD," Matt explained, "is it affects everyone differently. Symptoms manifest themselves in a certain commonality—hyperalertness, always making sure you have a way out, and assessing threats based on my experience as I evaluate these threats. I'm on alert constantly."

Since coming back from his deployment the third time, he has worked for the marketing company. He still thinks about Afghanistan. "I do worry about the Afghan people," he said. "I went back because I figured I had unfinished business. I saw a lot of Afghans die, and I thought I could help them out again. It was rougher than I thought it would be. They're under great socioeconomic and military hardship. It's generations of people.

"My focus right now is to get myself better. If I can't take care of myself, there's nothing I can do for America, let alone Afghanistan."

His third tour ended in mid-2006, and about eight months later he moved to London to attend school. He was with a friend near the subway entrance when an example of his hyperalertness came into play. He heard a *pop, pop, pop* sound as people headed out of the subway. "I pushed my friend into a newspaper stand, as cover for her. It was just some teenagers popping balloons."

Gracie has helped him cope with his anxiety and post-traumatic stress. After she ranked third in a dog training program at a Hollywood obedience class, Matt joined the Animal T.A.I.L. service dog program.

A few months later, Matt noticed Gracie had begun to limp during their walks, so he took her to the vet. "The diagnosis was that the ACL was probably all the way torn," he said. Surgery, the vet said, should repair it. Once Matt and Gracie return to Los Angeles, they'll resume service dog training with T.A.I.L.

"For me," Matt Preston said, "it's more than the fact that Gracie is able to calm me down whenever something happens that gets me agitated. She's very much my best friend in many ways—one of the friends I can count on most. She's a dog, and she does that very well. She's come light-years from where she started, but there's a lot more to go, and we're on that walk together. Before I got Gracie, I would hole up in the apartment for weeks on end, and the only thing I would do would be to go out, get fast food, and come back. That would be my only interaction with a person."

"I'm single right now," he said, "but if I find someone dumb enough to get involved with me, it'll be, 'Love me, love my dog.'"

Former Navy Seabee Paige Lipham doesn't look at herself as disabled, even though she's been diagnosed with PTSD. "To me, PTSD is not being able to adapt to new places. I think a lot of us don't see ourselves as disabled."

She was released from the service a year earlier than expected after serving in Afghanistan and Kuwait. "When I came home, I went on vacation and visited my family."

It would turn out to be anything but a vacation.

"It was the first time I got to see my family in a little over a year," she said. "While I was there, my heart started racing for no reason, and I was paranoid. It was a very strange time. I didn't know what was going on, and my family didn't either."

After she returned to base, it got worse. "I started passing out from panic attacks. Minor events, like traffic, would throw me into this manic stress mode. At first they thought something was wrong with my heart. But an outside specialist said it was PTSD."

She was just nineteen or twenty at the time. "I was scared that it was something to do with my actual heart," she said. "To know that it was PTSD was bad, but it also didn't mean open-heart surgery."

As time progressed, it got worse.

Veteran Rainier Schroeder and his service dog Tundra.

Slate glances back at the casket of his former teammate Brian Coutch at Arlington National Cemetery.

New Jersey assemblyman and veteran Bob Andrzejczak brings Maddie to his office each workday.

Veteran Joe Modica and wife Mary at home with their beloved Barney.

Veteran Joe Buzay and his best friend Frankie.

Frankie, once abused, is now a service dog.

Service dog in training Rascal with Linda Wiedewitsch and Linda's mother, Nettie Momb.

Service dog Auggie picks up
veteran Lance Weir's keys.

Service dog Auggie stands on Lance Weir's feet.

Rick Kaplan's daily walk with his service dogs.

Bobo shows off that handler Rick Kaplan brushes his teeth.

Rick Kaplan pauses to connect with service dog Diva.

Veteran Ronald Goosman shops with Nickel.

Puppy Twister in training at Susquehanna Service Dogs.

Brutus goes through light-switch training at Susquehanna Service Dogs.

Soldier Dave Wilkins with service dog Orvis at his side.

Pilot goes through training exercises at Susquehanna Service Dogs.

Puppy Corporal Stanley and Ellie Lynn Coty at the National Museum of the Marine Corps.

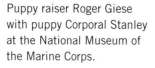

Puppy Corporal Stanley and Liam Schiele at the National Museum of the Marine Corps.

Puppy raiser Roger Giese with puppy Corporal Stanley at the National Museum of the Marine Corps.

Puppy Corporal Stanley will one day be a working service dog for a veteran.

CCI trainer Sarah Koch during daily playtime.

CCI trainer Becky Miller with Blade.

CCI puppy raiser Jan Ford with four-month-old Porter.

Marine sergeant Carlos Cruz training his service dog Logan at Wounded Warrior Battalion West headquarters.

Meeko takes a break during a training outing with her puppy parents.

Denise Costanten training Bodie through Brigadoon Service Dogs' prison program.

Veteran Kevin Brackney takes Nyma to work at the Philadelphia VA hospital.

Veteran Terry Henry and his service dog Chaney.

Veteran Adam Campbell with his service dog Kenan.

4 Paws for Ability trainer Jennifer Lutes practices walking down steps with Saxby.

4 Paws for Ability Trainer Shelby Bottger takes Jinx to a library to acclimate him to public places.

Paws4people service dogs in training: Sherman, Shaw, and Darby.

Veteran Adam Campbell's service dog Kenan.

"When I was home, I walked outside of my house at night with my friends," she said. "We were going out. All of a sudden, I jumped down on the ground and laid down, because I thought I saw a laser. I told everyone, 'Duck! Get down.' They were confused. I wound up not going out. I was too freaked out."

Although her friends thought she'd lost her mind, it was posttraumatic stress, rearing its ugly head.

"If I hear backfiring or fireworks, I hide behind a tree," Paige noted. It's no wonder. "I was around a lot of gunfire. My whole job was engineering in combat zones."

Her psychologist has tried to give her medications, Paige said, but she won't take them. "One of my very good friends in the military died while we were both still in," she explained. "He was having symptoms and he was trying to find a spot to kill himself. They gave him medication. He was drinking. He fell asleep and died."

Instead of meds, Paige is training her own dog Dakota to become her psychiatric service dog through the Animal T.A.I.L. program. Dakota is a German shepherd and coyote mix she had for about four years before she began training her, ever since she was a puppy.

"She's always been a really loyal dog, but since the training, she's even more so," Paige said. "If I'm upset or getting a little anxious, she'll get up on the couch and lay on me or lick my face. She makes me feel much better. When I'm upset, she nudges my hand. She knows. She's trying to take my focus off of it. I say, 'All right.' When I'm frustrated, she gets me right out of it. She didn't do that before. I could be crying or angry and she didn't pay any attention. She was mainly concerned with herself. Now she's focused on me."

Paige takes her to her college classes. "When we're not in class, we go hiking." Or they go to the grocery store. "She's solid on retail stores," Paige said. "She's got those down."

After Paige left the service in 2011, she saw an ad in the paper for puppies. "A woman had a female German shepherd who was in heat, chained up outside. She said she got caught up with a coyote and had four puppies." The ad read, "I want these abominations gone."

When Paige arrived at the house, two puppies were left. The owner was going to take them to the pound. Paige took Dakota home with her, to Simi Valley in Southern California.

Paige learned about Animal T.A.I.L. when she interned at Veterans Affairs. "Sheri came in to give a presentation about her program and I met her there," Paige said. "I thought, 'I have a dog. I love my dog. If she could go everywhere with me, I could do more things.' I wasn't doing anything new without being scared," she said. "I went to work and I went to school. That was it."

Before she and Dakota entered the program, Paige had already taught Dakota basic commands. In the summer of 2014, all the veterans and their dogs worked on water training. Today, they're in the advanced training phase, and even closer to Dakota becoming a certified service dog. "I work with her almost every day. I have a best friend who I know will go with me wherever I want, will always be there for me, will comfort me, She's given me more freedom."

～～

Rick Kaplan found his way to training rescued dogs to be service canines in the same way as Sheri Williams: through training his own dogs to be of personal service. In Rick's case, a decade earlier his dogs Freddie and Ginger had pulled him from retirement and into full-time work in a second career as a dog rescuer and trainer.

He'd retired from a New York City diamond-and-jewelry business, where his dogs went to work with him daily and even carried and delivered packages. Once retired, he relocated to Myrtle Beach, South Carolina, where he spent much of his time on the golf course. But he wanted more meaning in his life, and he knew he wouldn't find it on the greens. He found that purpose through matching service dogs with disabled veterans.

It was during a walk on the golf course that Jan Igoe met Rick—a chance meeting that changed the direction of her working career.

Jan, then a reporter for *The Sun News*, had been assigned to look into a potential story that included a nearby golf course and reports that "a guy was wandering around a golf course with two bears."

The "bears" turned out to be Rick's chocolate Labrador retrievers, brother and sister Freddie and Ginger, whom he had trained to assist him from the time they were puppies. Because of an injury, Rick suffered from seizures and understood the need for a service dog. Freddie and Ginger went everywhere with him. "They could detect his oncoming seizures," Jan said.

Some dogs, for reasons scientists have yet to discover, can learn how to detect epileptic seizures in people, often before they occur. According to Canine Assistants, a nonprofit organization in Atlanta, Georgia, that trains service dogs for people with physical disabilities or other medical conditions, some of these "seizure dogs" are trained to bark loudly, while some are taught to activate an alarm to alert people that their owners are in the midst of a seizure. Other dogs lie next to the person having the seizure to keep them from injuring themselves.

Once a person and a Canine Assistants seizure dog develop a strong bond, a large number of them—about 87 percent—can go on to predict seizures before they happen, alerting the person by whining, pawing, pacing, jumping, barking, or some other unusual behavior.

Such was the case with Rick's dogs, which he trained specifically to alert him about an impending seizure.

Jan went out to the golf course as her editor had instructed her, looked for the "bears," saw Rick and his service dogs instead, and interviewed him. They became fast friends and stayed in touch.

In 2010, Rick founded Canine Angels to provide service dogs for veterans and first responders.

"I was writing an article for a magazine about service dogs, looking for more service dog organizations, and saw that Rick had just started Canine Angels," Jan said. She contacted Rick, and then watched over the following months as he struggled to get content onto his website and catch the attention of the media about his organization.

Jan was also ready for a change.

"I'd had it with newspapers," she said, "and was able to make the shift to freelancing. I'm happy doing freelance work and donating my time to help Rick. I used to run an advertising agency, so I was able to bring a lot of skills to his organization. I can design, I can write, I can photograph, and I can talk to the media."

Most of all, she said, "I love what Rick is doing. I have never met anyone who lives his life without regret, without worry. He doesn't waste his time and energy. If something doesn't work, he says, 'Let's fix it.' He reminds veterans that there's no clock ticking. There's nothing that's putting limits on them or rushing them. Whatever pace they move at is perfect. It's a journey."

That journey has included Rick's first service dog placement: matching Barney, a chow-Labrador mix, with a veteran—although not a recent one.

Barney and then-ninety-four-year-old Joseph Modica, who served during World War II, graduated in 2011 from Canine Angels' service dog program. Barney, who was seven years old in 2014, never lets Joe leave his sight unless it's to alert Joe's wife, Mary, or his caregiver that Joe needs assistance.

Like so many rescued dogs, Barney has his own story. He was taken to a veterinary hospital and left behind with a request from his owner that he be euthanized. Rick Kaplan, who happened to be in the vet's office for a visit with one of his dogs, met Barney.

"The owner was dying of cancer and couldn't bear the thought of his dog living without him," Jan explained. "Rick saved Barney from euthanasia."

That was good luck not only for Barney, but also for Joe, who has dementia. Today, Joe depends on Barney. "Barney lets Joe's caregiver know when Joe needs something by notifying his wife," Jan said.

When a visitor was welcomed into the Modica home, Joe was prepared. He proudly donned three ties and six wristwatches—three on each arm. He enjoys dressing himself; it's harmless, and his wife and caregiver don't interfere.

To Joe, his dog Barney is as much a soldier as Joe once was. One of the first things Joe pointed out to his visitor was the emblem stitched onto Barney's vest. "He's a service dog," Joe said proudly as he pointed to the cloth patch on Barney's vest. "I was in the service too."

Indeed, Joseph Modica served in World War II as an army sergeant, spending time in North Africa driving large trucks. One day, Joe stopped the truck to get water at a well and inadvertently drove over a land mine, tipping the truck over and landing himself in a German hospital for six months.

"The blast threw him and a couple of the other guys to kingdom come," said his wife Mary. "That's when Joe's hearing started to deteriorate. The blast did it." His body, she added, "is full of shrapnel."

It's clear that Joe's service record speaks for itself. Joe read aloud from his discharge paperwork, noting that he received a Purple Heart and an honorable discharge.

His wife Mary said when they take him to the mall, Joe sits in a scooter while Barney walks at his side and a little bit ahead. Outside the mall, she said, "Barney leads. He doesn't look at other dogs. He doesn't try to go to the grass. He walks straight ahead. He knows his place."

Barney also provides companionship for Joe. "We keep him loved and safe," Mary said as she ran her hand over Barney's dark fur, "and he keeps us loved. He's our baby." Sitting in their home, Mary talked about a neighbor's dog, Sammy, who was the reason they got Barney.

Every day, Joe and Mary's neighbors allowed their dog Sammy— a large, fluffy mutt—to wander the neighborhood. And every day, he would go to the Modicas' house and let himself in through the dog door that was installed there.

"The dog adopted Joe," Mary said. He sat at his feet and followed Joe around the house. Eventually Sammy stopped going home and spent most of his time with them. He was an older dog, she said, and after a couple of years, he passed away. "Joe missed Sammy something awful when he died," she said. So they looked into getting a replacement dog, but one with the skills to assist Joe.

At that point in the conversation with the visitor, Barney got up and walked across the room.

"C'mere, Barney," Joe said, and Barney immediately turned around, walked over to Joe, and sat at his feet.

"He's a good boy," Joe said. Then, proudly, "He's a service dog. I was in the service, the army, and my dog is a *service* dog."

Joe's memory isn't very good at times, but when it comes to anything to do with Barney, his face lights up. "We talk to each other," Joe said.

"It's true," Mary chimed in. "When I move Joe from his wheelchair to his regular chair, Barney talks to him, doesn't he, Joe?"

"He does," Joe agreed.

"Barney's vocal. He runs to me when Joe needs something."

———

While Joe Modica has a larger dog from Canine Angels, Chris Skinner, a native of North Carolina's Outer Banks, has a six-pound Yorkshire terrier for his service dog. Despite her size, the tasks and services Zoey performs are no less valuable.

Chris was a member of the Army National Guard assigned to the 11 Bravo Infantry as it readied its members to ship out. Chris was also attending Radford University in Virginia and was a self-described partying member of a fraternity.

On June 10, 2000, before deploying, he and a friend attended a wedding, where they drank. They were headed home, and just before his friend lost control of the car, Chris had unbuckled his seat belt. He was thrown from the vehicle. The impact broke his neck and rendered him a quadriplegic, landing him in a wheelchair.

After the accident, Chris said, "I grew up really fast. I had to."

At a Virginia rehabilitation center, Chris went through lengthy and intense rehab therapy. His physical therapist, Suzie, became his best friend. His outlook improved, he returned to school, and, in 2002, he graduated from Radford. His relationship with Suzie became romantic, and by 2004, the couple had married. In 2007, they had children—a set of fraternal twins named Alethia and Caleb.

His children, he said, don't see their father as disabled. "I've always been in a wheelchair," Chris said. "They have no idea I'm paralyzed. It's hilarious."

During the week, while his children were in school and his wife was at work, Chris was left alone without companionship. It was suggested to him that he look into getting a service dog to assist him, because his injury had left him with limited use of his arms and hands, and no use of his legs. A service dog, he was told, could help him with everyday tasks.

Chris soon visited Canine Angels. Just one dog—a small one—caught his attention, and vice versa.

"Every time I went to Canine Angels, Zoey would jump in my lap, and she did it so naturally. I thought she was so cute. Each time I went there looking for a big dog, the next thing I knew, Zoey would be on my lap, looking up at me as if she were saying, 'I'm going to be your dog.'"

That's the philosophy at Canine Angels: The dogs choose the veterans. And so it was that Zoey went home with Chris.

Their work together had only just begun.

"We had a larger dog in mind for him, with enough strength to open the fridge and fetch hefty items," said Jan Igoe, Canine Angels' communications manager. "But Chris fell in love with our six-pound Yorkie, who never leaves his lap."

Chris points out that she's the perfect-size dog for his needs. "My paralysis is such a high level that I'm paralyzed from the collarbone down," he said. "If I had a big dog, my wheelchair would be a barrier. My six-and-a-half-pound wonder dog—and she is a wonder dog—is able to jump up on my lap and come up to where I have feeling, up around my face and neck."

Zoey was abandoned by her owner on the steps of a local shelter, with one broken leg and a torn ligament that happened in a dog attack. Rick Kaplan, who heads Canine Angels, rescued the small Yorkshire terrier and adopted her as his pet. He never expected Zoey to become a service dog, but that was before Chris and Zoey met.

The year 2014, Chris pointed out, marked fourteen years since he'd been injured. "My health is not as good as it used to be," he said, "so it's been a lot tougher to be alone. Never in my entire life have I been in a situation where I was completely alone. I was starting to feel kind of down. When I got Zoey, she absolutely brought me out of it. I immediately felt great. She got me outside. She got me talking with people again. I'm an extroverted person, but for some reason I shut down. She makes it inviting for other people to approach me."

And while Zoey is small in stature, she's a giant when it comes to what she does for Chris. "If I drop my wallet, she'll bring it back up to me," he said. "Besides everything she does for me, she is my companion, first and foremost."

Brushing and petting Zoey has helped to strengthen Chris's arms. His voice is much stronger too, Jan points out. "It used to be a whisper, because his diaphragm muscles were compromised by his injury. But Zoey has given him a new sense of obligation and responsibility. He wants to take care of her better than anyone else could. And he's succeeding."

Zoey has also brought him out of his shell, so much so that Chris has become a motivational speaker, helping veterans who find themselves in similar positions. Zoey, of course, travels with him.

"She comforts me," Chris said.

Rick describes what Zoey has done for Chris and his family as "beyond amazing."

"Zoey is special because it's not the size of the dog, but the size of the fight in the dog," Rick said. With Chris, "there was always a concern that he'd drop something and wouldn't be able to get it. This is a six-pound dog who jumps off the chair; she sleeps at the crook of his neck when he sleeps and wakes him up out of nightmares. She's a twenty-four-hour caretaker. He's not alone. He's receiving direct service from this little being. That's what it's all about."

Retired US Air Force firefighter Ronald Goosman also has a big heart for a small dog, this one a hearing canine.

It was 1958 at Biggs Army Airfield in El Paso, Texas, when Ronald worked a flight line of B-47 bombers.

In the midst of the Suez crisis, ships had strategically blocked the Suez Canal, which put US military forces on alert. Ronald and his fellow airmen were on call twenty-four hours a day during this diplomatic and military confrontation between Egypt on one side, and Britain, France, and Israel on the other, with the United States and United Nations urging Britain, France, and Israel to withdraw.

The B-47s had to be ready to go at a moment's notice, so the booster fuel pumps were regularly changed and tested. Ronald and the other airmen were only sixty or seventy feet from the planes when they revved their engines. The noise, according to Ronald, "was unbearable."

That turned out to be an understatement.

"At that time, a B-47 was really a flying gas tank," Ronald explained. "They had booster tanks with very high rpm." Ronald and the other airmen stood by during a seven-day period where pilots were testing takeoffs and landings and flying B-36 bombers in and out. These were the days before protective gear and earmuffs, and Ronald ended up permanently losing a good portion of his hearing as a result.

Over the years, his hearing continued to worsen. His wife Thelma urged him to seek help.

"My wife got tired of hollering at me," he said, "so I went to the VA and they told my wife, 'He's 'bout deaf.'"

After the hearing evaluation in 1964, Ronald was sent to Walter Reed Army Medical Center for forty-two days. "There wasn't anything they could do for me," he said. "We were here in Texas. I went to the VA and they gave me a hearing aid."

Once he was discharged from the air force in 1967 with a 40 percent disability because of his hearing loss, he had a tough time finding work.

"I was unemployed, and no one would hire me because I couldn't hear that well," he said. "I worked for my brother as a gofer—go for this, go for that. Then I worked as a welder." Ronald eventually retired.

The hearing aid he used wasn't enough. He knew he needed more. Help came in the form of a small Lhasa apso named Billy Bud, a hearing dog from Dogs for the Deaf, an organization based in Central Point, Oregon.

Billy Bud changed Ronald's life. "Before I got a hearing dog, I didn't feel like I could go anywhere," he said. "I'd hold my hands on the phone so I could feel it vibrate. I didn't want to miss a call."

Billy Bud became Ronald's ears and alerted him to sounds by pawing at him. The dog also became Ronald and his wife's protector. When Thelma fell, Billy Bud was there to find help.

"I hollered to Billy to go get Ronald, and he left me and went to Ronald," Thelma said. "Another time, we were outside and the toast in the toaster oven burned, and we didn't know it. Billy alerted me to that."

The Goosmans had Billy Bud with them thirteen years. Their daughter, Peggy, wrote a touching tribute to Billy in the summer 2011 edition of *Canine Listener*, Dogs for the Deaf's newsletter.

"Billy was a hearing dog by trade, but a true family friend by life," Peggy wrote. "He was as lucky to have my dad and mom as they were to have him. They took good care of each other for the thirteen years they had together. It was only as recently as last year that Billy's health began to irreparably fail, and the roles that had been long established were reversed as my dad became Billy's aide. My parents cared for Billy, and he could not have found a better home anywhere. There never was a dog as loved as Billy, and his passing has left a hole bigger than Texas in our hearts. You trained a wonderful dog, and he was part of our family to the end. You will never know how much Billy helped my dad. We will miss him more than words can ever tell. My father is so lost without Billy."

No dog can replace another, but when Billy Bud died, Dogs for the Deaf found another canine who passed their initial assessment, appearing to have the confidence, interest in people, and drive necessary to become a hearing dog.

Nickel, a pug mix, was found wandering the streets in Fresno, California, picked up by animal control, and pulled from the shelter by Animal Rescue at Fresno, or ARF. That's where Dogs for the Deaf met Nickel, when a couple of trainers were in the area to deliver a service dog and stopped at the rescue center to evaluate some dogs. They took Nickel back to Oregon and trained him to be a hearing dog.

Ronald, after losing Billy Bud, was sad, but he also missed the independence a hearing dog gave him. He was pleased to learn that Dogs for the Deaf had found a good candidate in Nickel.

Thus, two months after losing Billy Bud, the floppy-eared, copper-colored, twelve-pound, eager-to-please dog with a prominent underbite moved in with the Goosmans, who split their time between Washington State and Texas.

"Nickel's got lots of energy," Ronald said. "He alerts me to sounds. My first dog hit me with his paws. Dogs for the Deaf, based in Oregon, taught Nickel to tap me with his nose. I have a balancing problem, and if I'm in the computer room and my wife calls me, Nickel will come and get me and walk with me."

For a hearing-impaired person, alerting for sounds is paramount.

When Ronald shops at Walmart, Nickel stands on a small dog bed Ronald attached to his wheelchair's footrest. Facing forward, "Nickel puts his head up like he's leading and telling me where to go."

Nickel has made a difference in Thelma's life as well. "Our service dog has made life easier for me," she said, "because I can call Nickel and say, 'Do you want to go and get Daddy?' And he goes in and taps Ronald. This dog knows what we're saying. At five o'clock, I don't care where Nickel's at, he'll look at me, and I'll say 'Are you hungry?' He's very smart. He understands a lot."

Billy Bud and Nickel have brought not only practical help to the Goosmans, but also a great deal of joy to their lives.

"Ronald has companionship everywhere he goes," Thelma said.

"I have enjoyed my life," Ronald said. "A service dog has made it one hundred and fifty percent better. For the longest time, I wore a sign that said, 'Face me. I lip-read.'"

With Nickel, he no longer has to wear a sign. "When they see I have a dog, they look at me."

A dog named Wendy, as with the hearing dog Nickel, has taken on tasks that former Navy and army veteran Richard Heath calls "simply amazing," such as putting on and taking off his socks and shoes, and pulling up his trousers. "The more she does, the happier she is," he noted.

At first, Richard's wife, Elaine, didn't believe that Wendy, trained by Patriot PAWS, could ever do the things the trainer said she could. "I was skeptical. We laugh about that now."

When Richard, who suffers from seizures and post-traumatic stress, occasionally falls, Wendy quickly steels herself and breaks his fall. On top of that, the large black Labrador and standard poodle cross pulls him off the floor and onto a chair.

Wendy did exactly that in the summer of 2011 when Richard, who saw his share of combat injuries while serving during the Vietnam War at an evacuation hospital as a combat medic, suffered a stroke, fell, and was stuck on the floor, unable to move one side of his body. He was in the house alone with Wendy, who dragged Richard to a chair and hoisted him onto it. Then she handed him the phone. When his hand didn't move because of the stroke, Wendy put it in his other hand and Richard was able to call for help. Beyond the valuable daily assistance his dog provides, Richard said he'll never forget that summer day. "Wendy," he said quietly, "saved my life."

# CHAPTER 16

# "The Right Stuff"

A medical prescription from a doctor for a service dog changed army veteran Ted Martello's future for the better. On Memorial Day 2012, Ted welcomed Buster, a honey-colored chow mix who was found on the side of a highway, into his life.

And he hasn't looked back.

Ted, a four-year veteran who was a tank mechanic in Badkifigar, Germany, and at Fort Seal, Oklahoma, twice deployed to Iraq, in 2008 and 2010, for a year each. Halfway through his second tour, the truck he was driving hit an IED. The impact threw him out of the truck. It didn't end his tour. He finished and went home with his unit. Something was wrong, and it took about two years for him to learn that it had a name.

Once he was diagnosed with PTSD and TBI, his psychiatrist recommended a service canine and wrote him the prescription. Ted searched for service dog groups and found a program that was within driving distance from his Arizona home.

Buster came to Ted from Canines with Careers, through the Best Friends Animal Society. Sherry Woodard, who runs the program, is an animal behavior expert and consultant, and she introduced Ted to some dogs. "I picked Buster out of the lineup. We bonded right away," he said.

When Ted got Buster, he was already trained as a service canine.

"Buster saved my life," Ted said. "Without him, I would have been one of the twenty-two veteran suicides a day."

At Catholic Charities, where Ted works, "Buster is the office mascot." When he's on the street in search of homeless veterans, ready to introduce them to programs for the homeless, Buster is with him. "I can honestly say to them, 'Hey, I know how you feel. I was homeless for six months. I looked for jobs, but I didn't have stable housing and they wouldn't hire me.'" A nonprofit group got him into veterans' services, which led to his job with the nonprofit Catholic Charities as a veterans' employment advocate.

Ted has worked to move on from his time in Iraq, although he still experiences side effects. Supermarkets continue to cause what he calls "brain overload," but he goes shopping during slower hours, gets just a few things he needs, and quickly leaves. At the store, if he stops, Buster sits and blocks people from getting too close to Ted. "Just having him with me helps," Ted said.

Buster is one of the hundreds of formerly homeless dogs working via Canines with Careers, some of whom are service dogs for military veterans.

"In animal shelters there are literally thousands of dogs who have the right stuff to be career canines," Sherry told the *Fayetteville Observer*. "Every day, thousands of dogs are dying in shelters across the country, simply because they are homeless. At the same time, millions of people with psychiatric or physical disabilities don't have the service dogs they need. The roughly 400,000 to 600,000 veterans suffering post-traumatic stress could benefit from having service dogs. The Institute of Medicine estimates [that] of the more than forty million people with disabilities, only about 1 percent of those who could benefit from a service dog actually have one."

Ted is now counted in that 1 percent who benefit from a service dog—namely, Buster, once homeless too. Buster is one of the success stories from the Canines with Careers program, where Sherry identified his potential and worked with him at the Utah sanctuary. Sherry immediately noticed that Buster was empathetic and in sync with people.

The connection between Ted and Buster "is as good as it gets," said certified applied animal behaviorist Karen London in an article on the

Best Friends Animal Society site. Karen partnered with Canines with Careers to continue training Buster in Ted's hometown of Flagstaff, Arizona. "Buster has a natural ability to be attuned to the environment, is able to scan what's going on around him, and alert his person."

Ted agreed, saying, "Our relationship is more special because we both were rescued. He rescued me, and I rescued him."

"Buster is my little buddy," Ted told the *Fayetteville Observer*. "If I get upset, he calms me down by nudging my hand, which distracts me enough to stop the bad feelings. If I'm having nightmares, he wakes me up. Because I have to walk him, it helps me to interact with people. Everybody in town knows Buster."

"To put it bluntly," he added, "if I didn't have Buster, I wouldn't be here."

———

Douglas Tiffin, who was medically retired as an army staff sergeant after twelve years, also received a dog from Canines with Careers, only his dog is still a puppy in training.

Shiva, a Great Pyrenees mix, is a playful pup who has been working toward becoming a mobility dog for Doug as she grows larger. Each day, Sherry Woodard said, "She's learning more and more with positive, reward-based training."

Size was one of the factors in determining her potential as a service dog, as well as in deciding what kind of dog would be a good match for Doug, who is six-foot-six and weighs 250 pounds.

"I have arthritis in almost every joint," Doug said, noting that he had some parachute accidents in Italy and at the Republic of Korea Ranger School. The intensive training, he said, "and my enthusiasm are mainly how my body got beat up."

In Korea, he worked in a covert position. While stationed in Italy, he was in an airborne unit for three and a half years. His official title was battlefield interrogator; he noted that this job "put me in situations where I was uncomfortable for a very long time," ultimately causing his PTSD. "I've had pain and psychological issues ever since I got out."

He described Sherry, one of his trainers, as "very patient" while both he and his wife learn to train Shiva.

Shiva, her parents, and her littermates were rescued from Navajo reservation land in the Arizona desert and placed in foster care before going to Best Friends. The pups were bottle-fed for three weeks after the mama dog lost her milk, Sherry said.

Shiva is not only important to Doug as she grows and learns how to be a service dog, but she's also important to his entire household, where they have two smaller dogs. "She's part of the family," he said.

The timing was right to take in a service dog in training. A dog they had had for fifteen years had passed away, and Doug decided it was time for a service dog. "Anybody in my situation goes through ups and downs," Doug said. "My condition is chronic, and it's progressive. It seemed like the right time. I know that as I get older, I'll get worse physically, and Shiva will get better with training."

Not to mention, he noted, "There's nothing like having a dog for a best friend."

# CHAPTER 17

# The Making of a Service Dog

Spend time with the people who train and work with puppies and young service dogs in training, and it's immediately clear the individual pups are being groomed to become a veteran's best friend.

When puppies are eight weeks old, they begin socialization and training with volunteer puppy raisers—or puppy parents, as some organizations call them. A large part of that socialization involves the puppy raisers taking the puppies wherever they go, including to work with them. Training also includes teaching the dog a basic set of cues, or commands, such as eliminating on command (or toileting), walking on a loose leash, and sitting quietly under a desk or table. These puppy raisers foster the future assistance dogs for the first eighteen months of their lives, until they are ready to move on to the next phase of training toward becoming working dogs.

Jenna Beatty, as an example, has Ira, the foster dog she's been charged to care for and train through Freedom Dogs, until he goes into a veteran's home. Each day, the English Labrador retriever accompanies Jenna to a San Diego law firm where she works as a legal assistant. Ira is well trained, but at just twelve months, still acts like a puppy.

"We're working very hard on harnessing his energy," Jenna said as she walked him through a variety of training exercises at an indoor training facility on the base at Camp Pendleton near San Diego. When Jenna stood talking to a fellow trainer, Ira sat down on one of Jenna's feet and leaned against her leg. The bond is evident between the puppy raisers and the dogs. It's difficult for them to realize they will one day have to say good-bye to them as they advance toward becoming service dogs. Still, they volunteer and take these dogs into their homes and train them for up to eighteen months so that the lives of people with disabilities can be made better.

It's the same for Kathy and Mike Bennett, who have raised several puppies and said good-bye to them so they could move on to serve others.

On a weekday morning at a public park in San Diego, Meeko, the Bennetts' puppy in training, nine months old at the time, walked on a cobblestone walkway during a training exercise.

"Up," Mike said quietly. Meeko jumped up with just her two front feet onto a three-foot wall. He gave the verbal command "up" again, and Meeko jumped the rest of the way, putting all fours on the wall. When he said, "Off," Meeko jumped down from the wall. "Good girl," Mike said as he gave her a treat as a positive reward. In order for a dog to learn how to turn on a light, they need to know the "Up" command, Mike said. He also asked Meeko to "Roll," which she did as asked. It's needed, he said, for whoever eventually gets paired with her and needs to easily groom her. On cue, she rolls on her back and on either side. The "Jump" command, he said, is used to teach her how to jump into a car. "Going up and down stairs is another thing we teach." When she was given another command, "Visit," Meeko sat next to Kathy and rested her chin on Kathy's leg, which is a comfort command.

After walking her about on a loose leash, Kathy, Meeko's puppy-raiser mom, said, "Hurry," Meeko's cue to take a potty break on the grass, which she also did as she was told. It's an important command, Kathy pointed out, because dogs need to learn they can't go into restaurants or other public places and squat to relieve themselves. It's part of their basic training to only take potty breaks when given the command "Hurry," which will help make them good citizens while in public places.

When Kathy sat on a park bench and Meeko was at her feet, Kathy said, "Lap." Meeko jumped up and, although a large puppy, plopped half of her body on Kathy's lap.

For Meeko and puppy in training Sirius, being trained by puppy raiser Cyndy Carlton, their place of work for many months has been the Space and Naval Warfare Systems Command, better known as SPAWAR. All told, they'll spend about eighteen months going to work each weekday with their puppy raisers. Sirius goes with Cyndy to her job as secretary for the Department of the Army, and Meeko takes turns going with Kathy or Mike to their respective jobs at SPAWAR. It's all part of exposing them to new situations so they get comfortable in a variety of circumstances.

When asked if it will be difficult to let Meeko go when the time comes, Kathy said, "It's like your kids. You raise them and you love them, but you know they'll be leaving home one day. These dogs have a purpose."

This was particularly true of Erica, one of the dogs that Kathy trained. She didn't go on to be matched with just a single veteran; instead, she became the first facilities dog to be placed in an acute psychiatric ward at a veterans' hospital. At the Veterans Affairs Hospital in Fresno, California, she helps veterans with PTSD by giving them comfort.

Once they leave their puppy raisers' homes after finishing up to eighteen months of basic commands and socialization, they head to the Canine Companions for Independence training center, where they will live for the next nine months, learning skills and advanced commands.

"The puppies are smart," Mike Bennett said, adding that it takes repetition and patience, plus understanding that they're still puppies. They don't focus only on work—thus, the planned social playtimes in a backyard with fellow puppies in training.

The time for Meeko to be turned in, at eighteen months old, came in November 2014 at CCI's Oceanside campus. Mike and Kathy's tenure as her puppy raisers ended as they handed off Meeko—one of forty-one dogs moving on to the next level—to a trainer for what they called "college": nine months of advanced training to become a full-fledged service dog. Katie Malatino, with CCI's public relations department, calls the training "summer camp" for dogs. There, the dogs learn to switch lights on and off and open and close doors and cupboards, among other specific tasks. When retrieving items, including wallets, cell phones, telephones, and keys, they're taught to do it gently, so their teeth won't damage the items. "We teach them to hold the item calmly and to be able to walk with it," said Becky Miller, a dog instructor who was working at the time with a yellow Labrador retriever named Sprugel. She sat in a wheelchair, along with two other instructors who were also in chairs, to train Sprugel on retrieving items and handing them to her while she sat in the chair.

Becky also worked with Biscuit during the same training session and noted that Biscuit is happy to be working. "When we start working with them, we don't start with difficult items. We do it in increments. We start with an easy item, a water bottle, and graduate to more difficult items, like a wallet." At the end of the nine months, the dogs become adept at picking up items as small as a quarter and as awkward as a prosthesis.

Instructor Sarah Koch, working with a yellow Lab named Kenny who had already advanced to more difficult items, had him retrieve a cell phone. "Kenny, get," she said. When he picked up the phone with his teeth touching the sides, not the face and back, she said, "Attaboy, Kenny. Good boy." All the while, Kenny's tail never stopped wagging. He too appeared to enjoy "working."

"They love to be around people, and they love to please," Becky pointed out. Whenever one of the dogs completes a task successfully, the trainers cheer in unison, and the dogs keep wagging their tails. "The instructors reward them with pats on the head and by praising them," Katie explained.

On the campus is a grassy, enclosed area housing two bunnies named Stu and Zeke, and hanging around the campus is Bob the cat—all so the dogs get used to seeing and being around other animal species.

"It's fun watching them grow up," said Madison Ormond, an instructor who has a college degree in behavioral science. Madison said she has always wanted to be a dog trainer, ever since she was a child. "I want to make a difference. They are such special doggies."

If they don't qualify as service dogs, they may go into law enforcement. "One dog went to the US Border Patrol," Katie said.

———

Becoming a service dog is similar at Susquehanna Service Dogs. Their Labrador retrievers are bred to become service dogs. At the group's center in Pennsylvania, trainer Ryan Dolan and a three-month-old puppy named Twister, walked outside for some one-on-one time during a basic-training session.

As part of their socialization, puppies in training are taken by their puppy raisers and trainers to public areas, so that one day they'll be able to comfortably and confidently go with their human partners into airports, restaurants, shopping centers, and other public places. Their puppy raisers and handlers put them through various exercises in these locations. On one such training outing, the puppies and their trainers took a field trip to a large home-improvement store.

A light snow had fallen just before one training pair stepped outside of the store for a break. Twister, because of his calm demeanor and willingness to learn new tasks, already showed promise at a young age of eventually moving on to advanced training.

Outside, another three-month-old puppy named Drizzle had a sudden case of the "zooms" and ran around a tree trunk, picked up a stick, and then flipped it in the air. Twister, barely moving a muscle, watched dutifully and calmly as Drizzle played, undaunted by Drizzle's silly antics. He didn't join in, because he'd already learned that when his vest is on, he's in working mode, and all potential distractions are ignored.

Inside Susquehanna Service Dogs' facility, trainer Amanda Nicholson ran Brutus through a light-switch session of turning a light switch off and on. And then she taught Pilot how to focus on her through hand-to-paw touching. They're regular exercises the puppies go through daily, to learn skills that one day will assist wounded veterans and other disabled people.

On an outing to the National Museum of the Marine Corps near Quantico, Virginia, then-nine-month-old Corporal Stanley, a black Lab pup, was accompanied by his puppy raiser, Roger Giese, a volunteer with Warrior Canine Connection. They walked around the museum as Roger used the opportunity for training exercises by having Stanley first pick up his leash. Then Roger dropped his wallet and cell phone. Stanley picked up the items one at a time and placed them in Roger's hand.

The exercises caught the attention of passersby, and soon a crowd was watching as Stanley performed the tasks. Unfazed, Stanley completed each of the exercises. Roger then turned to the small crowd and explained that one day, with Stanley's promising skills as a service dog in training, he would no doubt assist an injured returning veteran, not unlike the Marines pictured in the photographs at the museum.

A young girl, Ellie Lynn Coty, and a boy, Liam Schiele, visiting the museum with their parents, dropped to their knees to hug and pet Stanley, who lapped up the attention. It was yet another opportunity for socialization, this time with children.

By July 2014 Roger was confident that Stanley, at thirteen months old, would "most likely" continue on to the puppy enrichment center for advanced training in June 2015. "He's maturing quite well," he said. The dogs need to be able to adjust to a variety of conditions and people, which is what the outings are all about. "I take him to work with me every day," said Roger.

Roger is a technology specialist at a school. For Stanley, a Labrador retriever with dark eyes and a sleek, black coat, it's yet another outing, which keeps him busy and socialized. Because Stanley is an English Lab, his head and body are fuller than his American counterpart, giving him an aristocratic look.

Roger and Stanley also attend puppy-training classes each week, plus the two regularly go on special outings to greet Honor Flights arriving at Washington, DC, airports, on golf outings, and trips to the Potomac River. The recreational field trips help to acquaint Stanley with a wide range of circumstances. As a result, "Stanley adapts quickly and comfortably to new events and surroundings," Roger pointed out.

Knowing that one day Stanley will be matched with a veteran makes the time spent training him worthwhile. "Having been in the service myself, I have a great love for the military and a love for dogs." Roger was Navy Seabee in a construction unit. "We built facilities for the navy during Vietnam," Roger said. "We served all over the world. My son, Steven, a special ops guy in the army, made trips to Iraq and Afghanistan. There are still troops over there."

After Roger served in Vietnam, he was at a navy hospital from 1963 to 1964. He met a man on his ward who had been one of the first prisoners of war in Southeast Asia. "He had been incarcerated so long that he had agoraphobia," Roger said, adding that veterans like this POW can feel more secure with a service dog, because dogs know when they're about to have flashbacks and seizures. "A well-trained dog will sense the onset of these episodes, and help them come out of it quicker."

"This is my way of giving back—not only to my son, but also to all of our military men and women. When they come home after getting injured, if it weren't for these special service dog organizations, we'd lose twenty-two troops every day to suicide, because of post-traumatic stress. There aren't enough dogs to be trained quick enough for them," Roger said, referring to the urgency to train more dogs—whether they're specially bred or rescued canines—to get them into the hands of veterans, thereby helping toward preventing suicides.

❦

Because Jan Ford, Porter's puppy raiser, has a day-care business in her home, this puppy in training spends his days with children. As a result, Porter enjoys kids, which is obvious when he interacts with them.

In early 2014, the handsome, then-four-month-old yellow Lab and golden retriever mix, Jan's eighth puppy in training, was already learning to fetch items. What seemed like a game to him at this age will become a vital skill later on for a disabled person, should Porter make it to the final stage of advanced training.

During a practice session, with cues from Jan, Porter shook hands, sat, and went into the down position. After going through these exercises, Jan acknowledged that she'd gotten attached to Porter, just as she had with her previous puppies in training. "It's hard let them go," she explained as she sat in her Santee, California, living room with Porter, "but Porter was never mine." After a pause, she added, "He's only mine to give to someone else as a gift."

Golden retriever Ora, a former service dog in training raised by Jan, moved on to advanced training, but only stayed for three months. She was eventually released and returned to Jan. "She's my 'keeper' dog." Instead of a service dog, "she is an outstanding therapy dog."

At a nearby puppy social later in the day, Jan noted the importance of keeping in touch with fellow puppy raisers, in order to support each other.

As the puppies played in a backyard at the meet-up, Jan made plans with fellow puppy raiser Cyndy Carlton to pet-sit that evening for Porter and Ora. "It takes a village to raise these dogs," Jan said. "I'm going out tonight, and my two are spending the night with Cyndy and her dogs." Having fellow puppy raisers sit for each other's dogs also gets the pups used to more than one handler, Jan said.

At around eight months, Porter moved from kinder-pup class to basic school, where the puppy raisers, with the guidance of an instructor, work on new skills and perfect the ones learned in the earlier class. At the age of ten months, in July 2014, he weighed in at eighty pounds, and was the largest dog in his puppy class. "You can't help but love the big goof," Jan commented.

At eleven months old, he'll move on to an advanced puppy class to prepare him for advanced service dog training at the CCI center.

While no one can predict the outcome for certain, Jan seemed confident that Porter would graduate from advanced training. "As long as Porter has no medical issues," she said, "I can see him going all the way. He definitely has the right temperament."

Ultimately, it will be up to Porter; although the dog is confident now, Jan said, "when the bar is raised, who knows?"

Until then, she said, he's a happy boy, eager to continue learning.

# CHAPTER 18

# Pups behind Prison Walls

Orvis, a big yellow Lab–golden retriever cross, spent a year in a Texas maximum-security prison with a woman inmate. In May 2013, Orvis left the prison for advanced school, a process described by Canine Companions for Independence as "matriculating" to its training center.

In the meantime, US Army sergeant Dave Wilkins was undergoing rehabilitation for challenges resulting from a combat-related injury he received while serving in Afghanistan, after what he called "several combat tours" in Iraq and Afghanistan. The injury meant he needed a cane to steady his gait and help him with equilibrium and balance issues. Dave also needed a large dog to help steady him. Orvis, nicknamed "the Great White" at the training center, fit the profile.

After being officially matched as a team, Dave and Orvis graduated together in November 2013 from their two-week residential training course.

Orvis was up to the challenge. The tasks he performed for Dave looked seamless. Dave, resting on a park bench with Orvis at his side, described his dog's skills in one word: "Amazing."

Orvis has helped Dave in many ways, including when they go out in public together.

"He loves women," Dave explained, especially since Orvis was raised by a female inmate inside a Texas prison. "When women come around, Orvis lights up." Like so many other service dogs, Orvis has served as an icebreaker for him.

With nine years in the military and three combat tours in Iraq and Afghanistan, Dave was badly injured while in Fallujah toward the end of his final tour. He was Medevac'd from Iraq to the Landstuhl Regional Medical Center in Germany, the largest American hospital outside the United States. From there, he went to Walter Reed and was later transferred to Balboa Naval Hospital in San Diego. He was diagnosed with traumatic brain injury, along with post-traumatic stress, hearing loss, and fibromyalgia. His body also contained shrapnel that could not be removed surgically. All told, he was hospitalized for nearly three years.

With the TBI and PTSD came major vestibular vertigo. "It's like having vertigo times a thousand," Dave said, sitting on the park bench with Orvis and talking about the events that had led him to welcoming a service dog into his life.

While he was recovering, his buddy, Calvin Smith—a retired sergeant from the US Marine Corps, with his own service dog named Chesney—suggested that Dave check into getting a canine to help him with balance. Because Dave's injuries to his back and leg from being knocked around during a mortar attack, along with the shrapnel that remains in his body, caused mobility limitation, Calvin thought a service dog could help Dave retrieve items he couldn't reach on his own, among other things.

After rehabilitation, and while still a sergeant in the Marines—he medically retired in late 2014—Dave applied with CCI, was accepted into the program, and was ultimately matched with Orvis. The matching and graduation came after Orvis had advanced from puppy school, through a prison program at the Women's Correctional Facility in Bryan, Texas. After training was completed, Orvis left the federal prison camp and his temporary home with an inmate for "college" at CCI.

"The little things, like getting out of bed, we take for granted—until we can't do them anymore," Dave said. Orvis helped pull Dave up and out of bed each morning, wearing a harness that has a strap attached to it. With the tug of a strap attached to the oven door,

Orvis opened and closed it for Dave, as he did with the refrigerator door. Orvis acted as a stabilizer when walking beside Dave, who uses a cane. "Picking up the cane was a little bit harder for him, but he can do it," Dave said as he told Orvis, "Get." Orvis picked it up and on the second try, kept it in his mouth as he placed it in Dave's hand.

"I never knew dogs could do that," he said, petting Orvis's side. Besides being a helper, he describes Orvis as "my best friend."

Sadly, keeping Orvis with Dave was not to be. About a year after he became his service dog, Orvis was retired. "Unfortunately Orvis's placement did not work out," said Katie Malatino, public relations coordinator for CCI's southwest region. "He started exhibiting some inappropriate behaviors that were not apparent in training, and the decision was made to remove him from service."

The good news is that the instructor who trained Orvis adopted him, and Orvis goes to work at CCI with her daily, as her pet. Dave, she said, may visit him anytime he likes.

"I love Orvis," Dave said. "It was tough. He was like a family member."

About three months later, another young yellow Labrador, this one a female named Pim, was matched with Dave, picking up where Orvis had left off to become Dave's new helper. "She's an amazing dog. You name it, she does it," Dave said.

Dave Wilkins entered the service fit, directly after getting a bachelor's degree in engineering from the University of Florida, where he played basketball and football for the Gators. Before college, he'd had an active outdoor sports life in Hawaii, on the windward side of Kaneohe, Oahu. "I'm so fortunate to have grown up there," he said, adding that the best things about Hawaii were "the weather, food, family, sports, wildlife, and clean air—not necessarily in that order. It was a carefree life. I grew up surfing, scuba-diving, kayaking, and rowing. Anything to do with water, I did it. But mostly, I surfed."

After college, one of his buddies joined an ROTC program and told him about it.

"I wasn't sure what I wanted to do," Dave said. "So I went and saw a recruiter and enlisted instead of going in as a commissioned officer through the ROTC."

Dave did three tours—one in Afghanistan for a year, and two tours in Iraq. While in Iraq for a year the first time, his vehicle was hit by incoming fire and it knocked him out, which is when he suspects the first brain injury occurred.

The second Iraq tour was cut short at ten months when he was on foot in Fallujah with four other Marines, and a mortar blast hit. "The other guys didn't make it," Dave said quietly. "We were like a family."

Dave was transported to recovery in Landstuhl, Germany, in 2011. After his physical wounds had healed, he joined the Wounded Warrior Battalion at Camp Pendleton.

Because of balancing issues due to TBI, he used to fall down occasionally.

"I've had a couple of spills," he said. "I've fallen down, and people have told me I should stay away from alcohol. It's embarrassing when people think you're drunk." With a service dog who wears a vest that includes a stabilizing handle for Dave to hold on to, his chances of falling have decreased.

After his injury, he said, "I had a really bad speech impediment, and I couldn't hold a cup at my mouth and drink." That's no longer the case. With speech therapy and the security provided by both of his service dogs, it's now easy to understand what Dave says. "They made me not feel like a little kid," he said. "I feel like I'm my old self again. A service dog is a huge confidence booster."

—◆—

Like Orvis, a black Lab named Nyma was also raised in a prison environment. She now lives with retired army sergeant Kevin Brackney. "She's changed my life," said Kevin, who talked excitedly about his relationship with his service canine.

Nyma, who goes to work each weekday with Kevin at the Philadelphia VA hospital, knows more than eighty commands, including

"Block," which means she either lies or stands in front of Kevin to do just that: block someone from approaching him too closely.

Upon hearing the command "Watch my back," Nyma looks out for anyone approaching him from behind. It's her favorite command, Kevin said, "where she stands on my left side and she faces backwards, and if anyone is coming from behind, she'll notify me."

Kevin, an Operation Iraqi Freedom army veteran who twice deployed to Iraq, often found himself up in the turret on a convoy—a sitting target, because the turret gunner was typically the first person the insurgents aimed for. "They didn't put people who were married up in the turrets," said Kevin, who was single when he served.

During his first rotation as a turret gunner, "we'd roll out trucks in threes. I'd have four guys with me." It was dangerous work, but he felt like he wasn't alone. "My father passed when I was fifteen and my grandmother died the same day. They were definitely looking out for me."

After his months of combat, Nyma brought peace back into his life, especially at night when he tried to fall asleep. "It got to the point that after I came back I would have to play the opening scene of *Saving Private Ryan*, because I needed the noise of the field to fall asleep."

At eight weeks old, Nyma was placed with a youth offender at the Fishkill Correctional Facility in upstate New York. For a time, it didn't look like Nyma would graduate, because of her shyness. But she remained in the program.

While Nyma was still being trained in prison, former sergeant Kevin Brackney, who sports a clean-shaven head that makes his hazel eyes even more prominent, had learned from his wife, Gianine, about service dogs helping veterans suffering from post-traumatic stress.

"My wife watched the *Extreme Makeover: Home Edition* show when one of the homes they rebuilt was for a guy with extreme PTSD. They donated a service dog to him. My wife told me it was something I should look into."

At that point, however, he didn't feel prepared, physically or emotionally, to take on a dog. He'd quit his job as a crane operator and enrolled in graduate school. "Once I finished grad school, I got a position as a veterans' services rep," he said, "and then I applied for a service dog and qualified. I've had Nyma for a year now."

Nyma got past her shyness issues, and about twenty-four months after going to prison, she graduated. During the placement period, Kevin went to the prison and met Nyma's puppy raiser. "He told me he felt unconditional love for the first time, from Nyma," Kevin said. He was released from custody and landed a job as a dog trainer for the organization he'd volunteered for on the inside.

Now Nyma watches over Kevin and helps him when his PTSD symptoms are triggered. "Nyma watches my back," Kevin said. Before he got his service dog, "it got to the point where I wouldn't go out. I felt as if I was on a convoy. I had that mentality. I had to watch people. It felt like it was outside the wire in a combat zone. When you go outside the wire, you're leaving where there are guards, and you're wide open, trying to get from point A to point B without any incidents. It was exhausting. It was upsetting for my wife. We didn't get to go out a lot. It caused a lot of strain in our relationship." Since then, they've had a daughter, Gianna, who is just a month apart in age from Nyma. "Gianna and Nyma play a lot," he said. "They plot against each other and hide each other's toys. My daughter is quick to tell people that Nyma is a service dog."

He and his wife met on MySpace and corresponded for about three years before they met. "We started out as friends," Kevin said, "and it grew from there. My wife is very supportive."

While there are still moments of stress for Kevin, the difficulties for him and his wife as they adjusted to his post-traumatic stress and a new marriage are less. "Most recently, we've been able to start going out more. We went to a George Strait concert, and that was a really big step. I was a lot better at the concert than I thought I would be. There were a lot of loud noises. Nyma nudged up against me. She made me feel okay. Nyma can sense when I get anxious. She'll even moan to get my attention and ease my stress."

With Nyma by his side, he's able to ride a train to his job at the VA hospital. "I'm sixty percent disabled," Kevin said. "Some veterans aren't able to work. I've been fortunate. I have an ability now to remain calm when other people get upset. I look at it as Nyma taking on my stress. That's one of the great effects of a service dog."

He looks at himself, as so many other wounded warriors with service dogs do, as an ambassador of sorts. At the VA hospital, when he meets Vietnam vets, he has Nyma acknowledge them.

"I always say that we stand on the shoulders of the Vietnam veterans," Kevin said, "because of the stuff they went through and had to fight for. My father-in-law was a mechanic in the military. My father was in the Air Force. You can't not appreciate them."

Nyma, he said, has public interaction commands: "Make a friend," to which she responds by wiggling her body; "Shake," for shaking hands with people; and "Salute." "At the VA hospital, if I see a Vietnam vet," he said, "Nyma salutes them and they salute back. That sense of pride never goes away. We're the public face of this, to show that even though we have PTSD, we can contribute to society."

In West Virginia, Terry Henry and his daughter Kyria Henry send puppies to prison for six to twelve months through the paws4people nonprofit organization. Afterward, the dogs go to "college" for advanced training by students, who spend a good part of their time accompanying them to public places. "They take all the skills they learned in prison and take the dogs out to the real world so they can go places, like restaurants, stores, movie theaters, aquariums, and the beach," Terry explained.

The Henrys founded the prison program in 2007 with four dogs and eight inmates. By 2014, their dogs were in six correctional institutions, state and federal, with 150 inmates training between eighty and ninety dogs at any given time.

In 2010 the Naval Consolidated Brig at the Joint Base Charleston-Weapons Station paired Jada, the facility's first prisoner-trained service dog, with former Marine sergeant Brian Jarrell, a wounded veteran, through Carolina Canines for Service, a nonprofit organization in Charleston, South Carolina. The group trains rescued shelter dogs as assistance canines for wounded warriors.

The inmates form bonds with the puppies that live with them for anywhere from six months to a year. One unidentified prisoner says Carolina Canines for Service's program not only helps the dogs and injured service members, but also helps to rehabilitate inmates too. "These dogs help calm us down," he said. "They give us an outlet. This is the best therapy you could ask for."

Corporal Tyler Deckard, a Marine brig liaison, agreed, calling the training program a win-win situation: "It helps the prisoners with problem-solving skills and teaches them patience and how to work through things without using anger. Not having problem-solving skills is nine times out of ten what got them in here in the first place."

The dogs, which have $40,000 invested in them upon graduation from prison, are given to wounded warriors at no cost.

Across the country in Washington State, another nonprofit, Brigadoon Service Dogs, runs a similar prison program but takes both rescued and in-house-bred dogs—seven at any given time—to Cedar Creek Corrections Center in Littlerock so inmates can train them.

Denise Costanten, founder of Brigadoon Service Dogs, was thrown when her brother, a promising student studying law before he deployed to Vietnam, returned a broken man who ended up homeless, suffering severely from the effects of post-traumatic stress. Back then, service dogs weren't available to veterans, and the psychological injuries had not yet been identified.

For many years Denise wanted to help other veterans like her brother, who took a decade to return from the streets. A personal dog trainer, she decided in 2005 to jump in headfirst and train service dogs for adults and children in need. Later she expanded and began laying the groundwork for the prison-training program. Around 2012, the Cedar Creek puppy-training program was in place.

"Cedar Creek is out in the middle of nowhere, and we are way up north," she said. "It's one hundred seventy miles from my door to theirs."

Despite the mileage, each week Denise makes the trip to oversee the inmates' training. She said she's driven by her desire to help veterans by improving their daily lives as well as inmates who will eventually be released, giving them tools to obtain a possible job on the outside.

To be eligible as Brigadoon trainers, inmates cannot have any prison infractions and must be in the last four years of their sentences.

"They stay at the prison for six to eight weeks," she said. "They learn the basics—Sit, Stay, and Lie Down—and they learn to not greet other dogs or people, and to walk without pulling on a leash. A couple of the inmates are pretty good at teaching advanced tasks—'Retrieve,' opening refrigerators, and turning lights on and off."

Because of her firsthand experience seeing the havoc post-traumatic stress does to a wounded veteran's life, Denise pays it forward by collecting no salary so that donated funds go directly to the program.

Once the dogs are matched with veterans, "we spend two weeks training them how to be with their dogs in public, teaching them the basic tools," she said. "It's about training the dogs and the people."

Bodie, a Labrador retriever and one of the first dogs to go through Brigadoon's prison program, graduated in 2012. "Bodie was paired with a navy veteran from Desert Storm who lives in Arizona," she said. With dogs trained primarily for PTSD and balance, Denise noted, "the veteran no longer has to have a family member go places with him, because now he has his battle buddy with him to 'watch his back,' as he told me. He was depressed and didn't want to go anywhere. Now he's living a full life.

"I find that this is the biggest thing these dogs give these veterans—the confidence to leave their house again."

The inmates, Denise said, bond with the dogs, which appears to have caused a nice side effect. "The interesting thing I found, because we deal with positive reinforcement training," she pointed out, "is that the inmates become nicer to each other. They treat each other with more respect now. The dogs live in the cells with them. They're in there twenty-four hours a day. They sleep in their cells with them. Corrections officers have told me the environment is much better, and everyone loves the dogs being there."

Denise's husband, Leon, served three tours in the Army special ops in Vietnam and retired a lieutenant colonel. As a veteran, he understands her motivation. "My husband allows me to do what I love to do," she said. "He's still working at seventy-six so I can do this. This is my passion, so I'm not paid. Because I'm not paid and the inmates aren't paid from Brigadoon, it helps us get more dogs out."

As for her brother, "he never went back to school, but he made something of himself and retired. He's happily married. My husband got him out of Southern California and helped him become a home inspector. My brother pulled himself up by his bootstraps."

---

A dog named Kenan, raised inside a prison, was matched with retired army staff sergeant Adam Campbell, who applied for a service dog to help him with traumatic brain injury, post-traumatic stress, and the symptoms that often go with each.

"I was only there two months when I was injured," he said. "We all got injured. If you were on the ground, you got concussions, you got bruises, you got scratched. This was the reality of what we lived and what we did." He served two tours in Iraq and two in Afghanistan. A fifth tour was cut short after two months when he was injured. For his service, he was awarded four Purple Hearts and a Bronze Star.

Adam was dedicated to the military. He joined the service at age seventeen through a high-school J-ROTC program and was in training to be an officer when the September 2001 terrorist attack occurred. "I liked the camaraderie," he said. "It gave me a sense of self, a sense of belonging, and a sense of pride. When September 11th happened, we got closer in our squad. We all understood that ACU—army combat uniforms—were in our future. I went from serving my country to serving with a purpose."

Adam was part of the infantry that made the initial push into Baghdad in March 2003 during Operation Enduring Freedom.

During a May 2006 tour in Iraq, he was "blown up two times in three minutes" by a roadside bomb that was immediately followed by a rocket-propelled grenade blast, he said. It threw him thirty feet against a wall. His spinal column was dislocated, along with two hairline cracks. It rendered him unable to walk for nine months. He didn't yet know about service dog programs for veterans. Even if he had, he wasn't ready.

"I was questioning life in general," Adam said. As for a service dog, "I wasn't thinking about taking care of another life, let alone my own."

He was medically discharged from the service. "I was pretty much released. There was no money, no benefits, no nothing. I didn't have a network. I didn't have the VA. I didn't have anything for two years. I went to the VA for the first time in 2009. I was trying to get work. My mother's neighbor was a war veteran, and one night at dinner said, 'This is what you have to do. Go to the VA.' I did. My mom helped me."

He was accepted into a VA program, and his benefits began to kick in. It was there that he met a veteran and his dog, Sadie, and observed all that the dog did for his fellow vet. "He started talking about what the dog does for him," said Adam. "It sounded like something I wanted to try. I'd just gotten a federal job with the Warriors to Workforce Program, and I could afford to have a dog," Adam continued.

The dogs Adam ended up meeting were started out as puppies in prison, raised and trained by inmates at the Lakin Correctional Center in West Columbia, near the Ohio border. It was a daunting visit for a veteran suffering from the psychological wounds of war. The dogs at Lakin are paired as puppies with prison inmates who have completed extensive K-9 training. Behind the barbed-wire fences and metal gates, the puppies get daily training and round-the-clock care. The prisoner-trained dogs emerge with the skills necessary to help military veterans suffering from PTSD and TBI, as well as children with disabilities.

The inmates' training and certification can lead to jobs on the outside once they've been released. Lori Nohe, warden of the Lakin Correctional Center, said that roughly 30 percent of the women housed at the facility suffer from PTSD as a result of traumatic childhoods, violence, and abuse, meaning that the trainers also benefit from the comfort the dogs provide.

"Everyone has to have a purpose, and this brings that back for these inmates," Warden Nohe told the *Saturday Gazette-Mail* newspaper in Charleston, West Virginia.

On this day, the inmates who had trained the latest group of dogs brought seven of them into a gymnasium-like room to meet Adam and a few other candidates, who were observed by a panel of people. "It was uncomfortable being in a prison, let alone sitting in front of these people," he said.

Each veteran was matched with a prison-trained service dog by having the dogs choose their human partners. And Kenan chose Adam.

Before Adam was officially matched with Kenan, their first meeting revealed an undeniable connection. Kenan, a handsome golden retriever, immediately walked over to Adam and leaned against his leg. Adam felt an instant bond. "It was the way he looked at me as he leaned into me and I pet him," Adam said. "It is a moment I will never forget. Kenan and I clicked. One of the people in charge walked over to me and told me, 'He wants you.' I said, 'Yes, ma'am, he does.'"

But Kenan couldn't go home with Adam just yet; it would be a couple more months. They needed to go through training together, as a team. "They purposely put me in uncomfortable positions and showed me what Kenan could do for me. One of the biggest examples was in stores. I always think about what's going on around me; my mind works a mile a minute, and I'm hypervigilant. It's not necessary."

Three trainers and their dogs went with him and made sure he focused on Kenan and not on what was going on around him in the store. "I was thinking about Kenan," he said. "After one or two times, it taught me how to use the energy in a positive way with Kenan. They got me out of my comfort zone more than a little bit. There were a lot of people, a lot of distractions, in places where I wouldn't go on my own."

Today, "I go to stores all the time. My wife clips out the coupons, hands them to me, and I go with Kenan to the store. I can pretty much go anywhere with him. He's with me twenty-four hours a day, seven days a week."

Shopping in a busy store is just one example of how Adam's service dog has changed his life for the better. "When I get stressed and I don't know what to do, I get very angry, very fast, or I get frustrated very fast. I was in the army. I could adapt. That didn't happen to me in the service. That's how my mind works now, and it's very hard to keep it in. I kept everything in and eventually it exploded."

In the middle of a regimen of college courses and training for his new federal job, it became overwhelming for him. "I was changing my life from being a blue-collar uneducated person to a white-collar educated person," he explained. "There were a lot of challenges. I was lost. I was away from my family, away from my support structure, and I had this dog with me. I went to my apartment and went to bed. I started bawling my eyes out. Out of nowhere, I feel this cold nose under my hand and he crawls into my personal space and lays his head on my chest. Nothing else mattered. He got me out of it. That was paramount, and it slowed me down and allowed me to breathe and say, 'You know what? This is small. Why am I thinking about this?' It was the first moment of clarity that I had had with Kenan."

Adam, who still sports a military-style buzz haircut, and who has earned his college degree, worked in management positions at fitness centers and home-improvement stores before going to work as an intern for the Department of Veterans Affairs, through the Warriors to Workforce Program, which transitioned him back into the workforce.

For Adam, Kenan has played a major role in that transition. When talking about Kenan, it is with "excitement and happiness," Adam said, adding that he has difficulty expressing just what his dog means to him.

"I can simply say that Kenan is amazing and has changed my life. I smile," he said. "Before I had Kenan, yes, I smiled. But the smile I have now is very different. I'm more relaxed. I am a happier person, because no matter what, I'm reminded every day to go for a walk. I'm reminded there's never a day too busy to not go throw a ball. No matter what memories I have, tomorrow is a new day, and my dog is going to need to be walked, and he is going to need to be petted. It's a whole different world with Kenan. He is the biggest lottery that I've ever won."

Prison-trained service dogs both inside and outside prison walls also changed Dave Burry's life for the better. He went from being an inmate who trained service dogs to working as a trainer on the outside, heading up the outreach program.

At the Bureau of Prisons, Dave worked with dogs daily as a prison trainer. He took the job so seriously that when he was released in December 2010, he went to work for paws4prisons. What attracted him to the program was when he realized that instead of benefiting inmates, it benefited someone else. He thought to himself, "Now here's something I can really sink my teeth into for the last few of years of my time in prison."

One of the dogs Dave worked with after his release was Bourke, who lived with Dave for five months during Bourke's transfer training and when Bourke was placed temporarily with veteran April Cook to also help train him. Dave and April learned to use the dog's natural talents to help April handle her PTSD symptoms.

Dave was a white-collar offender who was desperate to keep anyone from knowing that his business was failing and to maintain an extravagant lifestyle that included a beautiful home. To cover up the bad decision that had caused his business to spiral out of control, he borrowed money from friends and family.

"Within months, a snowball effect took control, with mounting interest payments," Dave said. "I made up additional transactions and borrowed to conceal the fact I was using this money to pay off prior commitments. This continued for several years, ending in machinations so unfathomable that even now when I look back, I cannot imagine the enormity of this scheme and how it was able to continue for as long as it did." He makes no excuses for his bad decisions and the resulting negative consequences for others.

When the pyramid scheme collapsed in April 1999, his family, friends, and business associates had difficulty grasping the enormity of the damages he had caused. "The guilt and humiliation I felt were overwhelming," Dave said. "Within hours, I was transformed from what some perceived as a successful business- and family man into a deceptive charlatan, with my family and friends the victims of my crime."

Dave Burry has been making amends ever since, beginning with the paws4prisons program in the Federal Prison Camp in Hazelton, West Virginia. Through paws4people's in-prison training program, he worked to train puppies toward ultimately becoming certified service dogs.

The paws4prisons program at the Hazelton penitentiary and others like it help inmates transition back into society. "They get to give back," West Virginia University professor Jeri Kirby told *WTVU 5 News* after inmates with puppies visited students on campus. Such has been the case for Dave.

He continued his work outside the prison walls. It has become his calling in life. "This program is something of noteworthy substance," he said, "and I knew I wanted to be a part of it." After his release in June 2010 from what he calls "government housing," Dave and his daughter Ashley O'Hara began PAWS Training Centers, with 100 percent of their profits going to its paws4people and paws4vets programs.

"When teaching a new command and observing these dogs," Dave said, "it is rewarding to eventually see them figure out exactly what you want them to do. It's good to know that what we're doing is comforting. The dogs become so happy when you praise them as they discover the association between the command and the act that you want them to perform."

Thinking back to high school, college, "the first years of my marriage, raising two beautiful children, the wonderful memories of times spent with my family, and throughout the growth of our business, perhaps the most unpredictable thing about my life is that I have spent nearly one-fifth of it within the confines of prison. No one would have guessed; there was no category in our high-school yearbook for 'Most Likely to Spend Time in Prison.'"

Today, Dave Burry lives in West Chester, Pennsylvania, with two golden retrievers, a cat, and two horses, and he runs the dog training service with his daughter Ashley. From the onset of his release from prison, he said his plan was to volunteer and be involved with public-access training, helping clients in the training of their service and assistance dogs. And that's what he's done.

"I have seen firsthand how these dogs transform the lives of those they ultimately go to live with," he said. And the dogs, he said, have turned his life around for the better. "The gratifying feelings are enough reward," he noted.

# CHAPTER 19

# Active-Duty Troops

Recovery groups are available for wounded warriors who return from combat and remain in the service. These groups, such as the Wounded Warriors Battalion West at Camp Pendleton Marine Corps Base in North San Diego County, are located at military bases across the country. Service members who join the battalion straight from the battlefield are provided with the tools they need to integrate back into daily life. One of the tools they are offered is information about service dog programs.

Ace Hoyt, a board member of the Freedom Dogs group that has collaborated with the Wounded Warrior Battalion West program, explained the two-pronged approach. "We are told by health-care professionals in the Naval Hospital and participants in our own program that having the full-time responsibility of a dog can spiral them down instead of helping them during their early stages of recovery," he said, pointing out again that should a Freedom Dogs program participant decide to take in a dog permanently, "then we give them one."

That's why the group offers two options, Partners Program and Partners for Life.

"Perhaps one of our best successes is a young Marine who was going to be retired from the Marines and decided that he would like to have a Partners for Life Freedom Dog. We were well into the transfer process when he was found to have recovered so well that the Marine Corps found him 'fit for active duty,' which is what he wanted. His plan is to be a career Marine. He is now back on active duty, stationed in

Hawaii, and had to return his Freedom Dog to us since he could not have a dog on active duty. This was a win-win for the young Marine and the Marine Corps, and the dog is now back in our program, ready to be assigned to someone who needs a Partners for Life dog."

—◦—

Former Marine sergeant Carlos Cruz, who took in a Partners for Life dog, began the healing process with the help of a canine while he was still on active duty. He progressed from refusing to participate in daily living to his dog, Logan, a yellow Labrador retriever, making a dramatic difference in his life. He credited Logan with pulling him out of what he called the "combat theater" in his head.

One of those milestones was transitioning from being a Marine in the military to becoming a dog trainer with a service group. That journey began after Carlos met renowned dog trainer Karen Pryor, who founded the Karen Pryor Academy. He announced to her that he hoped to become a trainer through her academy. Impressed with his enthusiasm and the fact that he was a wounded warrior with a service dog, the academy granted Carlos a scholarship. He enrolled and graduated in 2012 with dog training certification, and later became a volunteer trainer for Freedom Dogs.

Today, Logan lives with Carlos and his family in Oswego, Illinois.

—◦—

Service dog Charlie, who has greatly assisted many active-duty wounded warriors and was mentioned in chapter 1, began working with Marine sergeant Mark Plummer in 2010. "He's my friend," Mark said in a tribute video that he posted on the Freedom Dogs website, in honor of his helper dog after the Red Cross of San Diego named Charlie a Hero Among Us in 2010.

"He's helped me get through a very rough battle," Mark continued. "I'm a firm believer that Charlie is a reader. He can tell exactly when you're sad, when you're mad, and he knows exactly what to do every time."

While in Iraq, Mark was hit by a vehicle-borne IED. "I hit the side of the door and it knocked me unconscious," he explained. "But the chain reactions of so many I've encountered have led me to where I am today."

Beth Russell, founder of Freedom Dogs, sings praises about service dogs, especially Charlie, and the difference they make for troops returning home with symptoms of PTSD. "They don't go out of the house," she said during a training session with wounded warriors at Camp Pendleton. Once these soldiers have the help of dogs like Charlie, "there really are no words to express the joy you feel when you watch these young men and women return to school, participate in their families' lives, smile, become active members of society, and, mostly, return to the amazing young leaders they were before their setbacks with PTSD and TBIs."

Mark did not become a statistic. "What Charlie has done for me— he has become a friend, but also distraction," he said in the tribute video. "He knows exactly what to do every time. For that, I think he's a hero."

Ace explained in a telephone interview that "Charlie was paired with Sergeant Plummer during his recovery and then moved on to help other wounded warriors," just as he had helped Richard Gonzalez and so many other active-duty and veteran military personnel.

Charlie passed away in August 2014. "His passing," Ace said, "has left a huge hole in all of our hearts. He was the first dog in the Freedom Dogs program and helped dozens of America's heroes struggle back from their hidden injuries from PTSD. We will miss him very much, and dedicate the mission of Freedom Dogs to his memory."

Beth added, "Charlie can never be replaced, but he will live forever in our hearts and the hearts of those he helped."

# CHAPTER 20

# Looking Forward

Wounded heroes like Nico Marcolongo and his dog Tali, Lance Weir and Auggie, Richard Mosley and Captain, and handler David Balentine and Erica—as well as many others across the country—are now ambassadors for service dogs and the groups that train them. They are getting the word out to ensure that service canines are not only available to veterans and service members, but that the groups that provide them free to veterans will continue as long as there is a need.

Veterans agree that they want fellow wounded warriors to know that healing help is available through service canines, and that there is a service dog group in their area of the country.

The wounds of war have been eased by the presence of service dogs like Chesney, Yazmin, Dakota, Charlie, Gunner, Leo, Hillary, Liz, and so many others in these wounded service members' lives. They are examples of the healing power that canines have provided for military men and women over the years. The unbreakable human-canine bond these partners share is also testament to the fact that keeping trained dogs by their sides can be a vital therapeutic step for veterans as they pick up the pieces of their shattered lives.

One of the ways dogs are helpful is for them to be a part of their human partners' working lives as well as their personal ones. The results of the bond between service dogs and military veterans is irrefutable: Veterans with PTSD are finally able to sleep, they're less afraid of going out in public, and they are better able to deal with stress, all with the help of their service canines.

"So many people say, 'Oh yes, that seems to be very helpful as integrative medicine, but it can be easily dismissed as warm and fuzzy,'" Rick Yount, executive director of the nonprofit Warrior Canine Connection, told the *Stars and Stripes*. "If we can prove with hard science that what we're doing is effective, non-pharmaceutical, [and a] safe, available intervention that can mitigate symptoms of post-traumatic stress, it's likely it'll be more widely accepted, and we can benefit more wounded warriors with invisible wounds."

In November 2013 the Department of Defense funded a three-year study, at a cost of $750,000, to allow military medicine researchers and Warrior Canine Connection to better understand the science behind exactly how dogs are able to help wounded warriors deal with PTSD. Researchers will examine changes in the veterans' "physiology, perception, moods, and biochemical markers for stress." According to the *Stars and Stripes* article, forty service members will be recruited, twenty of whom will undergo service dog training. The other half will interact socially, but not with a dog. Researchers will compare the two groups, examining heart rate, changes in response to stress, and other markers.

"We think that the dogs are the catalyst that helps release the anti-stress chemistry that improves symptoms of PTSD," Rick told *Stars and Stripes*. "We're trying to connect some dots that haven't really been connected. It shows the dogs release oxytocin, and now we want to prove cause and effect."

In discovering why dogs help wounded warriors, the goal is to eventually standardize treatment for healing the invisible wounds of PTSD without the use of drugs.

———

The policy of employing man's best friend to help veterans and active-duty soldiers and their families is on the rise. And the good news is, it appears that the service dog organizations that place canines with veterans and soldiers are successful.

Allowing dogs to accompany their human partners to the workplace is becoming more commonplace; a good example is the fact that psychiatric service dog Erica and her handler, David Balentine, are allowed inside the locked psych ward at the Fresno VA hospital.

In order for service dogs to be more easily embraced by society, it's important that everyone who trains them abides by the Assistance Dogs International (ADI) standards, approved by the Americans with Disabilities Act of 1990. "My recommendation to any veteran is just wait, be a little patient, and get an accredited dog, and the VA will support you," said Lori Stevens with Patriot PAWS.

That's exactly what Mary Cortani, a CNN Hero and founder of Operation Freedom Paws, has suggested. She's made it formal by presenting it to the California state legislature and through a petition on Change.org.

---

Serious service dog proponents and the groups that provide dogs to the disabled say that in a perfect world, buying a so-called "service vest" online would be nearly impossible. That's not yet the case. Go online and for a nominal fee, people can buy a fake certificate, along with a service dog vest, a badge, and an ID card that allows their dogs to go anywhere with them.

The problem with this is that owners don't have to show proof to these online companies that their dogs have good manners and are properly trained and certified as service canines, to be able to accompany them into businesses and public places. Therein lies the problem.

Kyria Henry of paws4people suggests a plan that she feels is simple, albeit not necessarily easy to implement.

"How do you get a driver's license?" Kyria asked, hypothetically. "You have to pass a test." A similar process could be required in order to receive official service dog paperwork, she explained.

"You would just need to pass a public access test and demonstrate to a trained, neutral professional, at your county office or animal control, or wherever they decide it should be, that you have a dog who behaves well in public, and that you justifiably need that dog to mitigate whatever issue you have," she said. "The person giving the test could ask, 'What is your disability, and what is the dog trained to do to help you?' It's the basic equivalent of a canine good-citizen test, but it's done in public, and that's it.

"We can't just go out and drive because we have the basic skills, nor should a dog be a service dog because it can walk into a store. A dog can't just go with you because the dog makes you feel better. That doesn't cut it. Just like with your driver's license, you take a test and then they say, 'Here's your driver's license. Renew it in three years.' It could be the same with a service dog. You take the access test and they hand you an ID and say, 'Here's your dog's standard ID. You have to renew it in three years.' That's the only thing that's going to keep shenanigans from happening."

Rick Kaplan with Canine Angels has suggested another solution to weed out real service dogs from those that haven't gone through ADI training: Enforce the ADA laws already on the books. He relayed his reasoning in a letter to the editor published in June 2013 by *The Sun News* in Myrtle Beach. "We do not have a national registry for service dogs, a national certification test, or even a dress code," he wrote. "At Canine Angels and other service dog organizations, canines wear vests to identify them as working dogs, and their owners carry certification tags, but the law does not require it. That leaves room for confusion and fraud. When dog owners pass their untrained pets off as service dogs, the result is liability for well-intentioned businesses, a disaster for the service dog community, and an insult to everyone who relies on working dogs for their independence. Representing a pet as a highly trained service dog with a fake license and vest, easily procured online, is not a victimless crime.

"With the help of our veterans, Canine Angels is working to raise awareness of ADA law on a local and national level. As more wounded warriors return with physical and mental injuries, encountering service dogs in public places will become more commonplace. We owe it to our nation's heroes to support the rights guaranteed them by ADA law. More laws aren't the answer. Let's tighten up the ones we have and enforce them."

While Rick has suggested educating people about the ADA law and the rights it affords service dogs, and Kyria believes an access test for service canines would solve the problem of ferreting out untrained dogs, Mary Cortani, a retired Marine, has taken it one step further. She has pointed out—through a Change.org petition—that a national database is already in place and could be used as a registry for bona fide service dogs. It's the Department of Motor Vehicles, which already includes handicap placards for people with disabilities.

The issue at hand, Cortani said in a video on the Change.org petition page, "is real service dogs versus fake service dogs. The simple solution is to modify a system that already exists throughout the United States—your driver's license and ID. The Department of Motor Vehicles throughout the United States issues handicap placards based on a letter being provided to them stating that the individual is disabled. The same thing can happen with presenting a letter to them and adding a puppy paw to their ID or driver's license, therefore removing any influence by individual organizations, and not requiring a need to create a separate national service dog register."

By piggybacking onto a database that's already in place, "it would make it simple," Mary emphasized, "for those who have a need to have service dogs."

What she has proposed is a "legal identification that all disabled people can easily obtain." By modifying the existing process to obtain handicap access, namely handicap placards, "disabled people with real service dogs can complete a form, have it signed by a physician, submit it to the DMV, and receive a small paw-print sticker or something similar on a driver's license or ID card to signify a genuine and legal need for a service dog."

The petition, Cortani said, would be a first step toward solving the growing problem of fake service dogs.

The future is never assured for anyone, but systems can be put in place to guarantee that wounded veterans and active-duty service members who might one day need companion dogs will have access to them. As Mary Cortani and others fighting for access rights of service dogs have pointed out, society as a whole cannot help but benefit from the life-changing nonprofit groups that provide, at no cost to veterans, fully trained dogs who are valued at anywhere between $20,000 and $40,000, depending on the group and facility.

The dedicated service dog organizations, trainers, puppy raisers, and volunteers pay it forward every day. For wounded veterans, the dogs are invaluable, often lifesaving tools that will provide better lives for them and their families. For the dedicated service canines, they work tirelessly and happily to improve the lives of the disabled warriors they're matched with. Despite their continuing challenges, the dogs and the veterans press on together as teammates.

To repeat the words of Lance Weir, the former Marine reservist who is a quadriplegic, living independently solely because of his first service canine, Satine, and his current service dog, Auggie: "I wouldn't trade the life I have now for anything. I wouldn't take anything back."

# Appendix

## Service Dog Organizations and Groups

Animal Therapists Assisting in Living (Animal T.A.I.L.)
Founded in 2013, Animal T.A.I.L. trains dogs rescued from animal shelters as service dogs for veterans suffering from PTSD and TBI. The group also trains, as need be, veterans' own rescued dogs to become their service dogs.
Location: Los Angeles, California
Founder and President: Sheri Williams
animaltail.org

Best Friends Animal Society's Canines with Careers
Canines with Careers assesses and selects rescue dogs and then facilitates their training, and placement as canines for various careers, including law enforcement officers, dog handlers on search dog teams, first responders in emergencies, and service dogs to help people, including veterans, who are disabled.
Location: Kanab, Utah
Animal Behavior Consultant: Sherry Woodard
bestfriends.org

Brigadoon Service Dogs
Brigadoon Service Dogs, founded in 2005, trains various breeds of dogs to give assistance to veterans, children, and adults with physical, mental, and developmental disabilities. The dogs are from the group's breeding program, donated puppies, or rescued from animal shelters.
Location: Bellingham, Washington

Executive Director: Denise Costanten
brigadoondogs.com

Canine Angels
Founded in 2011, Canine Angels trains rescued shelter dogs to be service dogs for first responders and disabled veterans with PTSD, seizures, and hearing loss, as well as mobility and stability issues.
Location: North Myrtle Beach, South Carolina
Founder and President: Rick Kaplan
canineangelsservicedogs.org

Canine Companions for Independence (CCI)
CCI, founded in 1975, provides service, hearing, facility, and skilled companion dogs for people with disabilities. The organization breeds Labrador retrievers, golden retrievers, and crosses of the two, to become assistance dogs. CCI has five locations across the United States.
Headquarters: Santa Rosa, California
CEO: Corey Hudson
cci.org

Dogs for the Deaf (DFD)
Dogs for the Deaf, founded in 1977, takes rescued dogs from animal shelters and trains them to be service dogs for adults with hearing loss, including veterans, and children with autism. DFD also trains assistance dogs to work with counselors, physicians, and teachers.
Location: Central Point, Oregon
Finance Director: Janie Bol
dogsforthedeaf.org

4 Paws for Ability
4 Paws for Ability was founded in 1998 to provide service dogs for children with disabilities. Later, the nonprofit developed 4 Paws for Veterans, to help veterans with mobility problems or hearing loss caused by combat injuries.

Location: Xenia, Ohio
CEO and Executive Director: Karen Shirk
4pawsforability.org

Freedom Dogs
Freedom Dogs was founded in 2006 to train service dogs for wounded military members who need physical and emotional support as they return to civilian life. Breeders donate dogs to the program.
Location: San Diego, California
Founder and Director: Beth Russell
freedomdogs.org

Freedom Service Dogs
Freedom Service Dogs, founded in 1987, trains dogs from shelters and rescue groups for people with physical and emotional disabilities. Clients include children, veterans, active-duty military, and civilian adults.
Location: Englewood, Colorado
Executive Director: Sharan Wilson
freedomservicedogs.org

Love Heels Canine Partners
An all-volunteer, nonprofit group founded in 2005 that raises, trains, and matches service dogs with people in need.
Location: San Diego, California
Founder: Patricia Dibsie
loveheels.org

National Education for Assistance Dog Services (NEADS)
NEADS was founded in 1976 as the Hearing Ear Dog Program. In 1989, it expanded, with new services, and changed its name to NEADS. The organization provides service dogs for adults, children, and veterans who are deaf or have other physical disabilities. The dogs are donated by breeders or rescued from animal shelters.
Location: Princeton, Massachusetts

CEO: Gerry DeRoche
neads.org

Operation Freedom Paws
Founded in January 2010, Operation Freedom Paws trains veterans and others with disabilities to train their own service dogs. A nonprofit organization, it also matches dogs with individuals diagnosed with PTSD, complex post-traumatic stress, traumatic brain injury, and other physical, neurological, psychological, and mobility issues.
Location: Gilroy, California
Founder and Executive Director of Operations: Mary Cortani
operationfreedompaws.org

Patriot Assistance Dogs
Patriot Assistance Dogs was founded in 2011 to provide service dogs to disabled veterans who suffer from PTSD, TBI, and psychiatric challenges. The group trains dogs who are from animal shelters, are donated, or are bred for the group's program.
Location: Detroit Lakes, Minnesota
President: Linda Wiedewitsch
patriotassistancedogs.org

Patriot PAWS Service Dogs
Patriot PAWS was founded in 2006 and offers service dogs to disabled American veterans and others with mobility issues and PTSD. The dogs are from selected breeders, puppy raisers, local animal shelters, and rescue groups.
Location: Rockwall, Texas
Founder and Executive Director: Lori Stevens
patriotpaws.org

paws4people
The paws4people organization was founded in 1999 and trains service dogs for veterans, active-duty troops with post-traumatic stress,

traumatic brain injury, and military sexual trauma, as well as adolescents with life-changing disabilities. The group breeds golden retrievers, Labrador retrievers, accepts donated puppies from breeders, and trains rescued shelter dogs through its Shelter2Pet program.
Location: Wilmington, North Carolina
Founder and Deputy Executive Director: Kyria Henry
paws4people.org

Puppies Behind Bars
Puppies Behind Bars, founded in 1997, trains inmates inside prisons to raise service dogs for wounded war veterans and explosive-detection canines for law enforcement agencies. The inmates train Labrador retrievers for the group's programs.
Location: New York City, New York
President/Founder: Gloria Gilbert Stoga
puppiesbehindbars.com

Safe Humane Chicago's VALOR Program
Through the nonprofit's VALOR program, founded in 2008, dogs caught up in the criminal court system are rescued from shelters, trained, and paired with military veterans living with the psychological effects of combat. The group pairs five rescued canines a year with five veterans.
Location: Chicago, Illinois
Founder: Cynthia Bathurst
safehumanechicago.org

Stiggy's Dogs
Stiggy's Dogs, founded in 2010, is a nonprofit organization that rescues and trains shelter dogs to become psychiatric service dogs for military veterans suffering from PTSD and TBI. The organization was named after and dedicated to the founder's nephew, Ben "Doc Stiggy" Castiglione, who died while serving in Afghanistan.
Location: Howell, Michigan

Founder: Jennifer Petre
stiggysdogs.org

Susquehanna Service Dogs (SSD)
Susquehanna Service Dogs, founded in 1993, trains service dogs for veterans and civilians and is a service organization within Keystone Humane Services. The group also trains hearing, balance, and facility dogs, as well as in-home service and companion canines. They breed retrievers for their programs.
Location: Harrisburg, Pennsylvania
Director: Nancy Fierer
keystonehumanservices.org/susquehanna-service-dogs

Veteran's Best Friend
Founded in 2011, Veteran's Best Friend is a program created by K9 Coaches that teaches veterans to train their own dogs to become their personal psychiatric service canines. When the need arises, they assist veterans in finding trainable dogs at animal shelters.
Location: Cleveland, Ohio; training in Berea, Ohio
Coordinator/Trainer: Lisa Slama
veteransbestfriend.org

Warrior Canine Connection (WWC)
WWC was founded in 2011 and trains service dogs for veterans with PTSD and TBI. The organization uses service members and veterans suffering from combat stress to train dogs for fellow wounded warriors. WWC raises puppies to eventually become service dogs.
Location: Brookeville, Maryland
Executive Director: Rick Yount
warriorcanineconnection.org

# Acknowledgments

It is a cliché to say it takes a village, but throughout the course of writing this book, that is exactly what I found to be true.

First, I thank our steadfast agent, Scott Mendel, for his professionalism and dedication to this project, and Keith Wallman, editor extraordinaire at Globe Pequot/Lyons Press, for his enthusiasm and patience, and Meredith Dias, senior production editor, for her keen eye for detail.

Heartfelt thanks to photographer Clay Myers for his attention to detail and for finding so many of the organizations and groups that led us to the trainers, puppy parents, military veterans, and active-duty personnel who so generously gave of their time and knowledge. Clay passed on vital details from his photo shoots and helped with some interviews I was unable to attend because I was glued to the keyboard. Through his poignant images, he has captured the unique bond between military men and women and their service dogs.

Much gratitude to Bill Walton for taking time out of his busy schedule to write a beautiful foreword for this book. You are greatly appreciated.

Many thanks as well to Sandy Miller and Cassandra Lawrence for their editing and writing skills; they each played a role in this manuscript.

Special gratitude to my twin sister and brother-in-law, Cordelia and Bob Mendoza, for graciously putting us up in their beautiful coastal home when we worked for two separate weeks in San Diego County, interviewing and taking photos. The morning smoothies were a treat to wake up to.

Finally, I thank my own canine family—my rescued dogs, past and present—who have taught me the true meaning of friendship, loyalty, and love.

—Cathy Scott

Thank you to all who selflessly gave of their time to be interviewed and photographed. They saw it as an opportunity to help spread the word about how service dogs help all aspects of veterans' lives. The vets not only wish to help fellow veterans, but they also want to advertise the good work of service dog organizations. The groups have become part of their families, and the facilities are places where they can go and feel safe, appreciated, and understood.

Thank you to the active-duty troops and veterans alike who have served our country during war and peace. I especially thank Vietnam vets who have stepped up and welcomed home the returning troops from Iraq and Afghanistan. They know too well what it feels like to not be welcomed home as heroes. We were fortunate to meet several Vietnam vets while working on this book.

I could not have been a part of this project without my loving and supportive wife, Cathie. You were always there to boost my spirits during times when I was tired and felt overwhelmed by the scope of this project. You are an amazing, positive influence on me. Thank you, Cathie, for caring for our four dogs, two cats, and two rabbits while I was away, all of whom are rescued animals. They are lucky to have such a wonderful "mom."

I give special thanks to author Cathy Scott, who so eagerly became a major part of this project. Cathy and I have collaborated in the past, including in New Orleans in the aftermath of hurricanes Katrina and Rita, where we helped to rescue animals, and Cathy so eloquently told their stories. I knew she was the right person to team up with to make *Unconditional Honor* a reality.

Reflecting on the work for this book, I feel the need to celebrate the primeval bond between humans and dogs. We care for them in many ways, and in their way, they care for us. We laugh at the funny things they do and cry when they pass. I can't imagine a life without them in it.

Will Rogers said it best: "If there are no dogs in heaven, then when I die I want to go where they went."

—Clay Myers

# About the Authors

The saga of dogs helping military personnel is of special interest to both authors. In 2005, best-selling true-crime author Cathy Scott and Clay Myers worked together with a top national welfare organization to rescue animals in New Orleans following Hurricane Katrina, reuniting them with their families. Prompted by their lengthy stays, Cathy wrote the book *Pawprints of Katrina* (Wiley/Howell Book House, 2008), and Clay illustrated it with more than seventy photos from the field, with a foreword by actress and animal-rights activist Ali MacGraw.

Cathy is a prolific writer and author of nine other titles. Her latest true-crime book, *The Millionaire's Wife*, released in March 2012 by St. Martin's Press True Crime Library, has been an Amazon bestseller and was included on Amazon's "Hot New Releases" list. It was awarded No. 3 in *True Crime Zine's* Top 10 Best True Crime Books of 2012, which was decided by readers. And *Murder in Beverly Hills* (a rerelease of a book from Barricade Books) was a finalist in *ForeWord* magazine's 2013's Best Books of the Year in the true-crime genre.

Clay is a former marine who has a strong sense of camaraderie with active-duty troops and veterans. In addition, Clay and Cathy each spent more than a decade working full-time in animal welfare for Best Friends Animal Society's magazine and website—Clay as chief photographer and photo manager and Cathy as senior staff writer.

In 2009, artist Shepard Fairey used Clay's photo of a shaggy dog for a red-white-and-blue "Adopt" screen-print similar to the "Hope" poster Fairey created during the 2008 presidential campaign. The "Adopt" poster is used by thousands of rescue groups to promote shelter adoptions. Also, a compilation of Myers's work, titled *Captured Moments*, depicting the bond between people and their pets, was showcased in a 2005 gallery exhibit in the rotunda of the Russell Senate

Office Building in Washington, DC, attended by US senators Ted Kennedy and Elizabeth Dole, and covered by *Roll Call*.

Cathy, who has received dozens of journalism awards in California and Nevada, deployed with the military to Somalia while a reporter at a daily newspaper to cover Operation Restore Hope, experiencing firsthand the dedication of American troops. She also was in the pool of reporters who accompanied Margaret Thatcher for a day at Camp Pendleton as the prime minister welcomed home and met with troops returning from the Gulf War.

Coupled with Clay and Cathy's shared passion for animals is their deep admiration and empathy for the wounded service members who have sacrificed so much for their country. Through this book, they hope to bring positive attention to returning vets and troops saddled with mental and physical injuries, as well as educate readers about wounded warriors and their dogs.